'Without having to concur with every, that this is an important and timely book. Jonathan Bartley's erudite appreciation of what once constituted Christendom, his refreshingly objective view of the legacy of Paul and Augustine, and his appraisal of the contemporary challenges facing the State and the Church all make for a compelling read. He doesn't mistakenly hanker after a restoration of a largely non-existent golden age but his considerable appreciation of the role of groups like the Quakers and the Christians involved in the abolition of slavery point Bartley to radical conclusions about how new faith-led movements need to engage contemporary society on the whole gamut of issues: everything from religious hatred and penal reform to life issues and climate change. It was once imperative for people trying to understand political challenges to understand economics. In today's world they also need to be able to understand theology and the role of faith. This book provides a very helpful map and compass.'

David Alton – Lord Alton of Liverpool, Independent Crossbench Peer.

'At a time when the whole relationship between faith, government and public policy is undergoing a historic change in every part of the world, Jonathan Bartley has made a highly intelligent contribution to a debate which citizens of all creeds, and of none, ought to be following.'

Bruce Clark, *The Economist*

'How do Christians engage in religiously plural and sometimes aggressively secular society, now that the Church's authority is no longer universally accepted, or even respected and where its interventions in matters of morality, ethics, social work and education are often viewed with criticism, scorn and suspicion? With his background as a former political adviser at Westminster and now director of the Ekklesia thinktank, Jonathan Bartley, one of the smartest young evangelicals around, offers compelling insights and suggestions, based on deep thought and clear-headed research.'

Stephen Bates, Religious affairs correspondent, *The Guardian*

'In this excellent and accessible book, Jonathan Bartley invites us to reconsider the future shapes of politics and Christian belief in an increasingly complex culture. He writes with refreshing candour, and develops a powerful argument for a new paradigm of engagement between the churches and society. This is a well-judged and thought-provoking book, full of wisdom and insight. It deserves to be closely studied and widely read by churches, academics, students and faith-based organisations – indeed any who are interested in how Christianity might continue to have a say in transforming the world in an allegedly post-Christian era.'

Revd. Canon Professor Martyn Percy – Principal, Ripon College

'It is one thing to assert the death of Christendom and quite another to discover what alternative understandings might take its place. This book does not have the final word but it does help us on the journey of thinking through the complexities involved in being a witnessing minority within a world we do not control. The eddies and currents of contemporary Christian movements are well understood and exposed, with credible proposals as to how we might truly seek the common good.'

Nigel Wright – Principal, Spurgeon's College, London.

'On the way from Christendom to post-Christendom Christians need a guide to explain the unfamiliar terrain they are passing through, and the place where they are headed. Like the best guide books Jonathan Bartley's *Faith and Politics After Christendom* is concise, historically informed, imaginative and highly readable. I warmly commend it.'

Michael Northcott, Reader in Theology and Christian Ethics, University of Edinburgh

'Jonathan Bartley provides us with a map of the world after Christendom. In this confidently written and clearly expressed book he draws on his interests in history, theology and politics to critically analyse a church which settled down with a culture it complacently thought Christian. Now a marginalised Church has to recover its voice, and Jonathan Bartley sets out its options in a way which shows that the Church still has a future even if it must be subversive rather than conservative to enjoy it. This book should be considered essential reading by all those who care about the role of faith in civil society, whatever their beliefs.'

Roy McCloughry, lectures in ethics at St Johns College Nottingham and is a prolific author on contemporary social issues

'Free from the constraints of Christendom a host of fresh perspectives on the gospel become possible. It is a thrilling time for Christians. Books such as this feed our imagination so that a new understanding of "church" can blossom and vital new ways of expressing Christian faithfulness can emerge in these exciting but challenging times.'

Ann Morisy – community theologian

'The main churches in Britain continue to cling on to the wreckage of Christendom, and postmodern theology is increasingly neoconservative. This book is a clear and rigorous plea for Christians to face their situation more honestly, to seek a vision that is free of nostalgia.'

Theo Hobson, author of *Against Establishment: an Anglican Polemic* and *Anarchy, Church and Utopia: Rowan Williams on Church*

'Jonathan Bartley describes clearly and comprehensively the new situation in which Churches and all Christian groups find themselves in contemporary Britain – smaller, more marginal, confused about their political significance and political stances. He captures the excitement of the diverse Christian groups struggling to become a bolder, more confident and sometimes radical movement over and against government, and certainly cautious about being seduced by government money and government patronage. This will inspire Christians and Christian sympathisers to work, with integrity, towards coalitions of witness and shared actions for justice.'
David G. Deeks, General Secretary, British Methodist Church

'*Faith and Politics After Christendom* offers the reader a view of contemporary religion and politics that is both questioning and challenging. In a 'post Christian age', Jonathan Bartley questions the role of institutions both political and ecclesial. He bids us consider what it is to live in a multicultural, even secular society, where Christianity is stripped of its traditional protections of both establishment and its attendant political authority. This is not so much a book of answers but of pertinent questions. It deserves a wide reading.'
Rt. Revd. Peter Price, Bishop of Bath & Wells

'Jonathan Bartley gives us both a panoramic view and a microscopic dissection of the myriad issues Christians must address to rediscover an effective political voice post-Christendom. Very timely, very helpful, and a very good read.'
Simon Keyes, Director of the St Ethelburga's Centre for Reconciliation and Peace, London

'Jonathan Bartley is saying what urgently needs to be said. He's on a mission to remind Christians just what's written in their Bibles and has become a guiding light for those asking what Christianity might look like once it has given up the shelter of the establishment. Most important of all, he makes the Christian faith sound like a life-enhancing adventure. Always thinking about the bigger picture, I find it impossible to read his work without being challenged and inspired.'
Giles Fraser, vicar of Putney, lecturer in philosophy at Wadham College, Oxford and writer for the Guardian and Church Times.

'If we accept that post-Christendom is a process the outcome of which is still unclear, Jonathan Bartley expertly provides a guide to understanding the place that we may come to occupy as church in the political culture of our changing society. While helping us to come to terms with the new realities of the diminishing influence and power of a church on the edge, Jonathan leaves us in no doubt that faith and politics do have a long term future. Even if we do not always agree with his conclusions, he provocatively sets an agenda that we need to take seriously in both our practice and theological analysis.'
David W. Porter, Director, Centre for Contemporary Christianity in Ireland.

Faith and Politics After Christendom

The Church as a Movement for Anarchy

Paternoster:
thinking faith

Cover Design by 4-9-0 design.
Typeset by WestKey Ltd., Falmouth, Cornwall
Print Management by Adare Carwin
Printed in Great Britain by J.H. Haynes & Co., Sparkford

Contents

Series Preface

Many Christians have focused on the challenges of postmodernity in recent years, but most have neglected the seismic shifts that have taken place with the disintegration of a nominally Christian society. *After Christendom* is an exciting new series of books exploring the implications of the demise of Christendom and the challenges facing a church now living on the margins of Western society.

Post-Christendom, the first volume in the series, investigated the Christendom legacy and raised issues that are further explored in the books that follow. The authors of this series, who write from within the Anabaptist tradition, see the current challenges facing the church not as the loss of a golden age but as opportunities to recover a more biblical and more Christian way of being God's people in God's world. The series addresses a wide range of issues, such as social and political engagement, how we read Scripture, peace and violence, mission, worship and the shape and ethos of church after Christendom.

These books are not intended to be the last word on the subjects they address, but an invitation to discussion and further exploration. One way to engage in this discussion is via the After Christendom Forum hosted by the website of the Anabaptist Network:

Www.PostChristendom.com

Post-Christendom

The end of Christendom, where the Christian story was known and the church was central, invites Christians in western cultures to embrace marginality and discover fresh ways of being church and engaging in mission. Whilst the transition from modernity to postmodernity has received a huge amount of attention, the shift from Christendom to post-Christendom has not yet been fully explored. This book is an introduction, a journey into the past, an interpretation of the present and an invitation to ask what following Jesus might mean in the strange new world of post-Christendom.

- What was Christendom and how should we respond to its legacy?
- What are the prospects for the church in post-Christendom?
- What do mission and discipleship look like on the margins?

Drawing on insights from the early Christians, dissident movements and the world church, this book challenges conventional ways of thinking. For those who dare to imagine new ways of following Jesus on the margins, it invites a realistic and hopeful response to challenges and opportunities awaiting us in the twenty-first century.

Church After Christendom
by Stuart Murray

How will the Western church negotiate the demise of Christendom? Can it rediscover its primary calling, recover its authentic ethos and regain its nerve? Stuart Murray surveys the 'emerging church' scene that has disturbed, energised and intrigued many Christians. He also listens carefully to those who have been joining and leaving the 'inherited church'. Interacting with several proposals for the shape the church should take as it charts a new course for its mission in post-Christendom, the author reflects in greater depth on some of the topics introduced in Post-Christendom and the practical implications of proposals made in that book. *Church After Christendom* offers a vision of a way of being church that is healthy, sustainable, liberating, peaceful and missional.

Acknowledgements

Stuart Murray entrusted a great deal in allowing me to follow his two provocative and stimulating books. It has been a privilege, and I hope I have risen to the task. Stuart has been a constant source of help in reading and commenting on successive drafts – and in reassuring me that my ideas were not too outlandish.

Everyone at Paternoster, particularly Robin Parry, has been most patient in waiting for delivery of a book that missed its deadline by a long way. Huw Spanner was an absolute star in helping to bring things back on track with his expert editing of the manuscript. He also responded with many challenging and insightful questions, which have led to a much more coherent book.

I have been really grateful for the opportunity to float some of these ideas in talks at the Greenbelt Festival and to members of the Root and Branch network, in radio and TV interviews for the BBC and in training days for Continuing Ministerial Education (CME) for several dioceses in the Church of England. Everyone connected with the Certificate in Politics and Theology at Sarum College in Salisbury and the Workshop and Advanced Workshop courses run by the Anvil Trust, on all of which I have been fortunate enough to lecture and tutor, have been a continual source of inspiration and challenge – in particular, Lloyd Pietersen and Noel Moules.

Thanks also to Andrew Bradstock, and to Alan Kreider for his gentle correction on the early Christians.

Conversations with Giles Fraser on and off the golf course were also most stimulating, though sometimes a distraction.

I have saved my biggest thanks to the end, however. Simon Barrow, my colleague and great friend at Ekklesia, has been a rock and an inspiration. He has taken much of the workload to allow me to write this, as well as offering constructive critique and comment of the highest standard. And, of course, Lucy, Charis, Samuel and Thalia have, as ever, put up with more than they should have during the writing of this book.

I take full responsibility for everything in these pages. Those I have mentioned have undoubtedly made this book far better than it would otherwise have been, but they should not be held accountable for its contents.

Foreword

Secularisation was on the verge of triumphing in western culture, marginalising the churches and other faith communities, tolerating only the well-meaning moralising of religious leaders and privatised forms of spirituality that do not intrude into the public domain. What went wrong? Why is the fraught relationship between faith and politics, religion and public policy, firmly back on the agenda? Why is the daily news so often dominated by issues that have religious undertones and political consequences?

The inability of many politicians and much of the media to understand, interpret and interact with the relationship between faith and politics has been both hilarious and tragic. Nor have most churches worked out how to engage effectively in this rapidly changing context, in which there seem to be fresh opportunities but bewildering complexities and perilous pitfalls. So this book is timely. Jonathan Bartley, director of the Ekklesia think tank, draws on his experience in the media, politics and the churches to offer insights and resources to those who are struggling to come to terms with the relationship between faith and politics in a post-Christendom world.

Faith and Politics after Christendom is the third title in the 'After Christendom' series. In this series various authors, informed and inspired by the Anabaptist tradition, are exploring the implications of the demise of Christendom for church and society. The first book in the series, *Post-Christendom*, defined the terminology and identified the context: 'Post-Christendom is the culture that emerges as the Christian faith loses coherence within a society that has been definitively shaped by the Christian story and as the institutions that have been developed to express Christian convictions decline in influence.'[1] Subsequent books are investigating the consequences of this cultural shift.

Christendom was *both* a historical era in Western Europe, in which the relationship between faith and politics took various forms, *and* a mindset dominating church and society. Christendom has been unravelling since the sixteenth century but vestiges of this culture remain and its ideological influence is far from defunct. New expressions of Christendom are emerging in other places and in western societies the Christendom mindset continues to hinder (among other things) the development of an authentic and creative relationship between faith and politics.

Since the publication of *Post-Christendom* one of the questions I have most frequently been asked is whether the only future for the church after Christendom is withdrawal, accepting a marginal status and giving up any hope of participating in the renewal and transformation of society. This is the charge regularly brought against the Anabaptist tradition (and some Anabaptists have undoubtedly advocated such a stance). But this is *not* the perspective from which the 'After Christendom' authors write. The demise of Christendom certainly means Christians must not engage in politics (or evangelism, social action and many other activities) in ways that are anachronistic and counter-productive. However, post-Christendom offers new opportunities for creative and responsible social and political engagement. *Faith and Politics After Christendom* steers a course through this relatively uncharted territory, reflecting on the past and learning lessons from recent attempts to integrate faith and politics, identifying principles for future engagement and offering a wealth of practical examples and ideas. Those who know the author will rightly anticipate a heady mixture of incisive analysis,

---

[1] Stuart Murray, *Post-Christendom* (Milton Keynes: Paternoster, 2004), p. 19.

provocative comments, imaginative proposals and passionate arguments. I am very grateful for Jonathan, for his sometimes disturbing but often prophetic insights, and for this helpful book.

Stuart Murray Williams
March 2006

Introduction

Post-Christendom is presenting us – churches and individual Christians (and adherents of other religions, too) and policy-makers both of faith and of no faith – with a series of puzzles that are hard to solve. Nowadays it seems that almost daily something hits the headlines that directly involves faith and politics after Christendom.

Most notable are the continuing activities of terrorists which are strongly motivated by religion (or a distortion of it) and are seen by some on both sides as a campaign in a war between Islam and an essentially 'Christian' West. The US president, George Bush, used Christendom language when he talked of a 'crusade' against terrorism. Both his administration and the British government tried to represent the invasion of Iraq as a 'just' war – indeed, the operation was initially given the codename 'Infinite Justice' – although many in the churches invoked the same criteria of just war to show that it was morally wrong. However, it is quickly becoming obvious that in the twenty-first century the old formulas are inadequate, and Christians among others are busy rethinking them. We are also starting to recognise how much violence is inherent in some manifestations of Christianity, as well as in some other religions.[1]

These examples alone show that the relationship between faith and politics is still a matter of life and death after Christendom, just as it was during it. But whatever one's views on the 'war' on

---

[1] See Simon Barrow and Jonathan Bartley (eds.), *Consuming Passion: Why the Killing of Jesus Really Matters.*

terror or the invasion of Iraq, there are also plenty of instances where Christianity in particular, and religion in general, can be seen as a political force for good, too. A case in point is the efforts by leading figures in government to 'make poverty history', inspired (at least in part) by ideas of debt forgiveness and 'jubilee' that hit the public policy agenda in the 1990s. Much of the pressure behind this movement has come from development agencies and other groups with explicitly Christian bases, as well as numerous local churches and even whole denominations.

Many people around the world who face religious or political persecution find refuge in the post-Christendom societies of western Europe; but there are many in those countries who are fearful of what these refugees and other immigrants may bring with them, particularly different values and norms which are often dictated by religion. The concept of multiculturalism is now being questioned. Governments find themselves seeking to limit immigration and combat religious extremism, while introducing new laws to protect religious minorities that seem increasingly vocal and influential.

In a culture that is secular in theory but in fact pluralistic, many Christians feel that supposedly Christian institutions such as the family and even the rule of law are under threat. At the same time, however, the British government, aware of the inadequacies of penal policy, is exploring the concept of 'restorative justice', whose roots lie in alternative Christian ideas of crime and how to deal with it. Church groups have realised that they can now win tens of millions of pounds in funding for 'faith-based' welfare projects, and they are being invited to play a part in shaping social policy and even to run institutions such as prisons and the new city academies.

Meanwhile, the front pages of our newspapers have been dominated by stories of a very different character which are nonetheless also related to the issue we are discussing. There has been debate about whether a divorced prince can marry again, given his future role as 'Defender of the Faith'. There are panics and protests about 'blasphemous' depictions of Jesus, God and Mary (as well as Mohammed). There are outcries over the removal of religious language and symbolism from public and private places. Many Christians feel that not only have they lost the privileges of Christendom – not least the political influence the church once enjoyed – but they are now being unfairly discriminated against.

Of course, not everyone shares this perspective. While many Christians now lament their powerlessness, other people who are committed to secularism are protesting at what they see as undue religious influence on political decisions. The churches may no longer play a part in government, but they still have significant clout.

The leaders of the three main political parties have all gone out of their way to address Christians on issues of 'trust' and 'respect' during a recent general-election campaign in which churches and para-church organisations encouraged Christians not only to vote but to join political parties. But Christians are also seen as potential enemies as well as allies. One European commissioner was recently removed from office because of his religious convictions, and there are continuing calls for the disestablishment of the Church of England. Meanwhile, Christian activists have opposed governments on a range of issues from abortion and religious freedom to the war in Iraq and the commercial arms trade.

What all these – and many other examples I could mention – have in common is that they only really make sense in the context of post-Christendom. I hope that this book provides a convincing account of why these things are happening now and what connects them, and also explains why certain specific elements of society, most notably Christians, are reacting in the way they are. Post-Christendom is a transitional phase, however, and most of all I hope that this book gives a sense of where the relationship between faith and politics may be heading.

1

On Leaving Government

'I'm leaving the House of Commons to concentrate on politics.'[1]

So said the MP and former cabinet minister Tony Benn on his retirement from the British Parliament. Although many disagreed with his political positions, few disputed the wisdom and knowledge he had acquired from five decades of playing a part in democratic systems and observing how they worked. He was considered one of the twentieth century's foremost parliamentarians – and yet it was his conviction that a narrow understanding of politics, which takes as its starting-point government or the activities of Parliament, is inadequate.

His sentiments have since been echoed by a number of figures who hold high political office – perhaps most significantly Gordon Brown, who has declared that elected representatives cannot deliver what development agencies, churches and many others want for the continent of Africa unless there is a strong groundswell of support from wider civil society.

The words of Benn and Brown challenge the mantra of many (often less experienced) people in politics that 'you've got to be in it to win it' – that if you aren't playing an active role in party politics, standing for election or otherwise involved in efforts to gain power, you aren't going to make a difference. The political realities that these seasoned politicians testify to suggest is that such a

---

[1] This was a line Tony Benn used in a number of interviews in the broadcast media and the press after he announced his retirement from parliamentary politics in June 1999.

view is simplistic and naive. Politicians today operate within the limits set by the spirit of the age. Whatever decisions they have to make, their options have often been predetermined by others. They must choose a course of action within boundaries set by civil servants, constituents, think tanks, pressure groups, activists, academics, business interests, trades unions, the media and public opinion.

The realisation that the business of politics goes far beyond the ballot box and the division lobbies should be welcome to Christians. Like Benn, they too have been on a journey away from the seat of power. For many centuries, the primary political expression of Christians has been in and around the activities of government. This is not to say that church and state have been one and the same – sometimes the church has struggled and competed for political power, at other times it has been invited to take it, and often it has felt controlled by it. But exercise political power it certainly has, in various ways, throughout the Christendom era.

Christendom was a 'power structure'.[2] Its foundations were laid when the emperor Constantine 'Christianised' the Roman Empire following the Edict of Milan in AD313 and Theodosius I made Christianity the only legal form of religious worship in 381. Ever since then, a central, if not defining, feature of Christendom has been the church's relationship to government.

One of the most striking aspects of post-Christendom is the ending of the direct involvement of the church in the business of governing. This development can be seen to have begun some centuries ago. Christendom has been in decline perhaps ever since the time of the Reformation and the English Civil War, after which philosophers set about constructing theories of government that attempted to find alternative sources of authority for political power.

The process of removing religion completely from politics has been a slow one. Christendom was not only a power structure, it was also a culture. Theories of government may no longer have depended upon the authority of the Almighty but Christianity

---

[2] See Stuart Murray, *Post-Christendom: Church and Mission in a Strange New World*, p. 19.

was still integral to politics through its cultural influence. Post-Christendom is the culture that emerges in a society that has been definitively shaped by the Christian story as that story loses its power and the institutions that in many cases were developed to express Christian convictions decline in influence.[3] Of course, in Britain some remnants of Christendom remain: bishops still vote in the House of Lords, prayers are said each day before Parliament begins work and the Christian faith is protected from blasphemy by law. However, the church can no longer claim to play any direct role in governing the country. Instead, it must take its place alongside all the other commentators and campaigners.

Stuart Murray has identified seven transitions that characterise post-Christendom.[4] All of these involve a move away from a role in government.

- *From the centre to the margins.* In Christendom, the Christian story and the churches were often central to the business of government, but in post-Christendom they are marginal.
- *From majority to minority.* In Christendom, those who called themselves Christians comprised the (often overwhelming) majority, and so it was often easy for them to exert political power and influence, but in post-Christendom they are a minority.
- *From settlers to sojourners.* In Christendom, Christians felt at home in a culture shaped by their story. They aligned themselves with and took part in the activity of governing. In post-Christendom, they are aliens, exiles and pilgrims.
- *From privilege to plurality.* In Christendom, Christians enjoyed many privileges, often enshrined in law and often including the privileges of government itself. In post-Christendom, they are one community among many in a plural society.
- *From control to witness.* In Christendom, churches could exert control over society, perhaps most notably by legal means backed by sanctions for law-breakers. In post-Christendom, they have to exercise influence by witnessing to their story and its implications.

---

[3] Murray, *Post-Christendom*, p. 19.
[4] Murray, *Post-Christendom*, p. 20.

- *From maintenance to mission.* In Christendom, the emphasis was on maintaining a supposedly Christian status quo, often through the machinery of government and the law. In post-Christendom, it is on mission within a contested environment.
- *From institution to movement.* In Christendom, churches operated mainly as institutions, which made it far easier to be part of institutional government. In post-Christendom, they must become again a Christian movement.

But while we can see clearly what has passed, the vision of a new relationship between faith and politics that is emerging in its place is cloudy and often confusing.

What Comes Next?

As yet, we cannot really tell what will replace Christendom. The prefix 'post' means 'after' and indicates that something familiar is passing. It doesn't describe the relationship between Christianity (or indeed other religions) and government that will succeed it. Centuries of political theology and history lie behind us, and they may be helpful in making sense of the present situation. Approaches such as 'radical orthodoxy',[5] associated with the current Archbishop of Canterbury among others, have explored new ways of using old traditions. Certainly, a very different context is going to require such innovations.

'Post-Christendom' does not mean 'post-Christian', and it does not mean 'secular'. Although many nations are still regarded as 'Christian', the extent to which Britain has ever been so – and, indeed, whether there ever could be such a thing as a Christian country, nation or state – is disputed. Nonetheless, those who predicted that religious belief would die out in this country have proved to be wrong. Spirituality and religious conviction have flourished, and now a counter-process of desecularisation seems to be challenging old assumptions.

---

[5] See James K.A. Smith, *Introducing Radical Orthodoxy: Mapping a Post-Secular Theology* (Milton Keynes: Paternoster, 2005).

Post-Christendom is mainly the experience of western Europe, where it has found expression in particular political arrangements and ideas. From country to country, historical, socio-political and cultural differences have produced different forms in different locations and at different times. The movement of the church away from government, for example, has been faster in some countries than in others.

Post-Christendom is not the experience of the continents of Africa and Asia and of Latin America. Nor is it altogether the experience of the United States. Some parts of that country, and some aspects of its society, bear the hallmarks of post-Christendom, and then the language and the issues are recognisable and to some extent relevant to British Christians. But the form, the status and the experience of Christendom in the US have been significantly different from other Western societies.

How this will affect the transition to post-Christendom is unclear. In some parts of the US, despite the constitutional separation of church and state, a form of Christendom continues to thrive. This may persist far longer in the US than elsewhere in the West, and may even evolve into something still stronger. Some observers predict that the US will buck the general trend, even though church attendance in the north-west is already down to western European levels. However, the shift to post-Christendom is already evident in many urban areas across the States, and the US may only be lagging a generation or two behind western Europe.

Political concepts such as 'Faithworks', 'faith-based welfare' and 'values voters' have crossed the Atlantic to Britain, but uncritical adoption of US models of faith and politics will be of little help to the church in post-Christendom here, where it has to deal with a very different context.

Defining Politics

But nor does 'post-Christendom' mean 'post-political' as far as the church is concerned. Although one of the transitions of post-

Christendom is the movement of the church away from government, Christians have not ceased to be politically engaged. Indeed, as this book seeks to show, the church after Christendom is being radicalised. However, this is happening in different ways and for different reasons than in the past.

The term 'politics' has often been used to signify that sphere of activity that aims to employ the organised power of government[6] to achieve certain ends.[7] Others have attempted to draw a hard-and-fast line between politics on the one hand and social action, social concern, care for neighbours, stewardship, simple living and alternative community on the other. Politics, it is suggested, is 'what governments do and what we do in relation to them.'[8] For various reasons, however, such a definition may be too narrow in post-Christendom.

First, it is possible to influence, or engage with, government without actually meaning to. Modern democracies in the West involve many actors besides those who govern who have a consistent bearing on what government does. But while their actions have political consequences, not all of these aim to influence government: sometimes that influence is a by-product of what they do. For example, many Christians are procuring significant amounts of government funding for social-action projects, and in so doing they may be making statements about (among other things) the desirability of accepting such funding and working with government and about the targets and conditions that accompany such funding. These 'statements' exert a degree of political pressure, but wouldn't necessarily be seen as political in any traditional understanding of the term.

---

[6] Government is defined for the purposes of this book as the organisation that has the power to make laws and enforce them in a particular territory. It is distinct from the state, which here is understood as not only the government but also the people and institutions that help it to govern, such as the civil service, the police and the armed forces.

[7] See, for example, Linda C. Raeder, 'Augustine and the Case for Limited Government', *Humanitas* vol. XVI no. 2, 2003, pp. 94–106.

[8] Paul Marshall, *Thine is the Kingdom: A Biblical Perspective on the Nature of Government and Politics Today*, p. 11.

Second, for many people it may be unrealistic to aim to employ the power of government. For example, although at present there appears to be significant Christian political activity, the long-term trend suggests that the church's political influence is declining. Certainly, political activity does not automatically equate with political influence. In post-Christendom the church no longer has a role in government and indeed is increasingly distant from the centres of power. It may well end up with very little influence at all.

Third, politics can be understood in very different ways. As post-Christendom is a transitional phase, we don't know where the church will end up in terms of its political thought and action. Christian political thought is still developing, and is now doing so in a new and unfamiliar context. We don't know what the future holds. Systems of government, too, continue to change. It is conceivable that Christian political approaches that have yet to be developed will not fit with the aim of employing organised power.

Finally, some Christians may seek to oppose rather than work with government. Many have already done so, not only since the Christendom era but before and during it. For example, many in the early church rejected the violence employed by government especially in its functions of enforcing law and defending territory, and their lead was later followed by groups associated with the 'Radical Reformation' and others on the radical edge of the English Civil War.

To define politics as 'that which the state does' may shackle us to Christendom ideas that are no longer helpful. Such a definition may have suited a church that had a role in government (though not those people, including many Christians, who didn't), and it may still suit politicians who wish to emphasise their own importance or to control what politics is. It may not be helpful, however, for understanding faith and politics after Christendom.

Towards Anarchy

The inadequacy of a definition of politics as the employment of the organised power of government can be illustrated by consideration of one particular strain of political thought, mentioned in the subtitle to this book. Academics like to group political ideas under neat headings, tracing the development down the centuries of various ideologies – (new) right and left, conservative and liberal, Marxist and liberationist. However, one particular 'ism' often refuses to fit into such schemes, and that is anarchism.

Anarchism is accepted by political historians as a legitimate area of study, with identifiable thinkers – some of them Christian[9] – and an identifiable perspective or a set of perspectives that share certain political features. Nonetheless it sits awkwardly with other theories about the state and government. All the others accept the legitimacy of government to a greater or lesser extent[10] and seek to work through it, but anarchists reject the idea of government and often refuse even to use the power of government to achieve their ends. Few would dispute that anarchists are 'political', and yet many working within the anarchist paradigm would be excluded by a definition of politics such as the one cited above. The existence of anarchism thus draws attention to the important distinction between government and politics.

If we want an inclusive definition of politics, therefore, which takes account of the variety of political activities and perspectives that historically have been found both inside and outside the institutions of the church, it is better and more accurate to regard it as the sphere of *engagement with* the organised power of government, rather than simply its employment, to achieve certain ends.

The Church as a Movement for Anarchy

While Christians in post-Christendom could conceivably withdraw completely from the political realm, such a move seems highly unlikely, if not impossible – and of course even withdrawal would itself be an action or statement with political

---

[9] For example, Leo Tolstoy and Jacques Ellul.
[10] Some 'new right' thinkers, for example, would tend to see the state as less legitimate than others, even regarding taxation as theft.

consequences. The crucial issue is rather what form our engagement with government will take. This book does not set out simply to report where the church has been politically, or where it is
now. It is an attempt to imagine what faith and politics after
Christendom could be like.

My subtitle, 'The Church as a Movement for Anarchy', does
not imply that we should imagine a post-Christendom church
that goes around destroying things. The anarchist tradition, like
all the more radical traditions of Christianity, is much misunderstood. Anarchy does not mean violence. Indeed, there are thinkers
and actors within the tradition of anarchist thought who reject
violence as an article of faith and hold a pacifist position. Christian pacifist and anarchist perspectives have often been explored
as one and the same thing.[11]

What is meant by 'the church as a movement for anarchy' is
that the church's political perspective may be reimagined after
Christendom as something very different from what has gone
before, most notably with regard to its relationship to government. As Stanley Hauerwas has observed, an assumption shared
by left and right alike is that if you are in power you can do a very
great deal of good.[12] The church is no longer 'in power' and so it
has to think again about how it can do good in other ways.

Another pertinent characteristic of the anarchist political tradition is that it has always been marginal and contrary. In the
same way, there have always been around the edges of Christendom heretical and subversive communities that dissented from
Christendom and dared to imagine Christianity without it.[13] The
insights they provided continue to be inspiring as we imagine faith
and politics after Christendom.

A number of books have been written about Christian anarchy,
perhaps most notably by Jacques Ellul[14] – though some of them

---

[11] See 'Christian Anarchist and Pacifist Perspectives' in J. Philip
Wogaman, *Christian Perspectives on Politics.*
[12] Stanley Hauerwas, *After Christendom? How the Church is to Behave
if Freedom, Justice and a Christian Nation are Bad Ideas.*
[13] An observation made by Murray, *Post-Christendom*, p. 22.
[14] See, for example, Jacques Ellul, *Anarchy and Christianity, The Ethics
of Freedom, The Meaning of the City* and *The Politics of God and the*

use the term differently from the way I have used it in this book. Here the word invokes a number of key ideas, including the diminishing identification of the church with government and a commitment to the freedom of the church from the government and the government from the church. It also involves a view of government that sees it more as an enemy than as a friend,[15] and indeed perceives it as one of the 'principalities and powers' with which Christians are called to struggle.

Perhaps it also embraces the belief that one day we will see the reign of God without a government as we know it.[16] 'An-arkhos' in Greek means literally 'without a ruler'. Oliver O'Donovan has suggested that the opposite of 'secular' should be not 'religious' but 'eternal'. Secular government is 'secular' not in the sense that it is irreligious but in the sense that its role is confined to this age (in Latin, *saeculum*) that is passing away. It does not and cannot in any way represent the promise of the new age that comes in Christ. Applied to political authorities, the term 'secular' indicates that they are not agents of Christ and will inevitably be displaced when the rule of God in Christ is finally disclosed. For Karl Barth, too, the only real state was the future state to which Christians belong here and now.[17] Accordingly, faith can be something that challenges the social order and the government rather than supports them.

Anarchism also involves a suspicion of top-down notions of political engagement and a confidence in the subversive and creative potential of prophetic truth-telling and grass-roots action.

One of the features of post-Christendom is a church that does not align itself so closely with political institutions, parties,

---

[14] (*Continued*) *Politics of Man* and Vernard Eller, *Christian Anarchy: Jesus' Primacy over the Powers.*

[15] Vernard Eller has pointed out that 'anarchy' means being not so much against government as *not* government (see *Christian Anarchy*, 1) – but it does nonetheless include a sense of 'anti'.

[16] Oliver O'Donovan, *The Desire of the Nations: Rediscovering the Roots of Political Theology.*

[17] Karl Barth, *Church and State*, p. 38.

philosophies and ideologies. 'Anarchism' is a label given to a set of principles rather than a political ideology. Ellul has pointed out that his own anarchism puts him in opposition to the 'Christian Left' (as well as the Christian Right) who are intent on creating 'a new, Christian, social order'. This idea of moving beyond the right-left paradigm may have been new 20 years ago but it is old hat today – but it is worth adding that the word 'anarchism' also suggests leaving behind any 'third way'.

Faith and Politics After Christendom is not a book of theology, but it may provide some pointers towards theological approaches and it certainly deals with much of the political theology the church had embraced in the past. I hope it will prove to be a constructive contribution to the discussion of how Christians can be political in their new and still-changing context – and even beyond it.

Nigel Wright has pointed out that the real political challenge that faces the church is to witness to God's rule without itself ruling.[18] This book considers how the church can be political from a different position, on the margins rather than at the centre. It starts where the church is. Some may be disappointed that it is not more prescriptive, but Christians are only now beginning to explore what post-Christendom means politically. Behind us lie 1,700 years of political theology done from a particular position of power. We are only just beginning to discover what politics looks like from a very different position. Humility is called for.

This book gives an indication of where we may be heading – but our journey continues with an exploration of where we have been.

---

[18] Nigel Wright, *Disavowing Constantine: Mission, Church and the Social Order in the Theologies of John Howard Yoder and Jürgen Moltmann.*

2

Politics Pre-Christendom

To explore the relationship between faith and politics after Christendom, it is useful to identify what it was like *before* Christendom. This is not, of course, to hold the early Christians up as a model to imitate, or to indulge in nostalgia for a bygone age. It simply helps us to understand the politics of the early Christians, which will shed light not only on the changes that accompanied the journey to Christendom but also on how that journey was made. It will suggest why it was undertaken, and raise questions about how desirable such a course was. It will assist us in exploring and explaining the transitions of post-Christendom but it will also help us to imagine what lies beyond – both where we may want to end up and how we may best get there.

Interpreting What Has Gone Before

Various claims have been made:

* The early church had no political perspective.
* Its attitude to politics was ambivalent.[1]
* It regarded religion and politics as two distinct spheres.[2]

However, we have to be careful when we try to interpret the political views of the early church, for several reasons. First, such interpretations have often been made from the vantage point of

---

[1] David McLellan (ed.), *Political Christianity: A Reader*, p. 14.
[2] David Chidester, *Christianity: A Global History*, p. 93.

Christendom, and have brought to bear a particular political view or understanding of politics. As liberation theologians have pointed out, texts have always been read from positions of power and wealth and this has profoundly influenced their interpretation.[3] Christendom certainly had its own perspectives that significantly shaped its beliefs about and understanding of what preceded it.[4]

Also, within Christendom ideas of government on the one hand, and politics on the other, were conflated. The association of the two meant that other forms of politics, beyond government, were ignored. 'History' usually records the stories and perspectives of those in positions of power rather than the powerless. A conclusion that the early church was not 'political' may fail to take into account the fact that the interpreters' understanding of politics may have been formed in very different circumstances from those of the early Christians – or, for that matter, those the church in many countries finds itself in today.

The second reason to be careful is that interpretations of the early church have often been made from the perspective of our own modern politics. It is too easy to look at the church of the first few centuries in the light of our own democratic political systems and theory. Access to government is far easier today than it was then.

There is a third reason for caution. Scholars who have studied the early church's understanding of government have usually

---

[3] A good example is the parable of the ten minas in Lk. 19:11–27, which can be interpreted either as a lesson about good stewardship or as a political warning. The latter interpretation comes from a base community in Solentiname, Nicaragua – see Ernesto Cardenal (ed.), *The Gospel in Solentiname*, vol. IV, pp. 38–48. For a slightly different reading, which invokes the idea of a nobleman with retainers rather than a reference to the son of Herod the Great, Archelaus, see William R. Herzog II, *Parables as Subversive Speech: Jesus as Pedagogue of the Oppressed*, pp. 150–68. Both are quoted in Jonathan Bartley, *The Subversive Manifesto: Lifting the Lid on God's Political Agenda*.

[4] Lloyd Pietersen will explore how Christendom shaped interpretations of biblical texts in a later book in this series.

focused on texts that talk specifically about government, as if they were looking for an early Christian 'theory of the state'. This can be informative, but it can also be misleading. An alternative approach is to look at the early church more broadly, to get a sense of what Christians thought they were about, what prompted them to do what they did in the context of their society and what they believed.[5]

The New Testament

While there is debate about whether the early church can be considered 'political', almost every reader of the New Testament would agree that it has something to say that relates to politics[6] – even if that something is just that Christians should steer well clear of government, or simply obey it.

But in contemporary theological and historical scholarship, as well as in more popular writing, there has been a growing awareness, discussion and exploration of Jesus as a political figure.[7] While political theology from its beginning has considered the meaning of the Kingdom of God – the central theme of Jesus' ministry – it has often ignored the political side of Jesus.[8] Many early Christians, however, seem to have had an understanding of the political implications of Jesus' life and death at the hands of

[5] See, for example, Alan Kreider, 'Military Service in the Church Orders', *Journal of Religious Ethics*, 31:3, 2003, pp. 415–42.
[6] McLellan, *Political Christianity*, p. 5.
[7] See, for example, John Howard Yoder, *The Politics of Jesus*; N.T. Wright, *Jesus and the Victory of God*; Alan Storkey, *Jesus and Politics: Confronting the Powers*; Jonathon Bartley, *The Subversive Manifesto*; Ched Myers, *Binding the Strong Man: A Political Reading of Mark's Story of Jesus*; Walter Wink, *Engaging the Powers: Discernment and Resistance in a World of Domination*; and N.T. Wright, 'Paul and Caesar: A New Reading of Romans' in Craig Bartholomew, Jonathan Chaplin, Robert Song and Al Wolters (eds.), *A Royal Priesthood? The Use of the Bible Ethically and Politically*, pp. 173–93.
[8] A point made by both Yoder in *The Politics of Jesus* and Storkey in *Jesus and Politics*.

political leaders, as well as what it meant to become a citizen of the new kingdom he proclaimed.

Today, Christians on the margins, whose traditions were not close to government during the Christendom era, have also more readily seen Jesus in political terms. The contemporary scholarship that recognises and explores the political dimension of his life, death and resurrection represents a movement of such ideas from the margins into the theological mainstream.[9] There is a growing acknowledgement of the political language and message of the Kingdom of God. There is increasing recognition of the political context that Jesus lived and taught in, and of his engagement in contemporary political debates. There is more and more interest in the political expectations of Jesus *Christos* – the Messiah – accompanied by rigorous discussion of his view of political power and government.[10] Political meanings are being noted in parables and stories that were previously seldom recognised.[11]

Accompanying the rediscovery of the political Jesus there has been a re-evaluation of other figures in the New Testament, and especially Paul. The apostle has not traditionally been seen as a political radical – if anything, his opinions have been regarded as conservative and even oppressive. His letters have generally been supposed to endorse the political status quo, most notably with regard to slavery and the social position of women.

---

[9] Neil Elliott observes an emerging willingness by theologians to take the most likely historical explanation of Jesus' death – namely, that he was perceived as a political threat to the Roman order in Judaea – as a starting-point for theology. See *Liberating Paul: The Justice of God and the Politics of the Apostle.*

[10] His temptations in the desert are often now understood as political. See Storkey, *Jesus and Politics*, Yoder, *The Politics of Jesus* and Donald Kraybill, *The Upside-Down Kingdom* for different political interpretations.

[11] See, for example, Storkey, *Jesus and Politics*, Myers, *Binding the Strong Man*, Yoder, *The Politics of Jesus*, Bartley, *The Subversive Manifesto* and Richard Gardner, *Matthew (Believers Church Bible Commentary)* (Scottdale: Herald Press, 1991).

He has also often been viewed as someone who, belonging originally to the political as well as the religious elite, was prompted by his experience on the Damascus road to give up politics entirely.

However, such a perception of Paul usually fails to read his letters and sermons in the light of an understanding of Jesus as a political figure. Indeed, on the contrary, Jesus' teaching has often been interpreted in the light of a conservative understanding of Paul. In the last few decades, the notions that Paul held conservative views or lacked any political perspective have been challenged.[12] It now looks as if his political views were more radical than most had previously suspected.[13] We can see him as developing and elucidating the politics of Jesus. He identifies Satan as the architect of the oppressive (political) system from which the creation is now being liberated, and speaks of a new (political) struggle against 'principalities and powers'. And yet the politics he is proposing are not other-worldly: in his view, the new rule that Christians accept is manifested in a new political community.[14]

Commentators used to contend that Paul's emphasis on 'the spirit' rather than the law meant that he advocated withdrawing from the world to concentrate on the inner life of personal holiness. Now, however, a political reading of the apostle discovers that he was more of a radical who was 'against the law'. He spent time in prison. He made subversive demands for equality,[15] and

---

[12] Neil Elliott, *Liberating Paul*; Richard Horsley and Neil Asher Silberman, *The Message and the Kingdom: How Jesus and Paul Ignited a Revolution and Transformed the Ancient World*; Richard Horsley, *Paul and Empire: Religion and Power in Roman Imperial Society*, John Dominic Crossan and Jonathan L. Reed, *In Search of Paul: How Jesus' Apostle Opposed Rome's Empire with God's Kingdom*.

[13] See Richard Horsley (ed.), *Paul and Politics: Ekklesia, Israel, Imperium, Interpretation. Essays in Honor of Krister Stendahl*.

[14] N.T. Wright, *What St. Paul Really Said: Was Paul of Tarsus the Real Founder of Christianity?*

[15] 'Our desire is … that there might be equality … Today your surplus will meet their need; in turn their surplus will meet your need. Then there will be equality' (2 Cor. 8:13–14).

seemed to propose a primitive form of communism.[16] For him, the life of the spirit led to a freedom that abolished all distinctions of ethnicity, class and gender[17] and thus defied and subverted a social order that was actually built on them. Jesus represented for Paul the beginning of a new humanity and a new political community, a new Israel. And that community was called to observe higher ethical standards than the surrounding society.

Our new emphasis on Jesus' death as something engineered by the political authorities[18] also affects how we interpret Paul's preaching of 'Christ and him crucified'. The apostle aligned himself with a political threat to the state – and stressed that not only did his death make a mockery of 'the powers' but his subsequent resurrection constituted a conclusive victory over them.[19]

But what of his apparent insistence on obedience to the state? Verses from his letter to the Romans have formed the basis of a conservative ideology that defends the status quo and urges diligent submission to authority.[20]

However, John Howard Yoder, among others, has suggested that Paul was not propounding a theory of the state at all.[21] At least, that was not how the early church would have interpreted him. Some commentators have argued that the disputed verses do not lend legitimacy to the state because Paul was merely urging the Roman church not to confuse anarchy with revolution.[22] Others who have been re-examining Paul but read these verses in

---

[16] Not a communist state such as Marx proposed 19 centuries later but something more in line with the anarchist ideas introduced in the previous chapter.

[17] 'There is no longer slave or free, there is no longer male and female; for all of you are one in Christ Jesus' (Gal. 3:29).

[18] See Barrow and Bartley (eds.), *Consuming Passion*. Many of the essays in this collection highlight the political dimension of Jesus' death.

[19] Col. 2:15.

[20] This is explored by John Howard Yoder in *The Christian Witness to the State*, chap. 8, 'Theoretical Understandings of the State'.

[21] See Yoder, *The Christian Witness to the State*, p. 75.

[22] A similar point has been made by N.T. Wright in 'Paul and Caesar' in Bartholomew et al. (eds.), *A Royal Priesthood?*

a more conservative way have concluded that their sentiments are so at odds with Jesus' teaching and with much of the rest of the apostle's writings that they must have been interpolated by someone else.[23] Whatever the truth of this, the point is that there are a number of scholars who place Paul's thought within a radical political tradition.

Early Church Politics

What, then, were the politics of the pre-Christendom church? To what extent did they adopt radical political understandings of Jesus and Paul? It will be helpful to examine three aspects of some elements at least of the early church that distinguish them from what was to follow in Christendom:

- Their political community.
- Their attitudes to justice.
- Their social and political engagement.

A new political community

Many early Christians defined what it meant to be Christian not so much in terms of philosophy and doctrine than in terms of a shared way of life. 'Ekklesia', one of the commonest words in the New Testament that is translated as 'church', was originally a secular term that invoked the idea of people called aside for a purpose – namely, to make political decisions. As such, it agreed with the perception of the early Christians as a new political community. As Origen (c.185–254) observed: 'We recognise in each state the existence of another national organisation, founded by the Word of God.'[24]

Such a political identity seems to have arisen from a sense of being citizens of a quite different political order. Some early Christians called themselves 'foreigners' and 'strangers' to the state and

---

[23] See Elliott, *Liberating Paul*.
[24] *Against Celsus* VIII:75.

the society they found themselves living in. Origen noted that the church of Jesus had a different *politeia* or conception of citizenship.[25]

Baptism was seen as the point at which this new citizenship was acquired, and was dubbed an 'oath of allegiance' by the apologist Tertullian (c. 160–220).[26] This citizenship extended further, into what many may see as largely religious observances, but the liturgies of the early church and its acts of worship may often have been more political than those of the church today. Certainly prayers for the Emperor were offered during the Eucharist.[27] But it has also been suggested that the most important of the holy days in the new church's calendar was Passover, the celebration of liberation from oppression.[28] The baptised made an ethical commitment to live a just life.[29]

'The Way' was a popular term for the faith. One second-century believer, in response to a Pagan's question 'What is a Christian?', noted that Christians have a new citizenship and described the behaviour that resulted.[30] But the Way was not just a set of moral codes that governed personal conduct. It was sharply separate from the accepted, state-sanctioned norms and structures of society. It could involve the reordering of economic life, family patterns and social conventions. Tertullian described the church as a kind of rigorous counterculture distinct from and opposed to the practices and ethos of the Roman state.[31]

Some early Christians saw themselves as a new kind of family, overturning conventions of inheritance, wealth and honour. They shared their property. They ate communal meals together – and food was sent also to those who were absent because of sickness

---

[25] *Against Celsus* III:29–30.

[26] He was the first writer we know who used the Latin word *sacramentum* ('a sacred oath', as in the oath of allegiance required of Roman soldiers) to translate the Greek word *mysterion*.

[27] Chidester, *Christianity: A Global History*, p. 68.

[28] Chidester, *Christianity: A Global History*, p. 61.

[29] Hippolytus, *Apostolic Tradition* 16, pp. 42–3.

[30] *Letter to Diognetus* 5.

[31] *Letter to Scapula* 1–2.

or imprisonment. Hermas, a redeemed slave, observed that the rich could enter the church only after they had stripped themselves of their wealth for the sake of their poorer brothers and sisters.[32] This new family of Christ subverted traditional ways of allocating power and resources,[33] and in this way it followed Jesus' teaching, which had implied radical changes in the order and control of the family,[34] as well as the kin symbolism of 'brothers and sisters in Christ' that is found throughout Paul's letters.

Attitudes to justice

As I have already noted, the early church has faced the accusation that it was conservative when it came to issues of what we would today refer to as 'social justice', most notably slavery. It's evident that some Christians did own slaves, many of whom were also Christians. However, it's also clear that some Christians treated their slaves so well that their slavery became almost meaningless[35] – something that is also implied by Paul's statements that there are 'neither slave nor free in Christ'.[36] Others criticised the institution, and in some cases redeemed the slaves of others or set their own slaves free. In *The Shepherd of Hermas*, Christians are instructed to use their common funds to redeem slaves.[37] Some Christians may have even sold *themselves* into slavery or gone to debtors'

---

[32] *The Shepherd of Hermas*, 6.5–7.

[33] See Lisa Sowle Cahill, *Family: A Christian Social Perspective*.

[34] Household ties and kinship-related identity were relativised for the disciples, according to Stephen Barton, *Discipleship and Family Ties in Mark and Matthew* (Cambridge: CUP, 1993).

[35] 'Any male or female slaves or dependants whom individuals among them may have, they persuade to become Christians because of the love they feel towards them. If they do become Christians, they are brothers to them without discrimination' (Aristides, *Apology* 15,16).

[36] Gal. 3:28.

[37] See Carolyn Osiek, *The Shepherd of Hermas* (Minneapolis: Fortress Press, 1999), p.4 and also Dr Kimberly Flint-Hamilton, 'Images of Slavery in the Early Church: Hatred Disguised as Love?' (Stetson University, Dept. of Sociology and Anthropology Journal of Hate Studies, vol II:27, 2003) for a wider survey of attitudes towards slavery in the early church.

prison for the sake of others.[38] The money raised in these ways was used to provide such basics as food for the poor.[39] Some Christians regarded the affairs of the poor and marginalised as the affairs of the church.[40]

In some church communities, the overseer was required to be a friend of those who had least.[41] The private larder or storeroom was put at the service of guests and wanderers, and so was the common treasury.[42]

Some of the earliest Christian communities can thus be seen as 'catalysts for the incipient reconfiguration of important institutions of first-century civil society.'[43] While these communities were not always as easily identifiable as other political communities were on the basis of nation, territory, culture or language, the behaviour of some Christians would have presented a marked contrast to the society around them. Their counterculture, someone has suggested, imitated Jesus' 'detached involvement'.[44]

Although they were a small minority even at the beginning of the fourth century, Christians by then comprised perhaps 10 per cent of the population of the Empire.[45] Their care for the poor was sometimes recognised by the regime. Julian, the pagan emperor who in the fourth century was attempting to reverse the spread of Christianity, had to admit nonetheless that 'the godless Galileans feed our poor in addition to their own.'[46] In the year 250, the relatively small church in Rome gave regular support to

---

[38] The Pagan Lucian describes how the Christians helped prisoners in *Peregrinus* 13.

[39] *First Letter of Clement to the Corinthians*, c. AD94.

[40] See Justin, *First Apology* 67.

[41] Tertullian, *To His Wife* II.4.

[42] Tertullian, *To His Wife* II.4.

[43] See Cahill, *Family: A Christian Social Perspective*, p. 33.

[44] R.S. Giles 'The Church as a Counter-Culture Before Constantine', 1988 MLitt dissertation quoted in Nigel Wright, *Disavowing Constantine*, p. 15.

[45] A generally accepted estimate. See, for example, Alan Kreider, *The Change of Conversion and the Origin of Christendom* and Peter Brown, *The Rise of Western Christendom: Triumph and Diversity AD200–1000*.

[46] Macarius Magnes, *Apocritica* III.5.

one and a half thousand distressed people.[47] This kind of activity challenged the social order and the norms on which it was based. When some Christian women of rank gave away their property, Pagans deplored the fact that instead of commanding respect because of their wealth, they then became beggars, knocking at the doors of houses much less respected than their own.[48] Christians, it was once claimed, spent more money in the streets than the followers of other religions spent in their temples.[49]

Social and political engagement

In his teaching about the Kingdom of God, Jesus warned that his followers would be brought before governors and kings.[50] It was an experience that some early Christians came to know all too well. Initially, the opposition came from Rabbinical Jews, which perceived that Christians, like other heretics, had to be suppressed in order to preserve the integrity of the Jewish tradition. However, as the policy of the Romans was to protect Judaism, whereas Christianity was suspected of being a dangerous cult,[51] it was not long before the imperial authorities accused Christians of subverting the social order, just as at his trial Jesus was accused of (among other things) advocating non-payment of taxes.[52]

Much of this suspicion appears to have been unjustified and to have been based on misunderstandings of their faith. They were accused of incest because they married their brothers and sisters

---

[47] Bishop Cornelius in *Eusebius* VI.43, p. 183, calculated that the church in Rome spent vast amounts of money every year on relief for the poor. See Harnack ET, vol. I, p. 157. In the preamble to his letter to the Romans, Ignatius says that Rome 'presided in works of love'.
[48] Macarius Magnes, *Apocritica* III.5.
[49] Tertullian, *To His Wife* II.4.
[50] Mt. 10:18, 22.
[51] Robin Lane Fox, *Pagans and Christians* (New York: HarperCollins, 1987), pp. 268–73; Ramsay MacMullen, *Christianising the Roman Empire, AD100-400*, pp. 109–10. See also Chidester, *Christianity: A Global History*, chap. 4.
[52] Lk. 23:2.

in Christ. They were accused of cannibalism because they consumed the body and blood of Christ. They were accused of atheism because they refused to pay the proper respect or make sacrifices to the Roman gods and emperors.[53] They were also victimised by Nero, who in AD64 blamed them for starting the fires that swept Rome.

But is that all it was? Were they merely an unlucky community that was persecuted because people misunderstood them and politicians needed scapegoats? There are two other factors we need to bear in mind. The first is the ethical positions that many early Christians took, and the second is their attitude to idolatry.

Due to their marginal position in Roman society – often living in that world but not always being of it – Christians were particularly vulnerable to charges of being anti-social. The unwillingness of some to do military service, take positions in government, their subversion of economic norms and their strange ideas on the family threatened the values on which that society was built and which the Empire not only encouraged but enforced.

The other threat that Christianity presented was that while Rome recognised many gods – including its emperors – Christians believed in only one and insisted that he had supreme authority over human affairs. At a time when religion was important both to the authority of the state and to the cohesion of the Empire, this was deeply subversive.

Often scholars have considered the ethical positions Christians took on the one hand and their opposition to idolatry on the other as discrete and separate things. There is a continuing debate, for example, about whether the reluctance of many early Christians to do military service was due to their belief that they should not kill or because of the idolatry they would have had to participate in.[54] Perhaps it is better to take the two things together, however. The distinction between religion and politics that many people make

---

[53] Tertullian observed: 'We are charged with being irreligious people and, what is more, irreligious in respect to the emperors since we refuse to pay religious homage to their imperial majesties and to their genius and refuse to swear by them' (*To the Heathen*, 1.17).

[54] See Kreider, 'Military Service in the Church Orders'.

today was unknown in those days. The early Christians' opposition to idolatry and the ethical positions they took were intertwined. For the Empire, they constituted a threat to both the political and the religious order, the power structure, the social system and the moral foundations on which it was built, because of their whole mix of subversive attitudes, including their refusal to sacrifice.

As the Roman Empire spread, local gods tended to be accepted alongside the official pantheon. Different communities could continue to worship their own gods provided they also paid homage to Caesar. The Christian approach rejected this arrangement, asserting not only that the Roman gods were subservient to the lordship of Jesus Christ but that Caesar was, too. Such a claim, so different from many of the other religions, challenged the idea that the state was absolute, the sole judge of its own interests, laws and actions. As long as the Empire was omnipotent, Caesar could be worshipped and the empire and its laws regarded as culture, religion and morality. The Christians' claims – borne out clearly by their actions – undermined the system.

Public sacrifice, especially to the emperor, was a significant part of civic life, and the refusal of Christians to take part in it was an act of civil disobedience. At the same time, their refusal to show respect to Roman gods and rulers was thought to bring down divine wrath. War, civil unrest, crop failure, storms and earthquakes were all attributed to their impiety. They were charged with committing crimes not only against the gods but also against the polity.[55]

Their very commitment to their beliefs, even to the point that they were willing to be martyred for them, also seemed dangerous to the state. The fact that this was a revolution that did not involve violent insurrection perhaps made it seem all the more subversive. The threat was certainly made worse by the rapid growth of the

---

[55] 'Of those who introduce new religions with unknown customs or methods by which the minds of the people could be disturbed, those of the upper classes shall be deported, and those of the lower classes shall be put to death' – a legal decree, according to the second-century Pagan jurist Julius Paulus, *Collected Sentences* V.21.

Christian community, and the fact that it was encouraging people not to worship or sacrifice.[56]

Martyrdom was in fact a notable form of political engagement. Some early Christians celebrated the deaths of martyrs as acts of redemption – whereas many Pagans regarded their execution as a ritual sacrifice required to appease the gods and restore the harmony of the divine order that sustained the Empire. Martyrdom is often regarded as a purely religious event and its political dimension is ignored, but it was a way for people to engage with 'the powers' when their only other option was violent insurrection. It can be seen therefore as a way to gain direct access to the political system at a time when that was extremely difficult. Christians would be brought before the authorities and would then have the opportunity to bear witness – by both their words and their subsequent death – to the new regime they believed was coming. Of course, they also perceived that they were following in the footsteps of their Christ, who also appeared before the authorities and, through his death at their hands, and resurrection, was victorious over them.

It is perhaps a legacy of Christendom that until recently we have rarely seen martyrdom as a political act (though of course Islam has reintroduced the idea to the world). For some in the early church, however, it was one that bore witness to their citizenship of another kingdom. It was a statement of opposition to the state and its idolatry, violence and injustice, but also a proclamation of victory over it. It was also a demonstration of the new values Christians had been called to embrace, and the new way they had been called to follow.

Their View of Government

We have identified three political features of the early Christians: their new political community, their attitudes to justice and their

---

[56] 'He has persuaded many not to sacrifice and not to worship' was what the crowds shouted at Polycarp's trial (*The Martyrdom of Polycarp*, 12:2).

social and political engagement. But, underlying these, what was their understanding of government?

Many of them had a negative view of the Roman Empire.[57] Perhaps this is not surprising given that the state not only had put to death the founder and central figure of their faith but had also instituted laws against his followers and enforced them ruthlessly. But while their antipathy was undoubtedly strengthened by the persecution of Christians under such emperors as Marcus Aurelius, Decius and Diocletian, this is not sufficient to explain it. Although opposition to the existing political order was in a sense forced upon Christians, it was also deeply embedded in their developing tradition.

The apocalyptic visions of the book of Revelation encouraged Christians to see the Roman Empire as the Antichrist.[58] Some early Christians regarded the imperial government, and even the existing order of humankind, as a phenomenon that was already passing away, and they longed for the present age to end and the new order to arrive. They saw the state as the enemy of the gospel – the good news that God's new regime was coming – because it stood in the way of the new kingdom. But it was also an enemy because of what lay behind it: the political order was a front for demonic forces with which, as Paul had pointed out, Christians were called to struggle.

The values of the Empire were diametrically opposed to what the new kingdom stood for. For many early Christians, imperial 'justice' was something quite different from what they regarded as just. It relied on coercion and violence, whereas their justice relied on demonstrations of love and mercy, both to each other and to the wider society.

Tertullian was thus able to declare that 'emperors could only believe in Christ if they were not emperors – as if Christians could ever be emperors.'[59] A Christian could hold a high office that

---

[57] Tertullian's hostility was echoed by Origen, writing around 250.

[58] N.T. Wright notes that until recently the book of Revelation remained outside the implicit canon of many New Testament scholars, and even when they did consider its striking political significance, this was often limited to reflections on its 13th chapter. See *Paul and Caesar*.

[59] Tertullian *Apology* 21.

empowered him to adjudicate over the civic rights of someone else only if he did not condemn or penalise anyone, or cause anyone to be put into chains, thrown into prison or tortured.[60] Holding political office usually involved doing things that contradicted the justice of the Kingdom. As Paul had noted, Jesus' death on the cross confronted Christian understandings of justice with the injustice of the Roman state, symbolised by an instrument of torture and execution. By following in Jesus' footsteps and dying at the hands of the state, the early Christians too were confronting the old regime with the new one they proclaimed.

Their Engagement with Government

Jesus had commanded his disciples to love their enemies, and accordingly prayers were said for the Emperor and others in authority. But the early Christians' love for their enemies went much further. One of the most important strategies available to the early church was withdrawal. It was used to discipline one of their number: the community would withdraw from them in the hope that that person would change their behaviour and could then be welcomed back.

This idea of 'withdrawal' is often regarded as a kind of sectarianism, or as an abdication of the responsibility to engage. But those involved in non-violent direct action have noted that it is an important political act, particularly at times when people have no access to political structures and systems or no other way to express themselves. The withdrawal of labour in a strike is a good example of how such non-compliance works today. The early Christians withdrew through their refusal to sacrifice to idols. This challenged and undermined the political and social system, but it also invited the state to change, to set aside its political practices in favour of new ones.

This wasn't the only way in which their non-compliance manifested itself. They also found that their new citizenship called into

---

[60] Tertullian, *On Idolatry* 17.

question the legitimacy of working in certain professions, and especially in government or the army. This was not a matter of dogmatic legalism, it was just that the tasks they would be required to perform were incompatible with their faith. Some Christians suggested that they could join these professions but only if they could avoid doing the more problematic tasks. They could be soldiers as long as they didn't kill. They could be magistrates as long as they didn't govern.[61] They could hold a high office as long as they didn't condemn or punish anyone, cause them to be put into chains, thrown into prison or tortured.[62]

For others, however, such professions were ruled out entirely. Many early Christians found it impossible to take responsibility for any penalty or imprisonment, disfranchisement, power of life or death, exposure of infants, gladiatorial games, abortion or the carrying out of any death sentence pronounced by a martial or criminal court.[63] Christians therefore had to be prepared to give up their occupations.

We have to understand the account Christians gave of themselves, as people obedient to the law of the land, in the light of this dissent. Indeed, it was claimed that they went beyond the requirements of the law in terms of the high ethical standards they maintained.[64] Their stern condemnation of the dishonesty, impurity, violence and materialism in public life sometimes outweighed their acceptance of the existing order. 'Obedience' did not mean that they automatically obeyed the law. One of the hallmarks of their faith very often was their disobedience to the emperor when they refused to sacrifice.

Changing Attitudes

It has to be acknowledged, however, that there was a wide diversity in the political approaches of Christians before Christendom.

---

[61] Hippolytus, *Apostolic Tradition* 16, 42–3.
[62] Tertullian, *On Idolatry* 17.
[63] See *Epistle to Diognetus* 5.
[64] *Epistle to Diognetus* 5.

They debated many things[65] – indeed, it would be surprising if they didn't. When we talk about 'the early church', 'early Christians' or 'pre-Christendom', we are dealing with a period of time that spanned several centuries, when Christian communities were scattered over thousands of miles and there was little in the way of ecclesiastical organisation. We cannot simply lump all the Christians of this period together and consider them as one homogeneous group. What was true for one part of the early church may not necessarily have been true for another. Moreover, the church was growing significantly and, even as it tried to work out its relationship to the cultures around it, its social circumstances were changing.

It is undoubtedly true that there was great variety in beliefs, organisation and procedures, particularly between the eastern and western parts of the church. There was doctrinal diversity, and sometimes differences in 'worldviews'.[66] However, it's also important to note how the early church viewed doctrine on the one hand and behaviour on the other. While there was diversity in terms of belief as the first Christians tried to make sense of what had happened on the cross, for example, there was perhaps far less diversity in their political views.

The early Christians were far more concerned with general concepts, instructions and admonitions for following their faith in times of persecution (which, though occasional, could be intense). Of course, some did focus on the detail, but as Clement of Alexandra put it, 'those who are particular about words, and devote their time to them, miss the point of the whole picture.'[67] There seems to have been a far greater agreement in their behaviour, including their approach to political authority, than there was in their doctrinal beliefs, because the former was how they often defined themselves.

---

[65] See, for example, Kreider, 'Military Service in the Church Orders'.

[66] Chidester observes, for example, that the examples of Marcion, Valentius and Justin alone demonstrate that Christian religious discourse was marked by intense intellectual battles (*Christianity: A Global History*, p. 45).

[67] *The Stromata* II:1.

One thing we can confidently say is that there was less political diversity in the early church than there is in the church today. As we shall see later in this book, Christians today agree on very little politically and there is a wide divergence in political belief, thought and aspiration between different campaign groups, churches, traditions and denominations, and between individual Christians in different political parties.

There is no clear dividing line between pre-Christendom and Christendom. Although the actions of the emperors Constantine and Theodosius I in the fourth century are often regarded as significant, some scholars point to big differences between the very early church (that is, up to around 160) and what came after. The church was growing and changing. It was becoming more wealthy. It was beginning to form its own power structures. And by the end of the second century there are signs of what can be viewed as a more sympathetic approach to the state.[68]

As more political options became available to Christians, we see the church struggling with the issue of how to be involved in professions that seemed at odds with the gospel. How can Christians be magistrates but not govern? How can they be in the army but not kill? It's interesting to note, however, that in their apologies for a more sympathetic view of government church leaders more often appealed to the Hebrew scriptures and the writings of Paul than to the teachings of Jesus. Already, the political Jesus was beginning to be sidelined by some in the church, well before the time of Constantine.

We can also see emerging the idea that Christians would make better rulers, which would be developed in Christendom.[69] Christians began to assert that the councillors of their own communities would be capable of administering any large 'city of God' – if such a thing could exist in the present age – and contemporary rulers, with their bad character and poor performance, could not claim to be any better.[70]

---

[68] See the writings of Irenaeus, Bishop of Lyons, for example.
[69] See for example Origen *Against Celsus* III:29–30.
[70] Origen, *Against Celsus* III:29–30.

Of course, there was always a sense in which Christians believed that in the short term the state had a role to play. This was a matter not so much of doing justice as of limiting the unjust consequences of sin until the new kingdom arrived. In this task the state was ordained by God to be a bulwark against the most serious evils and it was thus a matter of conscience for Christians to honour and respect it. Scholars have suggested that this perception, though it grew stronger in later Christianity, was in fact never absent, even in the most radical circles during times of severe persecution.

Nonetheless, the key point to note is that at one time many early Christians clearly had a very different view of and approach to politics (as set out above) to that which was to emerge within Christendom. It is to these changes that we now turn our attention.

3

The Changes in Christendom

The notion that religion and politics shouldn't mix – or, perhaps more accurately, Christianity and government – arguably arrived in England at the time of the Restoration in 1660.[1] It was around that time that theorists set about formulating new ideas of political authority that were not dependent upon God or the church. Religious zeal seemed dangerous – it was considered to have killed a king – and so thinkers such as Thomas Hobbes, John Locke and John Jacques Rousseau, as part of the movement of the Enlightenment, developed ideas of government that tried to remove religious authority from the political picture.[2]

The underlying tensions that provoked such calls for a separation of church and state in fact began over a thousand years before. Christendom represented the bringing-together of two realms that many Christians had previously seen as being in conflict: church and empire. The foundations of Christendom were laid by the emperor Constantine. The Edict of Milan in 313 – a joint declaration with the ruler of the eastern Empire, Licinius – granted Christians formal freedom from persecution, and subsequent reforms gradually introduced Christianity as the imperial religion. Seventy years later, Theodosius I made a specific brand of Christianity mandatory, even requiring baptism as a condition of citizenship. Christendom had arrived.

---

[1] See, for example, the introduction to Storkey, *Jesus and Politics*.
[2] These thinkers have been seen as 'Deist' rather than 'Theist' in that, they acknowledged the existence of God, their theories of political authority did not depend upon God.

The leap of Christianity to the heart of government was both swift and unexpected, and it required a rapid and wide-ranging response from the church as it sought to adjust to its new position. In particular, it had to make sense of an apparent contradiction. Many in the early church had seen the Empire as something both hostile to and incompatible with their faith, so how could Christians come to terms with the fact that the church was now at its heart?

In practice, this new relationship was played out in various ways. Sometimes the church seemed to rule over kings and princes, most notably during the period of the Holy Roman Empire. At other times, different kinds of government had the mastery. It was not always easy to distinguish between church and state.

If Constantine laid the foundations of Christendom, its principal architect was Augustine.[3] In *City of God*, he set about trying to reconcile the new alignment of church and empire. Much of the subsequent history of Christian political thought has been the story of others building on his ideas as they struggled with the same enterprise. In what he has termed 'the doctrine of the two', Oliver O'Donovan has shown how Christians have explored what it means to live within the two societies – from a perception of a struggle between them in the patristic period, to a vision of a single society with two foci of authority in the Middle Ages, to a distinction between an inner self and its external roles in society at the time of the Reformation.[4]

However, not everyone in Christendom was satisfied by these various solutions to the puzzle. Radical groups pointed to their inadequacies, and especially the coercion and the lack of justice that such arrangements still involved. Some felt that allegiance to the Kingdom of God demanded a different approach. At the time of the Reformation and the English Civil War, groups such as the Ranters, the Diggers, the Levellers. The Anabaptists and the Quakers emphasised the radical equality of all people, often 'grounding their thinking in direct reappropriation of the

---

[3] Murray, *Post-Christendom*, p. 75.
[4] Oliver O'Donovan, *The Desire of the Nations*.

teachings of Jesus.'[5] It was many of these people who inspired and took part in the social unrest that in turn prompted the efforts to remove Christianity from the sphere of government entirely.[6]

From Citizens of Heaven to Citizens of the State

When Theodosius I made baptism a rite of citizenship in the Roman Empire, it represented far more than a religious or cultural embellishment. Baptism for the early church marked the point at which citizenship of the Kingdom of God took precedence over all other allegiances. The emperor's edict represented a challenge, but also signalled the beginning of a profound change in the church's political identity, in three crucial ways:

Christianity became associated with territory. Many in the early church had had a sense of being sojourners and even exiles in a foreign land, Christianity now became the official religion of cities and states, associated with specific territories. Distinctions between 'us' (Christians) and 'them' (Pagans) were made on the basis of geography and culture, rather than of faith and commitment. By the time of the Reformation, the principle *Cuius regio, eius religio* – 'He who controls the state chooses the religion' – was firmly established.

Discipleship became loyal citizenship. As Christianity became associated with territory, so being a Christian became less a matter of 'following the Way' and more a matter of being a good, loyal citizen. This manifested itself in ways that would have been anathema to many in the early church. For example, whereas once it had been unthinkable to many Christians to serve in the army, there were periods in Christendom when a man *had* to be a Christian in order to be a soldier.

---

[5] McLellan, *Political Christianity*, p. 45.

[6] Thomas Hobbes thought that belief in both the integrity and transcendent authority of the Bible and in the sufficiency and authority of the believer's faith was destructive of political order and authority. See Iain Hampsher-Monk, *A History of Modern Political Thought: Major Political Thinkers from Hobbes to Marx*, p. 3.

Citizenship of the Kingdom of God became other-worldly. New conceptions of citizenship changed the meaning and implications of citizenship of the Kingdom of God, which became associated with the afterlife rather than the here and now. The extent to which this was true can be seen in the observation by Christopher Hill of the ideas of some more radical groups who tried to introduce notions of the Kingdom of God at the time of the English Civil War: 'What was new in the seventeenth century was the idea that ... the kingdom of heaven might be obtainable now.'[7]

From Jesus to Elsewhere

What, then, happened to the ideal of justice and the life of discipleship that many early Christians believed in? It has been suggested that from the day the Empire began to embrace Christianity the church was faced with a difficult situation. 'Constantine was a Warrior king subduing and chastising opponents of truth by the law of combat. He gained absolute power and exercised it. He had no equal in battle and his wealth was beyond compare. Next to him Jesus was almost embarrassing.'[8]

There were a number of responses:

• *Spiritualisation.* It was suggested that Jesus' teachings were unrealistic as far as contemporary politics were concerned and applied only to heaven.
• *Reinterpretation.* Key passages were given new meanings. The parable of the banquet, in which people were 'compelled' to come in, and that of the wheat and the tares, in which the weeds were removed and burned, were used to justify coercion.[9]

---

[7] Christopher Hill, *The World Turned Upside Down: Radical Ideas during the English Revolution*, p. 17.

[8] Nigel Wright, *Disavowing Constantine*, p. 17.

[9] Dissidents in the Middle Ages also used the parable of the wheat and the tares from Mt. 13:24–30 to justify non-violence. Since the field was likened to the kingdom of heaven, they suggested that coercion must be illicit. See Donald F. Durnbaugh, *The Believers' Church: The History and Character of Radical Protestantism*, p. 39.

- *Privatisation.* Jesus was granted moral authority over people's personal behaviour but not over political or public affairs. This sometimes led to Christian soldiers being urged to love and pray for the enemies they killed.[10]
- *Clericalisation.* A distinction was made between clergy and laity. For Eusebius, pacifism was for clergy, monks and nuns, whereas lay Christians were obligated to defend the Empire with force.[11]
- *Separation.* An idea particularly prevalent at the time of the Reformation was that faith could be distinguished from works. It was the motivation behind people's acts that was important, not the acts themselves.
- *Marginalisation.* Sometimes the teachings of Jesus were ignored completely.

But the church was still left with a dilemma. If it was not going to look to the example and teachings of Jesus for its political ethics, where was it to turn? In fact, it found guidance and inspiration in a number of places. The Old Testament, with its histories of empires and kingdoms and its codes of law, seemed the most logical place to look. Augustine noted parallels between Israel and Christendom, and interpreted some Hebrew prophesies as foretelling Christian empire. As political thought became more sophisticated, others such as the German Calvinist Johannes Althusius turned to the polity of early Israel for insight. The Anglican reformers developed the theory of the godly prince, comparing the English monarchs to the kings of Israel. The flourishing of Hebraic studies during the Renaissance and Reformation periods produced a whole series of works on the Jewish polity as well as commentaries on the text of the Old Testament.[12]

---

[10] If a Christian killed an enemy soldier, even in a war that was considered just, he would have to do penance, usually by fasting and prayer for a year or more (Roland Bainton, *Christian Attitudes toward War and Peace: A Historical Survey and Critical Re-evaluation*).

[11] Louis Swift, *The Early Fathers on War and Military Service* (Wilmington: Michael Glazier, 1983), pp. 82–9.

[12] By, for example, Calvin, Junius, Peter Martyr and Johannes Piscator.

In the late sixteenth and seventeenth centuries, the Jewish commonwealth was a crucial model for the first modern political theorists.[13]

Even before the time of Constantine, there were some Christians in the army who appealed to the Old Testament – and possibly to other figures besides Jesus in the New Testament. They quoted the example of the centurion who believed, and pointed out that when soldiers went to John the Baptist he did not forbid them to kill but instead instructed them not to engage in extortion or threats but to be content with their wages.[14] Maybe such arguments were at first not common among the few Christians in the legions, but they were to become far more so once the empire was Christianised.

Paul's discussion of the law also seemed relevant. In particular, Romans 13 appeared to establish a basis for the authority of government (though the early Christians had often interpreted it in other ways) and there were also appeals to texts such as Romans 2:14–15, which seemed to suggest that everyone had 'the requirements of the law written on their hearts'.

Such texts as these were also employed to legitimise theories of government that had their origins outside the scriptures. Aristotle's ideas on natural law were developed by Thomas Aquinas and were still current at the time of the Reformation.[15] They also played a significant part in shaping the church's response not only to such issues as poverty but also to creation and what we now call 'the environment.' In his attack on Gnosticism in the second

---

[13] Lea Campos Boralevi, 'Classical Foundational Myths of European Republicanism: The Jewish Commonwealth', in Martin van Gelderen and Quentin Skinner (eds.), *Republicanism: A Shared European Heritage, Vol. I: Republicanism and Constitutionalism in Early Modern Europe* (Cambridge: CUP, 2002), pp. 247–262.

[14] Lk. 3:14. See Kreider, 'Military Service in the Church Orders', which quotes Tertullian in *On Idolatry*.

[15] Calvin defined natural law as 'that apprehension of the conscience which distinguishes sufficiently between just and unjust, and which deprives men of the excuse of ignorance while it proves them guilty by their own testimony.'

century, Irenaeus had worked out a theology of nature and the cosmic significance of the incarnation, death and resurrection of Jesus,[16] but this was never properly developed in Christendom.[17] With some exceptions within radical traditions, such as Benedictine practices that took up the notion of stewardship,[18] 'there was an assumption that the [environmental] status quo was natural and God-given' and that the task of human beings was to preserve it rather than manage it.[19]

From Radical Reform to Mediating Principles

In Christendom, Christians had to come to terms with another dilemma: the nature of the ethical demands that could be made of the Empire. For Augustine, politics could not be based on any genuine consensus regarding right and wrong, as there could be no agreement between the 'earthly' people who did not and could not know true justice, because they didn't know God, the source of all justice, and the citizens of heaven who did.

Before Constantine, some Christians had seen the church as a counterculture in the Empire, living out a radical rethinking of economic and family relations in a communal life marked by self-sacrifice and non-violence. But such an approach, which began with ideals of equality and justice, seemed unrealistic in the

---

[16] See C.J. Glacken, *Traces on the Rhodian Shore: Nature and Culture in Western Thought from Ancient Times to the End of the Eighteenth Century* (Berkeley: University of California Press, 1967), and also H. P. Santmire, *The Travail of Nature: The Ambiguous Ecological Promise Of Christian Theology* (Philadelphia: Fortress Press, 1985).

[17] R.J. Berry (ed.), *The Care of Creation: Focusing Concern and Action*, p. 25.

[18] Although the term may date back only to the seventeenth century. See Richard Bauckham, 'Stewardship and Relationship' in Berry (ed.), *The Care of Creation*; J. Black, *The Dominion of Man* (Edinburgh University Press, 1970); and also R. Attfield, *The Ethics of Environmental Concern* (Athens, GA: University of Georgia Press, 1991).

[19] *The Care of Creation*, p. 25.

context of the church's new alliance with government. The impetus towards radical reform diminished as Christendom brought with it a change of emphasis to principles of mediation designed to temper the negative effects of existing structures and practices.

For example, the practice of buying slaves in order to set them free became increasingly rare. In the seventh century Eloi, the wealthy Bishop of Noyon, bought British and Saxon slaves in batches of 50 and 100 so that he could liberate them. But this was rare. The church concentrated more on making conditions for slaves more humane. Indeed, it also endorsed, and sometimes even demanded, enslavement. When the Bishop of Le Mans transferred a large estate to the Abbey of St. Vincent in 572, ten slaves went with it. In the early ninth century, the Abbey of St. Germain des Prés listed 25 of its 278 householders as slaves. When Pope Gregory XI excommunicated the Florentines in the fourteenth century, he ordered that any of them that were captured should be enslaved. In 1488, King Ferdinand sent 100 Moorish slaves to Pope Innocent VIII for him to present as gifts to his cardinals and other luminaries of his court.

The church also set about drawing up guidelines for Christian politicians, economists, civil servants and military strategists with an empire to run and defend. One of the most significant ideas proposed was that of 'just war'. Originally conceived by classical philosophers such as Plato and Cicero, it was adopted and developed by theologians such as Augustine and Aquinas. Instead of the ideal of non-violence, it offered guidance for political leaders concerning the right way to act in times of potential conflict. The theory was intended not to justify war but to prevent it, but it was subsequently used many times to legitimise the use of force.

From Useless to Useful

The concept of 'just war' is one example of the way the church assisted governments by providing a way to justify their actions. Where once the emperor had found it hard to use to his advantage a community that was fast gaining influence in society, in

Christendom the church became helpful to political leaders. As Christianity attained pre-eminence, the ideas of theologians lent weight to the authority of the state. For example, Augustine's concept of original sin and his emphasis on the depravity of humankind validated its role in restraining and punishing the worst excesses of human vice. From the eighth century onwards the church anointed monarchs, who began to wear priestly vestments as a symbol of their sovereignty. It also took part in other state ceremonies, and often publicly blessed what the state did.

The church's enhanced position also opened up new possibilities for the control – by both church and state – of more radical groups which might threaten the status quo much as the early Christians had. The church's own interests now seemed to coincide far more closely with those of the state. When the Franciscans stressed the importance of poverty, this was considered potentially subversive and Pope John XXII declared it heretical to believe that Jesus and his disciples had no possessions.[20]

Much later, when a new brand of Christianity emerged from the evangelical revivals of the 1730s, its message of justification by faith apart from works was seen to undermine morality. The ecclesiastical authorities intervened and John Wesley was locked out of churches and obliged to preach instead in the open air.[21]

From Illegitimate to Legitimised

In the new relationship between church and state it was not just the role of Christians to offer guidance to political leaders, or even bless their activities. Many were political leaders themselves. As we have seen, some in the early church believed that Christians

---

[20] Chidester, *Christianity: A Global History*, pp. 263–4.

[21] Ironically, the revivals later came to be seen as one of the factors that helped England to avoid a bloody revolution. See William E. H. Lecky, *A History of England in the Eighteenth Century* (London: Longmans, Green and Company, 1921); Chap. 11, 'The Transforming Power of the Cross', in E.P. Thompson, *The Making of the English Working Classes* (London: Penguin, 1991).

could not hold political office; but there is evidence that, even then, there were those who did. Nonetheless, it was generally accepted that Christians could hold political office only if they were not involved in killing, imprisonment or coercion. The fact that the emperor now professed the Christian faith meant that, even as the foundations of Christendom were being laid, these assumptions had to be re-examined. The issue was now not *whether* Christians could hold political office but *how* they should behave when they did.

The principal solution was to draw a distinction between personal conduct on the one hand and the actions of someone in political office on the other. In Christendom, Christians were able to hold public office on the basis that different standards applied to their political actions. Indeed, as the functions of government increasingly were understood to have been ordained by God, Christians felt all the more able to justify their part in carrying them out. It wasn't long before it was accepted that if a Christian neglected a political duty – for example, to punish a wrongdoer, and even to kill them – they were being disobedient not only to the government but to God as well.

From Social Solvent to Social Glue

It has been observed that Constantine more likely embraced Christianity out of political expediency than as a result of conversion.[22] Whatever the truth of that, there is no doubt that his predecessors in pre-Christendom had been aware of the potential of co-opting religious ideas to shape the Empire, reinforce its institutions and unite its citizens.[23] Whereas in pre-Christendom Christianity had been regarded as a threat to the social order, in Christendom it came to be seen as glue that held society together.

---

[22] L. Verduin, *The Anatomy of a Hybrid: A Study in Church-State Relationships* (Grand Rapids: Eerdmans, 1976), p. 102. See also Nigel Wright, *Disavowing Constantine*, p. 15.
[23] Charles Villa-Vicencio, *Between Christ and Caesar: Classic and Contemporary Texts on Church and State*, pp. 4–5.

The church did little to discourage such a perception. When Rome was sacked by the Goths under Alaric in 410, many Pagans blamed the disaster on the fact that the Empire had abandoned its traditional gods. Augustine set about refuting this and, keen to find common ground between church and empire, argued that every society was bound together by certain shared interests. Generally, he said, the City of Man loves domination, but it also loves to rule in peace too – and such temporal peace is also beneficial to the citizens of the Heavenly City, because it provides a secure environment in which they can work out their eternal destiny. Church and state must co-operate to protect the fabric of society against conflict, disruption and disintegration.

The idea that Christianity should be the glue that held the social order together was in marked contrast to the views of many early Christians, whose practices challenged and undermined the economic norms, family patterns and religious conventions of the society around them – and yet this idea became dominant. Indeed, when from time to time Christians emerged who challenged the social order, attempts were made by both church and state to deal with them – often harshly.

In the fourteenth century, the preacher John Ball criticised the feudal system and angered the church hierarchy, which was supporting the nobles in their efforts to revoke all tenancy agreements and return the peasants to serfdom.[24] He was imprisoned on the orders of the Bishop of Norwich, and when on his release he carried on preaching, the Archbishop of Canterbury gave instructions that anyone found listening to his sermons should be punished.[25] In 1525, Martin Luther suggested in his tract 'Against the Robbing and Murdering Hordes of Peasants'[26] that anyone who killed a rebellious peasant was performing a service to God.

---

[24] See Chris Bryant, *Possible Dreams: A Personal History of the British Christian Socialists*, p. 2, for the location of John Ball within the historical tradition of Christian Socialism.

[25] Mark O'Brien, *When Adam Delved and Eve Span: A History of the Peasants' Revolt of 1381*.

[26] Quoted in E.G. Rupp and B. Drewery (eds.), *Martin Luther* (London: Edward Arnold, 1970).

Taking the side of the rulers against a variety of radicals who were forming alternative Christian communities, he aligned his own reforms with 'the interests of the cities.'[27]

From Function to Form

Augustine's focus on 'temporal order' was accompanied by a shift of emphasis from the 'function' of institutions (such as doing justice) to their 'form'. Whereas the early church had radically reordered institutions such as the family in the name of justice, now institutions were seen as things to be defended and the church became increasingly active in endorsing them. For example, at the end of the ninth century the benediction of a priest became a necessary part of a marriage ceremony.

Thomas Aquinas took up this theme, emphasising the importance of social order. For him, obedience to Government was crucial. The authorities were the chief guardians of the common good. Evil would flourish when order disappeared.

The theme of covenant that was later developed in the Reformed tradition also involved a distinctive vision of society that set out the proper relationship between institutions. Covenant theologians understood the whole community to be fundamentally bound to God as Creator, and thus bound to one another. This prior relationship to God, they said, must govern, order and constrain relationships between individuals and between, and within, social and political institutions. Althusius suggested that politics was the art 'of associating men for the purpose of establishing, cultivating, and conserving social life among them.'[28] He suggested that the function of the state was to protect and foster social life as it was expressed in five types of association: family, college, city, province and kingdom. Like Abraham Kuyper after him, he emphasised that each of these had their own integrity.

---

[27] Chidester, *Christianity: A Global History*, p. 321.
[28] F.S. Carney (tr. and abbr.), *The Politics of Johannes Althusius* (Indianapolis: Liberty Fund, 1995).

From Freedom to Imposition

If Christianity could hold society together and, indeed, protect its institutions, it made sense for governments to impose 'Christian' ideas, religious practices and moral standards, particularly in the sphere of personal conduct. Constantine had set an example by forbidding divination and magic even in private, closing some prominent temples and ordaining the death penalty for anyone who tried to prevent Jews from converting to Christianity. Many laws were to follow that placed restrictions on other faiths, and particularly Judaism. Specific religious observances were made mandatory and harsh penalties were imposed for immoral behaviour, especially sexual offences. Divorce was made more difficult.

As the church's views changed, laws were adjusted accordingly. Augustine, and most other Christian thinkers of his period, equated the practice of abortion with murder as long as the foetus concerned had become a 'fully formed' human. Subsequently, the church focused on the moment of 'quickening' (when the soul was believed to enter the body) and the first authoritative collection of canon law, which was adopted in 1140, enshrined the conclusion that early abortion was *not* in fact murder. The first references to abortion in English law, in the thirteenth century, followed the church's teaching and accepted its concept of quickening.

Laws also changed throughout Christendom as political arrangements changed, and many underlying patterns emerged. In England, for example, the death penalty was imposed for adultery and fornication.[29] In 1533, the Buggery Act introduced by Henry VIII brought sodomy within the scope of English statute law for the first time and made it punishable by hanging. There were also laws outlawing blasphemy.[30]

---

[29] The Adultery Act of May 1650 was introduced in the 'rump' parliament that repealed the statute that required compulsory attendance at church dating back to the reign of Elizabeth I.

[30] For example, the Blasphemy Act of 1697 in England, which made an offence of 'denying certain tenets of the Christian religion after having been brought up in, or having professed, that religion.' For a detailed account of the practice and punishment of heresy and blasphemy in both

From Persecuted to Persecutor

The Edict of Milan had promised Christians protection from persecution throughout the Empire. In practice, it was only the objects of persecution that changed. In an edict of 380, Theodosius I introduced measures that set clear boundaries around the church, excluding those not in communion with the Bishops of Rome and Alexandria. Christian groups that refused to accept this definition faced penalties including the seizure of their property and possessions.

Subsequently, both church and state were involved in persecuting not only people of other religions or of no religion at all but also those Christians who were judged to have erred from the 'true' faith.

Augustine appears to have been at first opposed to any sort of coercion of non-Christians, on the grounds that belief had to be voluntary. But later, it seems, he decided that coercion might produce genuine belief, by forcing people to listen to teachings they would otherwise have dismissed or ignored. When the church in North Africa came into conflict with the Donatists, a large and well-organised Christian movement, laws against heretics were applied to the movement. Augustine also advocated asking the Empire for protection against violence, but other bishops persuaded it instead to send its troops to compel the Donatists to embrace orthodoxy.

Afterwards, Augustine was struck by the fact that many of these people seemed grateful for their enforced change of heart and he wrote to another bishop, Vincentius, defending the policy.[31] He posed the question: 'Why ... should not the church use force in compelling her lost sons to return, if the lost sons compelled others to their destruction?'[32]

---

[30] (*Continued*) the past and the present, see Nicholas Walter, *Blasphemy: Ancient and Modern* (London: Rationalist Press Association, 1990) and also David Nash, *Blasphemy in Modern Britain: 1789 to the Present.*

[31] Letter 93, to Vincentius.

[32] *The Correction of the Donatists*, pp. 22–4.

Later, inquisitors of the Roman Catholic Church would travel widely to search out traces of religious error, superstition and heresy. The Waldensians, who challenged the church's monopoly on the right to preach and ignored its exclusion of women from the priesthood, were driven out of cities and excommunicated. During the Reformation and beyond, Catholics persecuted Protestants and Protestants Catholics. Luther took the side of the authorities not only against the peasants but also against radical reformers such as the Anabaptists.

There was persecution outside the Christian faith, too. Jews were consistently subjected to persecution. Constantine's son, Constantius, forbade them to marry Christians or to own Christian slaves. In 388, synagogues in Rome and Callinicum were razed by Christians. When Theodosius insisted that restitution be made, a leading churchman of the day, Ambrose, suggested that it would be sinful to help Jews in this way. The emperor yielded to the will of the church and withdrew his demand for justice. In 438, the emperor Theodosius II promulgated a new code of law that excluded Jews from all political and military service and reenacted a law which forbade the building of new Jewish synagogues.

Under the emperor Justin I (518–27), Jews were forbidden to make wills, to receive inheritances and to give testimony in court or perform any other legal act. Marriage between a Christian and a Jew was made a capital offence. By the end of the sixth century, Jews were being subjected to forcible baptism. By the beginning of the new millennium, Jewish communities were being massacred in Europe, notably in Rome, Orléans, Rouen and Limoges and throughout the Rhineland. In England, there was a horrific massacre of York's Jewish population in 1190. The Fourth Lateran Council in 1215 debarred Jews from owning land, and from all military and civil functions. It also required all Jews to wear distinctive clothing and obliged them to fast during Lent.

Between the beginning of the sixteenth century and the end of the seventeenth, many alleged witches were hunted out and either burned or hanged.

From Loving Enemy to Critical Friend

Although the early Christians acknowledged that the state restrained some of the worst excesses of sin, they often viewed it as an enemy they had to love. Christendom provided the context for a more accepting view of government.

Augustine's view of the Empire, like that of the early Christians, has been regarded as largely negative. He suggested that if the Fall had not taken place and sin had not entered the world, the institution of government would not have existed. He has been seen as the first major philosopher to reject classical conceptions of politics, including the idea that the state is the highest achievement of human society.[33] Neither did he have any illusions regarding the essence of political authority: coercion. Coercive rule was, for him, a necessary aspect of human existence but not one that deserved to be revered.[34]

However, his conclusion that church and state should work together to maintain the social order and his acknowledgement that coercion was a legitimate means were a marked departure from the beliefs of those early Christians who saw the social and political order as a front for demonic forces with which Christians were called to struggle.

---

[33] Linda C. Raeder, 'Augustine and the Case for Limited Government' in *Humanitas*, vol. XVI no. 2, 2003, pp. 94–106. To the classical mind, human flourishing was inextricably entwined with the flourishing of the state, and personal and political fulfillment were symbiotic and inseparable – although, as Raeder notes, 'Plato did share Augustine's aversion toward politics as such; on his view, it was an order of affairs intrinsically inferior to, say, philosophy and the contemplative life. This is just one of several similarities between their respective views that have earned Augustine the title of the "Christian Plato".'

[34] Raeder, 'Augustine and the Case for Limited Government'. Others, however, have suggested that Augustine actually had a more positive view of government, considering political life a substantive good that fulfilled a human longing for a kind of wholeness. See, for example, John von Heyking, *Augustine and Politics as Longing in the World* (Columbia: University of Missouri Press, 2001).

Augustine introduced a more positive understanding of the state that was subsequently developed by others. Aquinas, for example, suggested that states existed before the Fall. For him, obedience was what bound human society together, but with the Fall spontaneous obedience to the state came to an end. Accordingly, God had given rulers the important power to force people to obey.[35]

From Servant to Subservient

In Christendom, sometimes the church ruled governments and sometimes governments ruled the church – but whereas previously the church had not been subservient to secular power, at times in Christendom it certainly became so.

The early church had often seen itself as a servant of the state in the sense that Christ came to serve the world; but this meant that it was also prepared to disobey government when necessary. The church in Christendom was prepared to struggle with political leaders for power, Christians became far more *subservient* when it came to the laws of the region in which they lived. Because of the deals the church struck with the other powers of its day, it was often obliged to give its support to princes, kings and emperors.

Certainly, there were attempts to free some areas from government control, particularly as Christendom declined. The Reformers were at pains to keep matters of 'faith' under their own jurisdiction. John Calvin concentrated on winning the church autonomy from the civic authorities in Geneva. Luther suggested that there were limits to the duty of obedience to political leaders and matters of faith lay outside their remit. But this does not mean that he supported dissent against authority. On the contrary: princes were God's representatives, and whoever resisted them resisted God.

---

[35] Hence Paul's statement in Rom. 13:1–2 that authority comes from God.

From Barrier to Bridge

Whereas the Empire had been regarded by many in the early church as a barrier to God's new regime, Christendom encouraged an understanding of government as something that helped to promote the interests of the Kingdom of God. Augustine suggested that temporal authority helped to create the right conditions for the advance of the Kingdom. Aquinas went further: the state was necessary for people to reach their *telos*[36] – to become citizens of the Heavenly City. Governments were necessary and fundamental to God's purposes.

Often, the early church had seen Jesus as a liberator who came to rescue those who were oppressed under the law. As Paul told the Galatians: 'When the fullness of time had come, God sent his Son, born of a woman, born under law, in order to redeem those who were under the law.'[37] In Christendom, however, the law was seen less and less as something from which Jesus set people free and more and more as something good to be endorsed, supported and employed as a basis for government and an aid to God's purposes.

From Respect to Reverence

In Christendom, too, government was held in higher esteem. Whereas in the early church the idea was prevalent that the person who most wanted to lead was least qualified, Augustine and Aquinas both suggested that ruling power was given by nature to the best and most intelligent.

Luther may have had a low opinion of many politicians, but they were 'fools' or 'scoundrels' because of their lack of respect for God. The Reformers still ascribed great power to godly rulers, including the power to reform the structures of the church. Indeed, to our way of thinking they were remarkably reluctant to undertake the reform of the church on their own authority. They expected rulers to take responsibility both for the church and for the moral condition of the nation.

---

[36] A Greek word meaning 'end', 'goal' or 'purpose'.

[37] Gal. 4:4–5.

In England, the monarch, who was closely bound to the
Church of England by their coronation oath to preserve its established status and was consecrated to God by their anointing, was
endowed with an almost mystical status as 'supreme governor' of
the church as well as the state.

Conclusion

Whether it was deliberate or not, the moves made by the Roman
emperors in the fourth century followed an already classic political strategy: 'If you can't beat 'em, join 'em' – or, in this case, 'get
them to join *you*'. It has been said that Constantine's purpose was
to allow Christians to share power without making life difficult
for the powerful.[38] In this way, a potential threat to the Empire
was neutralised.

This did not mean that no threat remained. Christianity was
not always helpful to governments in Christendom. 'Who will rid
me of this turbulent priest?' Henry II asked, referring to his friend
Thomas à Becket, as he tried to bring the institutional church
under his control. There were times when political leaders were
subordinate to the church. Pope Gregory VII famously claimed
precedence as senior 'vicar' over the emperor Henry IV at
Canossa in 1077, and later Innocent III asserted that 'no king can
rightly reign unless he devoutly serve Christ's vicar.'

However, Christendom changed the nature of the threat the
church posed. Whereas it had previously been perceived as something that could subvert the political order, now the church was
sometimes a collaborator in it, at other times a rival. In pre-
Christendom, the Empire fought in vain to bring the early
Christians under its control: as N.T. Wright has put it, 'Rome …
could not cope, as history demonstrated, with a community
owing imitative allegiance to the crucified and risen Jesus.'[39] In
Christendom, the political battle moved to more familiar ground.

---

[38] Nigel Wright, *Disavowing Constantine*, p. 18.
[39] N.T. Wright, 'Paul and Caesar' in Bartholomew et al. (eds.), *A Royal
Priesthood?*

As political leaders struggled with the church, they were able to employ methods and techniques they were more accustomed to.

The arguments advanced by Augustine and others were often based on the premise that pre-Christendom political approaches were unrealistic given the new relationship between church and government. Certainly, Christendom forced Christians to face up to some hard political questions.

The early Christians perhaps had a broader perspective, believing that God would bring in the Kingdom and that all things would be made right again. In Christendom, such ideas were played down: things developed rapidly in an unexpected direction, and the focus of the church shortened and narrowed to the realities of government. The eschatological perspective of the early Christians often made them willing to sacrifice everything for the poor and needy and even to lay down their lives, in Christendom the church became far more concerned with defending what it perceived as its own interests.

Although it is unlikely that Constantine intended this, new opportunities arose for emperors, kings and princes to divide and rule the church. Once Christians had been united by a shared political understanding of their citizenship of the Kingdom of God, but now their loyalties were split. By the early fourth century, with widespread persecution of Christians at an end, their leaders began to dispute among themselves. Bishops in the big cities emerged as an élite and rivalries broke out over the status and prestige of churches.[40] Christians now persecuted Christians. They competed not only for political control over the church's doctrines but also for power and influence over the mechanisms of government. Christendom became the scene of something previously unthinkable: Christians killing one another, both within states and during wars between them.

Moreover, now that the political priorities of Christians had changed, successive political leaders were able to employ new incentives and penalties. Patronage became an option, for example, as governments often had a say in who was appointed to

---

[40] Chidester, *Christianity: A Global History*, p. 98.

particular positions in the church and how certain valuable resources were allocated. As the church sought to maintain, or improve its position at the centre, it paid more heed to the laws that the state enforced.

4

Opportunity Knocks

It might have been expected that the end of Christendom – something so defined and shaped by the alignment of church and government – would signal an end to, or at least a decline in, Christian political engagement. The Reformation brought with it a new distinction for many Christians between matters spiritual and temporal. The philosophical movement of the Enlightenment introduced a new basis for political authority that diminished the church's control. And certainly, in the death throes of Christendom, some sections of the church withdrew from political involvement.[1]

Absolute disengagement was short-lived, however. In fact, post-Christendom has been characterised by a flurry of Christian political activity as well as a fundamental change in the way the church has engaged with government. These are the most notable developments:

• *New para-church groups have emerged.* Organisations have been formed with the explicit goal of influencing government. Often bypassing denominational and church structures and recruiting support across denominations, they frequently

---

[1] Most notably evangelicals at the end of the nineteenth century. See David O. Moberg, *The Great Reversal: Evangelism versus Social Concern*, and also David Bebbington, *Evangelicalism in Modern Britain: A History from the 1730s to the 1980s*. However, the Reformers earlier also demarcated large sections of life as the preserve of 'secular' government.

appeal to both lay Christians and clergy, and set out to secure legislative change around single or specific sets of issues.

- *New political movements have emerged.* Distinct from parachurch groups, which often lobby government directly, movements have been formed that aim to mobilise Christians to political action in large numbers and bring about political change.[2]
- *Existing groups have expanded or created new political functions.* Organisations and church denominations, many of which were set up in Christendom, have initiated or expanded lobbying and campaigning activities.[3]
- *Explicitly Christian groupings within the main political parties have emerged.* Each of the three main political parties now has recognisable Christian groupings.[4]
- *Christian political parties have emerged.*[5]

It isn't easy to identify which of these are a response to the passing of Christendom and which are more a reaction to the changing nature of political engagement in wider society. Some Christian approaches may display some of the attitudes of Christendom, but (in the broadest sense of the term) whatever politics the church currently pursues is 'post-Christendom politics'.

Indeed, many of the developments listed above can be seen as having emerged during Christendom's decline. Glimpses of them could be seen even in the height of Christendom – Christian political movements have been a consistent feature of dissent within

---

[2] Examples include Faithworks, Jubilee 2000 and the Movement for Christian Democracy.

[3] The Evangelical Alliance is one good example of an organisation formed in the nineteenth century that now has an active public affairs department. Development agencies have also notably become more political in their focus. Even Christian media such as Premier Radio are engaging in campaigning.

[4] The Christian Socialist Movement, the Conservative Christian Fellowship and the Liberal Democrat Christian Forum.

[5] For example, the Christian People's Alliance, Operation Christian Vote and the Pro-Life Alliance (which, though not explicitly Christian, was set up by Christians).

Christendom from the time of the English Civil War.[6] One of the most famous of these was the movement to abolish the transatlantic slave trade.[7] Other para-church groups and movements, most notably those of evangelical character, as well as Christian Democratic parties on the Continent, were evident in the nineteenth century.

Many Christian political developments in the dying years of Christendom were undoubtedly reactions to change outside the church. Christian Socialism was articulated by F.D. Maurice and others in the 1850s, in response to early socialism. In 1891, Pope Leo XIII issued *Rerum Novarum*,[8] an encyclical 'on the condition of the working classes', following the Communist Manifesto of 40 years before. It addressed a society of 'immense wealth for a small number and deepest poverty for the multitude', and was the principal inspiration for Christian Democracy. New political ideas have also emerged. Pope Pius XI outlined the principle of 'subsidiarity' as a vital counterbalance to the centralising tendencies of both capitalism and collectivist socialism. In 1931, *Quadragesimo Anno* first introduced into Catholic teaching the term 'social justice', to be set alongside the traditional concept of natural justice.

Many of these developments have come into their own in post-Christendom, however. The *idea* of Christian Socialism may have been current for a hundred and fifty years, but the Christian Socialist Movement gives its own date of birth as 1960. Christian Democratic parties really took off after the Second World War. Many of the new groups are distinguished by the length of their agendas (which address groups of issues rather than single issues) and the breadth of both their appeal (from individuals and local churches to organisations and even whole denominations) and their financial support.

---

[6] See Hill, *The World Turned Upside Down*, and also Bryant, *Possible Dreams*, chap. 1, 'Posthumous Comrades'.

[7] See Robert Anstey, *The Atlantic Slave Trade and British Abolition, 1760–1810*.

[8] This can be translated 'Of New or Revolutionary Things'.

To some extent we can measure how far these characteristics are a consequence of post-Christendom rather than a result of wider changes in the way politics is done by drawing a comparison with places where post-Christendom is less strong. In the US, for example, no new Christian parties have been formed and there are not the same kinds of Christian grouping within the main parties – possibly because the Republicans are often considered 'Christian' anyway. On the other hand, just as in Britain, many of the Christian pressure, lobby and campaign groups that are active in the US are a response to the perceived decline of Christian influence on government, and they often use the same methods as their counterparts here. However, as Jim Wallis has pointed out, the agenda of the religious right in particular is limited to a handful of issues. Similarly, although many civil-rights movements of the last century were religious in inspiration, the Democrats have been reluctant to draw on the strength of religious groups.[9]

Above all, it is the collective mobilisation of Christians in large numbers across a wide range of issues to influence government that characterises the political changes that have accompanied post-Christendom. This represents a fundamental change in the political character of the church. Since post-Christendom has involved a perceived loss of political power and influence, Christians have reacted by creating or expanding explicitly political operations, groups, parties and movements to influence government. Indeed, such has been the explosion of political activity that some people are even claiming that the political fortunes of Christians are being reversed, and religion is now a much more 'significant and potent force' than it was 30 years ago.[10] However, the actual extent of that influence remains the subject of debate.

---

[9] Jim Wallis, *God's Politics: Why the American Right Gets It Wrong and the Left Doesn't Get It*.
[10] Submission to the House of Lords Select Committee on the BBC Charter Review from senior members of the faith communities, 2 November 2005.

Political Issues

There is almost no area of politics untouched by this new Christian activity. However, this is not always apparent to the public, as the kind of issues the media generally prefer to report are those that provoke 'moral outrage' – in which, admittedly, Christians are often involved.

So, for example, a good deal of attention has been paid to the furore surrounding abortion. Pro-life groups have campaigned against the 1967 Abortion Act and the way it is enforced. They have also sought to change public opinion, by explaining how 'terminations' are done and pointing out that an unborn child is a human being, and provide support for women deciding whether to have an abortion. The issues in this general area have multiplied as advances in medical technology hold out the promise of help to infertile couples and those who are injured or ill through the use of human embryos and clones. Many of the pro-life groups have objected to these developments and have become politically active on this front as well.

Likewise, Christians have had much to say about issues surrounding the end of life, from concern over the treatment of elderly people to euthanasia. In particular, there has been concern that the law on so-called 'mercy killing' will be liberalised.

Many of the groups and organisations engaged in these areas are also active in family policy and issues of sexuality. Christians have been involved in work around the repeal of Section 28 of the Local Government Act, the age of consent, civil partnerships and gay adoption. They have even gone as far as to examine the law on prostitution and the working conditions of prostitutes.

There has been much concern about the way the tax regime treats married couples and the way the law handles divorce. The treatment of children, too, has also exercised many churches and para-church groups – not only issues of poverty and protection but also the question of smacking, on which Christians have opposed each other. Education – and especially religious education – has often roused Christians to political action, as has the levels of violence in the media, and media standards in general.

But there are very many other issues on which Christians have been active that have not hit the headlines in the same way. The escalating numbers of people in prison[11] – and particularly women and black, young and elderly people – have moved Christians to respond. Some have advocated alternatives to prison, but others have objected that sentences are not long enough. There has been continual lobbying over successive criminal justice bills, and Christians have also had significant input in the debate over drugs policy (most notably the decriminalisation of cannabis) and gun control.

In the area of economics, Christians have focused especially on the impact of markets, and also on alternatives to them. They have also done work on questions of unemployment, personal debt, taxation and the redistribution of wealth, and there have been attempts to influence the government's budget.

In response to the threat of climate change, churches have become involved in international campaigns and have also examined how their own behaviour may be contributing to global warming. On animal rights, the church has been criticised for staying silent,[12] but bishops have denounced the buying and wearing of fur[13] and other Christians have protested against fox hunting, though some have leapt to the defence of such practices.

Churches and Christian campaign groups spoke out strongly about the introduction of the National Lottery, and have since issued statements on the subjects of age limits, debt and the size of the prizes.[14] They have also had significant impact on subsequent gambling bills.[15]

---

[11] In 2004, the prison population in England and Wales reached the highest level ever recorded.

[12] Andrew Linzey, *Animal Gospel: Christian Faith as though Animals Matter* (London: Hodder and Stoughton, 1998).

[13] Andrew Linzey (ed.), *Cruelty and Christian Conscience: Bishops Say No to Fur* (Nottingham: Lynx, 1992).

[14] See Keith Tondeur, *What Price the Lottery?* (Oxford: Monarch, 1996).

[15] Campaigns by the Methodist Church and the Salvation Army in 2005 resulted in major changes to the Gambling Bill, including the reduction

Christians have also been active on many international fronts. Development agencies such as Christian Aid have repeatedly become involved as advocates of behalf of the Palestinians in the Occupied Territories. Other Christians, often associated with Zionist positions, have lobbied on behalf of the state of Israel. Others have campaigned for or against sanctions against countries such as South Africa and Iraq, or have spoken out on behalf of people suffering in Burma, Zimbabwe and a host of other countries.[16] Overseas aid has been a constant concern and the subject of several campaigns. Closer to home, the welfare of immigrants and asylum seekers has focused Christian attention on a succession of bills going through Parliament.

The churches have also had much to say about wars such as the Falklands Conflict, the 1991 Gulf War and the recent invasions of Afghanistan and Iraq. They have also spoken out about the commercial arms trade, as well as issues of nuclear proliferation and disarmament. And they have contributed not only words but money and other practical help in response to bloodshed and violence in Rwanda, Darfur, Bosnia, Israel and the Occupied Territories and Northern Ireland.

They have continually addressed racial intolerance and prejudice, compiling their own reports and responding to other people's.[17]

As the notion of a 'Christian' country has lost currency and a more religiously plural society has emerged, issues have arisen around the treatment of religion under the law, especially in the areas of liberty, blasphemy and discrimination. Christians have pressed for freedom of worship for believers all over the world,

---

[15] (*Continued*) of the number of 'super-casinos' and the removal of fruit machines from 6,000 premises frequented by children. The campaign used a range of public-affairs techniques, PR tactics and grass-roots mobilisation. See 'Gambling Bill Strategy Pays Off', *Christian Herald*, 27 October 2005.

[16] Such as the press release from the Methodist Church, 'Methodist Church calls for action to end Darfur violence', 3 February 2005.

[17] Such as the MacPherson Report (Home Office, February 1999) which followed the inquiry into the murder of Stephen Lawrence.

and have also considered the place of religious festivals and holidays. Since the events of 11 September 2001, the 'war on terror' has intensified many of these debates and has also focused attention on the disaffection and alienation from the wider culture that religion can cause, and the violence these can engender.

Christian Approaches

Amidst the plethora of groups, issues and perspectives, a degree of coherence can nonetheless be observed. There is a growing awareness of how different issues are interconnected – how, for example:

- The arms trade relates both to debt and to conflict across the world.
- Allowing immigration may be a good way to deliver effectual aid to people in developing countries.
- Global development is linked to global warming.[18]
- The tax regime and the deportation of refugees[19] both are implicated in the break-up of families, which in turn has connections with rising levels of crime, which can also be attributed to wider social and economic changes.[20]

---

[18] In 1983, the World Council of Churches added the need to maintain the integrity of creation to its programme of pursuing peace and justice. See also 'Up in Smoke? Threats from and Responses to the Impact of Global Warming on Human Development' (London, New Economics Foundation: 2004). Endorsed by Archbishop Desmond Tutu, this report was produced by the Working Group on Climate Change and Development, which included a number of explicitly Christian agencies and campaigns including World Vision, Tearfund, Christian Aid and Operation Noah.

[19] See, for example, 'Breaking Up More Families: Case Studies of Families Facing Deportation', Churches' Commission for Racial Justice.

[20] See 'A Place of Redemption', a report issued in December 2004 by the department for Christian responsibility and citizenship of the Catholic Bishops of England and Wales.

Christian movements, denominations and para-church groups, as well as political parties, have practised 'joined-up' political thinking. In the run-up to the 1997 general election, the Catholic bishops of England and Wales produced a report, *The Common Good and the Catholic Church's Social Teaching*, which urged voters to assess the different candidates in the light of their church's social teaching about the dignity of the human person.

Others have hammered out political principles that offer a distinctive approach to politics and in some cases have given rise to political programmes. Notable examples would be the Movement for Christian Democracy and the Christian People's Alliance, who have both developed principles of Christian Democracy. The Jubilee Centre in Cambridge has pioneered a 'relational' approach to government as a framework, agenda and strategy for social reform.[21] Still others have developed values-based approaches, such as the 'justice and peace' groups of the Catholic church.

Another feature of post-Christendom politics is its global perspective. Many of the issues with which Christians are deeply involved – global warming, developing-world debt, trade justice, the need for cheap medicines in developing countries, the international arms trade, immigration and asylum, nuclear proliferation, support for the persecuted church – have worldwide implications, but churches are also seeking to develop perspectives and strategies that look further than our national borders. This could include, for example, recognising that every country in Europe faces a degree of poverty and social exclusion and asking how churches should respond.[22] Others have been looking at the impact of

---

[21] See, for example, Michael Schluter and David Lee, *The R Factor* (London: Hodder and Stoughton, 1993); Schluter and John Ashcroft (eds.), *Jubilee Manifesto: A Framework, Agenda and Strategy for Christian Social Reform* (Leicester: IVP, 2005).

[22] Herman Noordegraaf and Rainer Volz (eds.), *European Churches Confronting Poverty: Social Action against Social Exclusion* (Bochum: SWI Verlag, 2005).

globalisation[23] and exploring whether it can be made to work for the poor.[24]

Sometimes the churches' response has involved the formation of global partnerships. Both Jubilee 2000 and Make Poverty History mobilised Christians and others around the world in a concerted effort to influence the leaders of the G8. Micah Challenge, which was spearheaded by the World Evangelical Alliance (representing three million local churches in 111 countries) and a network of over 270 Christian relief and development agencies, urged Christians in a hundred countries to press their governments for action to halve global poverty by 2015. There has also been a growth in advocacy on behalf of Christians around the world who are being persecuted or oppressed.[25]

Clergy and laity are working more closely with each other and Christians are collaborating not only across denominational divides but also with people outside the church. They are also drawing inspiration from diverse sources. Those who opposed government proposals to outlaw incitement to religious hatred found common cause with comedians and secularists amongst others. The Keep Sunday Special campaign formed alliances with trade unions. The support of national newspapers has been enlisted in various campaigns – to cancel developing-world debt (*The Guardian*), for example, and to oppose the removal of religious symbols (the *Daily Mail*, *Daily Express* and *The Sun*).

Electoral Activity

One of the most notable features of post-Christendom politics has been the encouragement given to Christians to vote. At the 2005

---

[23] The Capitalism Project (September 2000–August 2004) at the London Institute for Contemporary Christianity gave rise to a collection of papers, Peter Heslam (ed.), *Globalization and the Good*.

[24] Andrew Bradstock and Paul Murray, *Global Capitalism and the Gospel of Justice: Politics, Economics and the UK Churches – Edited papers from the Ushaw 2001 Conference* (London: Christian Socialist Movement, 2003).

[25] Most notably by the Jubilee Campaign, Christian Solidarity Worldwide and Barnabas Fund.

general election, Christians were urged by many agencies to 'make their cross count' at the ballot box.[26] Many Christian groups express disapproval of failure to vote, which they equate with apathy.[27]

There are ever-increasing attempts to get politicians to recognise the influence of the church and take Christians' votes seriously, often at general elections.[28] At successive general and European elections during the 1990s, the Movement for Christian Democracy sent questionnaires to MPs to elicit their political views on a range of issues and then made the results public via telephone hotlines.[29] The advent of the internet has allowed a number of other Christian groups to take this further. Dozens of different election guides have been published by pressure groups, interest groups and denominations to help Christians to decide how to cast their votes. At the 2005 general election, the Catholic Bishops' Conference of England and Wales encouraged Catholics to question parliamentary candidates on a number of 'key issues' before deciding who to vote for.

One priority for Christian groups at elections has been to combat extremism. The Methodist Church has issued many statements urging people to oppose racist political groups and parties,[30] and others too have focused on how debates are conducted, criticising (for example) the use of asylum seekers as 'political footballs'.[31]

---

[26] Such organisations included, for example, the Evangelical Alliance, Churches Together in Britain and Ireland, Care and the Roman Catholic, Anglican and Methodist Churches.

[27] See, for example, 'Election Fever', *PQ* vol. 5 no. 8, 14 April 2005 from the Evangelical Alliance.

[28] See the press release from the Christian Institute 'Christians publish votes of MPs on moral issues', 23 May 2001.

[29] See David Alton, *Faith in Britain* (London: Hodder and Stoughton, 1991).

[30] 'As Britain approaches the General Election, when people exercise their democratic right and responsibility to vote, we restate the Methodist Church's conviction that political parties based upon racist policies are contrary to a Christian understanding of God's love' – press release from the Methodist Church, 'Statement on racism', 15 April 2005.

[31] Press release from the Methodist Church, 'Methodist Church warns against using immigration as a political football', 13 April 2005.

Christians are also being encouraged to join political parties[32] and get involved in party politics between elections.[33] They appear to be doing so in increasing numbers. Some organisations have set up internship programmes for graduates to make them more effective in a career in public life. There are now established Christian groupings in all the main political parties. Although they don't all divulge the number of MPs and peers that belong to them, it has been estimated that between one-sixth and a quarter of the members of the House of Commons are associated with the Christian Socialist Movement, the Conservative Christian Fellowship or the Liberal Democrat Christian Forum.[34]

Christian political parties have also sought funding for their councillors in local government, and have used political mechanisms to spread their message (such as putting up the requisite number of candidates to secure party election broadcasts). There was much controversy when the Pro-Life Alliance's broadcast, which showed a mid-term abortion, was banned by Channel 4.[35]

Methods of Political Engagement

Casting votes and joining political parties are just a couple of what are becoming firmly and established methods of political engagement for the church in post-Christendom. It is now clear that most of the standard political methods used by campaign and lobby groups in wider society are being used by Christians. Some are short-term, sometimes relating to key events such as summits,

---

[32] Care, through its Changeactivist programme, and Faithworks are two notable examples. Christians working within the main parties have also united to urge people to join them. See www.christiansinpolitics.co.uk.

[33] Press release from the Evangelical Alliance, 'Eric the Evangelical – the latest tool to get people interested in politics', 26 April 2005.

[34] This was an estimate made by Ekklesia before the 2005 general election.

[35] The abortion was eventually shown in a different context three years later – see Kamal Ahmed, 'Channel 4 to screen graphic film of abortion', *The Observer*, April 4 2004.

elections or the debate of bills in Parliament; others are longer-term.

Submissions. Para-church groups, denominations and individual Christians regularly make submissions in response to government papers and consultations as well as in evidence to select committees.

Letter writing. One of the principal ways in which Christians are urged to engage politically is by writing letters, on particular issues or in support of particular campaigns. They are also often encouraged to correspond more generally with their MPs, as well as writing to the newspapers.[36]

Petitions. Petitions have long been an accepted feature of British politics, and Christians have increasingly resorted to them. The Faithworks campaign presented a 70,000-signature petition to Downing Street.[37] The Movement for Christian Democracy presented a 100,000-signature petition about 'video nasties'. Such petitions increasingly use electronic and web-based formats as churches employ new technologies.

Commissions. Some lobby groups and campaign groups have set up their own commissions to look at specific issues, often recruiting theologians, ethicists and politicians to serve on them.[38]

Statements. Both the main denominations and parachurch groups often publish their responses to political events such as the Queen's Speech, the Budget and general election results.[39]

Reports. Many of them commission reports, on subjects ranging from unemployment to foetal pain.

---

[36] See, for example, the Methodist Church press release 'Church leaders call for action on nuclear non-proliferation', 4 May 2005.

[37] Faithworks press release, 'Faithworks delivers 75,000 signatures to no. 10', 19 June 2001.

[38] Commissions of inquiry into the effects of abortion and into foetal sentience were set up by Care. Their respective reports, 'The Physical and Psycho-Social Effects of Abortion on Women' (1994) and 'Human Sentience before Birth' (1996), are available from www.care.org.uk.

[39] For example, see the press releases from the Methodist Church 'The general election', 16 May 2005, and 'Response to the Queen's speech', 17 May 2005.

Surveys. Pressure groups often commission research of public opinion to bolster their campaigns, and may also select polls and surveys commissioned by others that fit in with their own political objectives.[40]

Lobbying. Many campaigners now regularly brief members of Parliament directly, often circulating briefing papers before key debates.

Resourcing churches. Denominations and para-church groups produce resource packs to help local churches and individual Christians to get involved in their neighbourhoods as part of their mission and ministry. These may include inspirational stories from church and community groups,[41] videos, PowerPoint presentations, suggestions on how to obtain funding and tips on how to exert influence and make a difference in the local community.

Protest. Churches now see protest as a valid method of political engagement. Christians have taken part in sit-ins[42] and marches[43] and even a human chain that ringed a whole city,[44] and some burned their TV licences outside the BBC Television Centre in protest at the screening of *Jerry Springer – The Opera*.[45]

Civil disobedience. As Christianity has become less and less identified with the social order and also with democratic participation, there have been more cases of civil disobedience. Recently,

---

[40] For example, the Methodist Church and the Salvation Army both cited the findings of the 2000 Gambling Prevalence Survey, and the Salvation Army also commissioned its own NOP poll as part of its award-winning campaign over the Gambling Bill in 2004–05.

[41] See, for example, 'Assets for Life', an action pack and report produced by the United Reformed Church in conjunction with Toc H; Steve Chalke and Tom Jackson, *Faithworks 2: Stories of Hope* (Eastbourne: Kingsway, 2004).

[42] Most notably by peace campaigners.

[43] For example, in support of Jubilee 2000 and against the invasion of Iraq and the government's Racial and Religious Hatred Bill.

[44] Organised by Jubilee 2000 when the leaders of the G8 met in Birmingham on 16 May 1998.

[45] Mike Collett-White, 'UK Christians burn TV licenses over Springer opera', Reuters, 7 January 2005.

a Catholic priest refused access to his church to police who had come to take an asylum seeker away, and the Catholic group Pax Christi has explored the subject of civil disobedience at some of its conferences.

Prophetic actions. A number of Christians have performed 'prophetic' actions, most notably in the area of disarmament and peace. Members of the Fellowship of Reconciliation and other peace groups have broken into Ministry of Defence property and disabled military equipment, often then giving themselves up, admitting what they have done and standing trial. Others, such as the Catholic James Mawdsley, campaigning for democracy in Burma, have allowed themselves to be captured and imprisoned by oppressive regimes overseas.

Active compassion. Still others have promoted practical projects of peacemaking and reconciliation both in Britain and around the world. This is part of a much wider movement social action, aid and care for the vulnerable, including people who are poor, displaced or persecuted.

Modelling. More and more churches and local groups are trying to demonstrate to government examples of best practice, and are now seeking statutory funding for this.[46] Oasis Trust has obtained millions to set up new city academies, and Care has also received substantial government funding to run remand fostering schemes. More and more church groups are securing Lottery funding not just for repairs to their buildings but also for work in their local communities. Others have won statutory funding for projects that serve asylum seekers or the homeless or meet a range of other social needs. More and more conferences have been held that aim to help Christians to get money out of local government.[47]

---

[46] For example, the press release from the Christian Institute 'Consultations to be held on independent Christian City Academies: Call to set up Christian schools', 13 April 2000.

[47] Press release from Faithworks, 'Faith in local government', 19 June 2002.

Conclusion

In post-Christendom, Christians seem to be politically active in a great variety of ways on a wide variety of issues. I have presented here only a snapshot of Christian political involvement, and there are many more organisations, programmes and initiatives I could have mentioned.

Informing all these developments is a growing awareness among Christians themselves of a distinct political identity that has found expression in many different areas. Seasons in the church's year have been used to political effect. The World Council of Churches has urged Christians to give up violence for Lent. Members of Christian Peacemaker Teams living and working in Iraq have appealed to the worldwide church to join a Lenten fast for justice and healing for detainees in that country, and likewise groups campaigning for religious liberty have called Christians to fast for the persecuted church. Advent calendars have been given a political dimension.[48] The story of Mary and Joseph has been used to highlight the plight of asylum seekers. Particular Sundays in the church calendar, such as Unemployment (now Poverty Action) Sunday and Racial Justice Sunday, have been used to focus the attention of Christians on specific issues and, often, also to witness to the wider society. Politics Sunday was a new arrival in 2004.

There has been an increasing politicisation of liturgy and worship. Churches have always prayed for political leaders in their intercessions, but new initiatives have emerged such as the Parliament and Whitehall 24-7 prayer week. Many campaigns have explicitly biblical themes, such as Jubilee 2000, Micah Challenge and Operation Noah. Denominations are openly urging their members to think about their politics in Christian terms.[49]

---

[48] Press release from the Methodist Relief and Development Fund, 'Advent calendar tells modern story of a mother's hope at Christmas', 26 October 2005.

[49] 'In a diverse society, and one preoccupied with celebrity culture, the bishops urge Catholics to think about how their vote might bring about a world shaped by the values of Christ' – press release from the Catholic

In local congregations and in whole denominations, there also seems to be a new awareness of the political implications of the way the church conducts its own life and an appreciation of the political message its policies send out. A report to the 2004 general synod of the Church of England led to the church adopting environmental policies. Many churches and church groups have consistently rejected Lottery funding, though this stand has weakened in recent years. Para-church organisations such as Christian Ecology Link encourage individual Christians as well as local congregations to switch their energy suppliers to make sure that the energy they use comes from renewable sources. Many churches now serve fair-trade coffee, and there have even been calls for sustainably-sourced palms for Palm Sunday services.

Often, pressure on the church has been applied by Christians outside its institutions. The Campaign Against Arms Trade Christian Network, ran a campaign urging the Church of England to disinvest from arms companies. Other groups have surveyed the problems of low wages and poor employment conditions in churches, Christian organisations and church schools.[50]

The growing politicisation of the church is intriguing and begs a number of questions. Why is it that Christians seem to be increasingly involving themselves in politics at a time when the church appears to be in decline? Why, now that Christendom has come to an end and religion and politics are supposedly so separate, does Christian political activity seem so vigorous? It is to these questions that we will now turn.

---

[49] (*Continued*) Bishops' Conference of England and Wales, 'Catholic bishops issue general election letter', 14 March 2005.
[50] Steve Cann, *A Living Wage Church?* (London: Church Action on Poverty, 2005).

5

The New Radicalisation

The continuing energetic engagement of Christians with government could perhaps be put down to new democratic opportunities and the changing nature of political involvement generally. It could be argued that Christians are simply part of a wider cultural and political trend involving campaign groups – but this doesn't explain why this explosion of Christian political activity has been so vigorous at a time when church attendance is declining and so many of the church's other activities have been scaled down. Nor does it take account of the reasons that many of these groups themselves give for their own existence.

Other developments also challenge the idea that Christians are merely conforming to wider social trends. While membership of campaign groups is strong in the wider society, voter turnout and membership of political parties are declining – but Christians appear to be bucking the trend. Statistics quoted by pollsters suggest that people who profess a Christian faith are significantly more likely to vote than those of other faiths or none.[1] Other surveys conducted within the church suggest higher levels of political participation than might be expected in the wider population.

---

[1] According to research conducted by Mori, turnout was higher among Christians than in the rest of the electorate at the 2005 general election, with 61% of Catholics and 65% of other Christians getting to the polls, compared with 56% of those professing other faiths and 55% of those who said they had no religion. These figures were quoted in BBC2's documentary *God and the Politicians*, broadcast on 26 September 2005.

One poll found that eight out of ten evangelicals intended to vote in the upcoming election – suggesting a high turnout compared with the population at large – and of these half said that they were active in their local communities, many as councillors or school governors.[2] People with a Christian faith are also over-represented in the House of Commons, and Christians are joining or even forming political parties in significant numbers at a time when others are leaving them.

It is post-Christendom itself that may offer some of the most convincing explanations for the new political activity and its timing and character. Two responses to post-Christendom in particular offer reasons for the new radicalisation. On the one hand there are those who see post-Christendom largely in negative terms, as a threat that invites – and indeed demands – a political response. On the other are those who see it in a far more positive light, perceiving new opportunities for the political expression of their faith.

Post-Christendom as a Political Threat

'The Church will go through a time of great persecution.'

Such a statement might have been expected from one of the many organisations that campaign for religious freedom in parts of the world where Christians face discrimination, harassment and even death at the hands of repressive regimes; but what made this warning surprising was that it referred to Britain. Nor was it voiced by someone who could be dismissed as a crank. It came, in fact, from Jayne Ozanne, a member of the Church of England's Archbishops' Council, who predicted that Christianity could soon be driven underground in the West.[3] Her words, which to many seemed extreme, expressed the feelings of many Christians

---

[2] A poll at the Spring Harvest festival quoted in a press release from the Evangelical Alliance, 7 April 2005.

[3] Ruth Gledhill, 'Church faces implosion and life underground, says senior adviser', *The Times*, 11 December 2004. See also the interview of Jayne Ozanne on Radio 4's *Sunday* programme, 12 December 2004.

in Britain,[4] across continental Europe and even in the US[5] who believe that persecution is not just a future possibility but a present reality.

The move toward an alliance of church and empire that began under Constantine promised an end to the terrible persecution that Christians had been enduring. In the US, too, the constitutional principles on which the nation was founded were, at least in part, a response to the persecution some had experienced in Europe. It should come as no surprise, then, that in post-Christendom, as the church moves away from its position of privilege and security, fears of persecution are re-emerging. Whether such fears are well founded, or even valid, is disputed, but this does not change the fact that they are deeply felt.

Open Season

Within weeks of Ozanne's warning of persecution came what many Christians saw as a classic confirmation of their fears: the BBC televised *Jerry Springer – The Opera*.

This is a raucous, obscene and gleefully offensive send-up of the record-breaking US television chat show, in which Jerry Springer hosts confessions, slanging matches and brawls among guests chosen for their low-life behaviour, attitudes and experiences. In the opera, things gets out of hand: Springer is shot, and in a semi-conscious state he has a delusional dream in which he is hosting a show in which Jesus, the Devil and other religious figures appear in warped perspective.

Christians objected primarily to the representations of Jesus, God and Mary. Although many others felt that the show was not in fact blasphemous,[6] it provoked outraged complaints from tens

---

[4] Rob Frost (ed.), *Freedom Fighters: Defending Freedoms in a Politically Correct Age* (Milton Keynes: Authentic Media, 2005).

[5] David Limbaugh, *Persecution: How Liberals are Waging War against Christianity* (Washington DC: Regnery Publishing, 2003).

[6] For example, the Bishop of Worcester, Dr Peter Selby and Christians involved in the production and the cast.

of thousands of people, even before it was shown.[7] The production had been running for several years in the theatre, but it was the decision to televise it on BBC2 that caused the outrage. It was seen as the promotion of blasphemous material by public service broadcasting. Money collected from the general public through the licence fee was being used to fund anti-Christian propaganda.

For many, this was weighty and compelling evidence confirming a trend. An editorial in a well-known Christian magazine claimed: 'This is the landscape we live in. Our faith is under attack in a way that it has not faced for hundreds of years. In the school playground, in the world of business, in university, in politics, in the workplace and on our TV screens, it is open season – we are fair game to be shot at. The prejudice against us is breathtaking.'[8]

It is often said that post-Christendom has ushered in an 'open season' against Christians. These are just the most obvious of the ways in which Christians now feel that they are under attack:

Humiliation. One essential element of the 'persecution' that Ozanne foresaw was increasing ridicule of Christians and their leaders and all they believed in – including God and Jesus and other figures in the Bible. The principal media for this ridicule are radio, television and film. In addition to *Jerry Springer – The Opera* and films such as *Monty Python's Life of Brian*, cartoons such as *Popetown* (a spoof sitcom which portrays the Vatican as a corporation and the Pope as its chief executive) and commercials that parody or make light of religious events or stories have provoked protests from both churches and para-church groups.

Marginalisation. Evidence that Christian faith is being marginalised is also interpreted by many as a sign of anti-Christian feeling. The television and radio schedulers appear to be moving religious programmes further and further away from prime time. Increasingly Christians are having to share the available

---

[7] The BBC said it received 65,000 communications, 96% of which were complaints about its 'Springer Night' on BBC2. Over 84% of these preceded the transmission of *Jerry Springer – The Opera* ('Finding by the Governors' Programme Complaints Committee: *Jerry Springer – The Opera*, BBC Two, Saturday 8 January 2005' [London: BBC, 2005]).

[8] John Buckeridge, *Christianity*, March 2005.

'godslots' with advocates of other faiths, and indeed of agnosticism and atheism. The Christian acts of worship in schools seem to be in decline, often having to give way to other faiths,[9] and the traditional Nativity play appears to be losing its Christian distinctiveness. The government is accused of spending more on observing Ramadan, Eid ul-Fitr, Diwali and Chinese New Year than Easter and Christmas.[10] Proposals to reduce the number of bishops in the House of Lords are taken as evidence of the churches' diminishing political influence. Many Christians see the deregulation of Sunday trading as a further displacement of their faith from the heart of our society, and likewise the removal of Bibles and crosses from public places such as hospitals and funeral parlours.

Criminalisation. Many feel that they are being criminalised for behaviour that had previously been considered 'Christian'. Churches and para-church groups objected to new child-protection laws that restricted the right of parents to smack their children, on the grounds that it would turn many ordinary people into criminals,[11] and protested that new measures proposed by the British government to outlaw incitement to religious hatred could criminalise evangelism. Alarm that Christian organisations could find themselves on the wrong side of the law if they refused to employ non-believers has prompted major campaigns, and there have been fears that religious adoption agencies will be breaking the law if they refuse to place children with homosexual couples, and that hospices will be if they don't publicise the views of pro-euthanasia groups.[12] Para-church organisations have

---

[9] Press release from the Christian Institute, 'Christian integrity not a multi-faith fudge', 11 February 1998.

[10] Dominic Kennedy, 'Christians "are being ignored" as ministers court other faiths', *The Times*, 10 February 2006.

[11] See, for example, the press release from the Christian Institute 'Christian Institute objects to executive's anti-smacking slant: Durkan's smacking ban proposals will plunge parents into fear and confusion', 25 January 2002.

[12] Press release from the Christian Institute, 'The right to sue a church should not be a human right', 9 April 1998.

suggested that their views on homosexuality may soon be declared illegal.[13]

Discrimination. A recurring theme is that churches and individual Christians are being discriminated against. A survey of over three thousand British churches revealed that one in five felt that their community projects had been refused government funding because of their faith basis.[14] High-profile cases reported in the media have also fed the belief that Christians are facing discrimination in many practical ways, such as being required to work on Sundays.

One example of discrimination that is often cited is the failure to appoint Rocco Buttligione as a European commissioner. When Italy's surprise choice as the EU's commissioner for justice, freedom and security made some remarks about homosexuality and the role of women during a confirmation hearing, it provoked objections from MEPs and sparked a small institutional crisis and his candidacy had to be withdrawn by an outraged Italian government. Ironically, the Vatican complained of 'a new Inquisition'.[15]

Many in the Catholic Church in particular saw this incident as further evidence of growing anti-Christian feeling. The Vatican has pressed the United Nations to recognise 'Christianophobia' as an evil equal to anti-Semitism or 'Islamophobia'.[16] A variant on this term, 'Christophobia', which claims that it is not merely Christians who are being discriminated against but Christ himself, was coined after the Co-operative Bank refused to allow one Christian group to hold a bank account because of its condemnation of homosexuals.[17]

---

[13] 'Suspending Judgement' in *PQ*, from the Evangelical Alliance public-affairs department, February 2004.

[14] Unpublished survey by Faithworks in 2001.

[15] Daniel Williams, 'Vatican is alarmed by political trend in Europe: Policies in many countries contradict church doctrine', *Washington Post* Foreign Service, 20 October 2004.

[16] Jonathan Petre, 'Vatican presses the UN to recognise "Christianophobia"', *The Daily Telegraph*, 7 December 2004.

[17] Press release from the Christian People's Alliance, 'Disinvestment campaign in Co-operative Bank launched by Christian party leaders:

Restriction. Many Christians feel that their right to free speech, and specifically their right to criticise and attack other religions and behaviours such as homosexuality, are also being curtailed, particularly in the area of broadcasting. Explicitly religious organisations have been debarred from holding a national radio licence, an ITV franchise or any of the new digital licences, and some Christians saw this as a form of deliberate discrimination. It has been claimed that it is 'easier to broadcast pornography than the Christian faith.'[18] But Christians also feel discriminated against when they are judged to have overstepped the mark in speaking about people of other faiths. A Christian radio station was given a 'yellow card' by the Radio Authority for breaching the rules on several occasions, for example by criticising other religions and by suggesting that the Koran and the Hindu and Buddhist scriptures were 'full of superstition and absurdities'.[19]

Similarly, concerns have been expressed over freedom of religion. I have already mentioned Christian opposition to government proposals aimed at preventing incitement to religious hatred, which many people felt would limit their efforts to evangelise. But there is also concern about restrictions on the expression of what some say are Christian doctrines. When the government introduced measures that prohibited independent schools from using corporal punishment, some Christian schools went to the European Court of Human Rights, claiming that the right to hit children was a 'Christian doctrine'. Its denial, they argued, was an infringement of their religious freedom.

Victimisation. While fears are growing that Christians are losing the right to criticise other religions, it appears that followers of other faiths are being afforded more protection than they are. In a poll following the screening of *Jerry Springer – The Opera*, nine out of ten Christians said they did not believe that the BBC would

---

[17] (*Continued*) "Diversity" has become a secular cover for Christophobia', 27 June 2005.

[18] Press release from the Christian Institute, 'Religious broadcasting bill welcomed', 10 July 1999.

[19] 'Christian radio station warned over content', *Media Guardian*, 25 October 2001.

show a programme that was offensive to Muslims.[20] In a subsequent report, the corporation noted that 'a recurrent point in correspondence was that the BBC would not dare to broadcast programmes which treated other religions (particularly Islam) in the manner in which Christianity was treated on this occasion.'[21]

When complaints by Christians are not upheld, it is taken as evidence that Christianity does not receive equal consideration. Peter Kerridge of the evangelical radio station Premier Radio criticised the decision of the Advertising Standards Authority not to uphold their complaint about an ad on Channel 4 that they said portrayed the Last Supper in an offensive way. Claming that there was one rule for Christians and another for everyone else, he suggested that if the ad had portrayed a sacred moment from the Koran 'you can be certain any complaints would have been taken seriously. Just like the BBC, the ASA (Advertising Standards Agency [*sic*]) have shown their reluctance to take Christians and their faith seriously in matters of prejudice.'[22]

Disempowerment. Alongside concerns that Christians are being treated unfairly in comparison with followers of other faiths, there is a growing feeling that Christians are themselves losing the right to discriminate. For example, it is common practice for CUs, often affiliated to the Universities and Colleges Christian Fellowship, to insist that the members of their steering groups not only are Christians but have signed UCCF's doctrinal statement, which lays down which beliefs are mandatory. The students' unions at both Hull and Birmingham Universities have insisted that membership of CU steering groups should be open to all, on the grounds that anyone can do the job whether they are a Christian or not.[23] UCCF has been joined by Christian pressure

---

[20] Press release from Premier Radio, 'Christians ignored again! Ad standards agency disregards "shameless" blasphemy complaints', 14 January 2005.

[21] 'Finding by the Governors' Programme Complaints Committee: *Jerry Springer – The Opera*, BBC Two, Saturday 8 January 2005' (London: BBC, 2005).

[22] Press release from Premier Radio, 'Christians ignored again!'

[23] Press release from the Christian Institute, 'Hull Christian Union banned for being run by Christians', 30 March 2004; Liz Ford, 'Student

groups in supporting the CUs' right to discriminate and has claimed that CUs are being denied access to university resources because they are 'run by Christians'.[24]

Christian organisations also feel they are losing the right to sack their employees. It has been said that church schools may no longer be able to get rid of head teachers who commit adultery or convert to another faith and may also be obliged to consider job applications from atheists or practising homosexuals.[25] Likewise, religious charities may no longer be able to dismiss people who fundamentally disagree with them on moral or doctrinal issues.[26] Aspects of the proposed European Constitution too were opposed on the basis that the treaty's requirement to integrate a non-discrimination strategy into all areas of EU law would prevent discrimination on the grounds of sexual orientation.[27]

The ways in which many Christians feel it is 'open season' against them, then, are many – and this feeling is eliciting a political response. Much of the perceived threat comes from government action and legislation, which need to be resisted politically.

A feature of Christendom was the introduction of laws that sought to impose Christian ideas of morality, particularly in the area of sexuality. As these have been amended, repealed or replaced, so alarm bells have begun to ring and calls have been made 'for the drift away from the Christian ethos in British public life to end.'[28]

---

[23] (*Continued*) union suspends Christian group', *Education Guardian*, 25 January 2006.

[24] Press release from the Christian Institute, 'Hull Christian Union banned for being run by Christians'.

[25] Press release from the Christian Institute, 'Church schools forced to employ atheists and practising homosexuals', 25 May 2000.

[26] Press release from the Christian Institute, 'The right to sue a church should not be a human right', 9 April 1998.

[27] Letter to Tony Blair regarding the draft treaty establishing a constitution for Europe from Prof Paul Beaumont, vice-chair of the Lawyers' Christian Fellowship, 6 December 2003.

[28] Colin Dye, 'Government policy and Christian Britain: A call for policy makers to take note that Britain is still a Christian country', *Revival Times*, April 2005.

Institutional Assault

A watershed for many British Christians was reached towards the end of the sixties, when (among other changes to the law) Parliament repealed the 1687 Blasphemy Act and passed both the 1967 Abortion Act and the 1967 Sexual Offences Act, which decriminalised homosexual acts between two men over 21 years of age. Since then, there has been a series of other changes to the law that have been interpreted as further evidence that Britain is abandoning its Christian roots. Some of the most high-profile and heated political engagement by Christians has surrounded issues often referred to as 'private' or 'moral'. These have generally come under the headings of 'life-and-death' issues (such as abortion and euthanasia), sex (such as prostitution and homosexual practice) or the family (including smacking and marriage law), but have also included gambling, drugs and standards in the media.

But a feeling prevalent among those who view post-Christendom with a sense of foreboding is that institutions are disintegrating as the Christian glue that has long held society together is itself disappearing. Some commentators have blamed the abandoning of conceptions of law based on the Ten Commandments in favour of 'faddish theories' or 'political correctness' for undermining social institutions such as the family, the criminal justice system and schools.[29]

A number of institutions, once seen as closely aligned with the Christian faith, are now often said to be under attack:

* *The nation.* Britain is regarded by many as a Christian country – according to recent surveys, 63 per cent of the population 'identify with the Christian faith'.[30] Immigrants and asylum seekers, often associated with the influx of religions such as Islam, are therefore seen as undermining the country's 'Christian' heritage just as secularism has.[31]

---

[29] Colin Hart, 'Repairing the moral fabric: How Christians can work against moral decay in society,' *Evangelicals Now*, December 1996.
[30] Populus survey published in *The Times*, 6 April 2004.
[31] See Dye, 'Government policy and Christian Britain', *Revival Times*.

- *The constitution.* The British constitution was described as 'Christian' by several churches and campaign groups in evidence to a House of Lords select committee charged with looking at religious offences.[32] The Christian faith, such groups suggest, 'is woven deeply into the fabric of the constitutional tapestry.'[33] The adoption of the European Convention on Human Rights, the proposal to ratify the European Constitution and moves to repeal the law against blasphemy (which campaigners say helps to buttress the constitution of this country[34]) or to disestablish the Church of England are all viewed as attempts to further undermine the country's Christian heritage.
- *Law and order.* It is suggested that the common law of England has its roots in the Christian religion and the Bible.[35] Crime statistics are quoted as evidence that the rule of law is breaking down. The problem is sometimes identified as a shift away from 'the protection of the public' and the 'concept of retribution' towards seeing criminals as victims.[36] 'The desire to

---

[32] See, for example, Christian Voice's evidence to the Select Committee on Religious Offences in England and Wales, 8 July 2002, but also evidence given by the Evangelical Alliance and the Christian People's Alliance for the clearest examples.

[33] Antony Bell, 'Moving the goalposts', *New Directions*, February 2003. Many others churches, church leaders and campaign groups have expressed such beliefs. See, for example, Fergus Sheppard, 'Cardinal in ethnic row over "Christian Scotland" remarks', *The Scotsman*, 12 January 2006; the submission from the Elim Way Fellowship to the Select Committee on Religious Offences in England and Wales, 4 July 2002; Jonathan Petre, 'Bishop's reminder: We're still Christian', *The Daily Telegraph*, 22 December 2004.

[34] The Evangelical Alliance has said that the retention of the blasphemy law 'would act as a largely symbolic reminder of the Christian basis to UK law' (undated memorandum from the EA to the Select Committee on Religious Offences in England and Wales). See also the evidence to the same select committee from the Christian People's Alliance, 24 July 2002.

[35] Bell, 'Moving the goalposts'.

[36] Hart, 'Repairing the moral fabric'.

"understand a little more and blame a little less"' is also identified as a problem.[37] Some would like to see the return of the
death penalty. Others associate sexual immorality with lack of
respect for law and order.[38]

- *The family.* Marriage and 'traditional models' of the family are
  often regarded as fundamentally Christian. Government moves
  to allow 'no-fault' divorce, abolish tax allowances for married
  couples and give legal recognition to gay partners[39] and
  cohabiting heterosexuals have been seen as further eroding the
  institution of marriage.[40] Research conducted by pressure
  groups suggests that married couples and 'traditional' families
  are also getting a rawer deal than cohabiting and gay couples[41]
  with respect to taxation and welfare benefits. This is taken by
  those same groups as evidence that the family is being
  undermined.

- *Schools.* A claim that is heard quite often is that schools and the
  education system at large are in trouble because they no longer
  promote 'one culture or one religious faith'. Not only the government is held to blame for undermining discipline and the
  teaching of right and wrong in schools but also 'union leaders,
  teacher trainers and educationalists'.[42] The sidelining of acts of
  religious worship in schools is also seen as symptomatic of the
  way schools are forsaking Christianity.

- *Economic systems.* Christian commentators have lamented the
  diminishing influence of Christian moral standards in business
  dealings. They refer to the assumptions of the economist Adam
  Smith and the sociologist Max Weber and suggest that the

---

[37] Hart, 'Repairing the moral fabric'.
[38] Charles Murray, *Charles Murray and the Underclass: The Developing Debate* (IEA, 1996).
[39] Press release from the Christian Institute, 'Peers must reject "counter-feit marriage"', 23 January 2002.
[40] Press release from the Christian Institute, 'Family Law Bill: A fundamental attack on marriage', 10 January 1996.
[41] Press release from Care, 'Is this really a budget for hard-working families?', 17 March 2005.
[42] Hart, 'Repairing the moral fabric'.

market system depends on certain values and non-market institutions in order to function properly. Some set out to show how Christian values are needed to underpin markets, whose roots they often trace back to the Judaeo-Christian tradition. Many also associate democracy and capitalism (and refer to 'democratic capitalism').[43] Democracy, they suggest, is in practice compatible only with a market economy, and both systems nourish one another.[44] Some believe that largely unregulated markets, and the values they reinforce and promote, are part of the problem. Some reckon that markets have intruded too far into schools and the National Health Service and have undermined institutions, replacing their fundamentally Christian ethos with a new managerialism.[45]

There are many more examples I could cite. We could consider specific institutions, festivals and holidays. There have been campaigns to 'keep Sunday special' and to 'put "Christ" back into "Christmas"' (coupled with concern that local authorities may replace Christmas altogether with a 'Winterval'). There has also been vigorous lobbying to have Christianity recognised in new contexts such as the preamble to the EU constitution. All these things have one thing in common: Christians not only are fearful about the discrimination and even persecution that they see accompanying post-Christendom but also are alarmed by the changes they see in the society around them. Things they have regarded as good, have equated with Christianity and would wish to retain, appear to be changing and even disappearing. And their desire to do something to prevent this has been radicalising them politically.

---

[43] See Michael Novak, *The Spirit of Democratic Capitalism* (IEA, 1982), and also Brian Griffiths, Robert A. Sirico, Norman Barry and Frank Field, *Capitalism, Morality and Markets* (IEA, 2001).

[44] Novak, *The Spirit of Democratic Capitalism*.

[45] A criticism quoted but answered by Brian Griffiths in his chapter 'The Culture of the Market' in Donald A. Hay and Alan Kreider (eds.), *Christianity and the Culture of Economics*.

Post-Christendom as a Political Opportunity

Birmingham doesn't have a reputation as a hotbed of political radicalism, but what happened there on Saturday 16 June 1998 will go down in the records as a significant political event.

'An emotionally charged, positive, uplifting, but also scary day'[46] was the verdict of Ann Pettifor, director of the Jubilee 2000 Coalition which was responsible for forming a human chain of some seventy thousand protesters around the city as the leaders of most of the most powerful nations in the world met.

Trains brought thousands from London, Cardiff, Nottingham, Manchester, Leeds, Newcastle and north of the border, and many thousands more came in coaches and cars and on bicycles. There were supporters from the US, from Finland, France, Germany and Austria. Development agencies brought people from Africa, Latin America and Asia who stirred the crowds with their speeches. Three thousand journalists covered the event and the calls for the cancellation of the debts of some of the poorest countries in the world. Celebrities, politicians and even national newspapers pledged their support.

What made it particularly remarkable, however, was that this was a campaign inspired by Christians who mobilised thousands of churches – as well as people who would never normally consider entering their doors – to political action. A radical Christian idea became a mass movement which put debt cancellation on the political agenda.[47] In the space of a few years, the question in the public mind changed from 'Should the debt be cancelled?' to 'How should it be done?'

While some Christians regard post-Christendom as a threat, others have a very different, at times even contrary, point of view. Many see it in fact as a wonderful opportunity – a liberation, which offers new chances to do justice, new possibilities of political expression, with new agendas, new concerns, new perspectives and new ideas.

---

[46] Quoted in 'Did the G8 Drop the Debt?', a report by Jubilee Debt Campaign, Jubilee Research and Cafod.

[47] See Will Hutton, 'Debt-relief campaign Jubilee 2000 can now claim its great victory, thanks to Leviticus', *The Observer*, 3 October 1999.

As we saw in Chapter 3, Christendom brought with it a tendency towards mediating principles rather than radical reform. One of the features of post-Christendom is that Christians are beginning to think in new and more radical ways, which draw on the resources of their faith, about how justice can be done.

While some look back on Christendom with nostalgia and dwell on the potential hardships of the new dispensation, others argue that Christendom was not without its problems. In particular, they point out that for many it, too, involved oppression, persecution, criminalisation, marginalisation and destruction.

- *Women.* A theology that identified the patriarchal social order with the divinely created order insisted that the proper relationship between men and women was one in which men dominated and women were obedient.[48] Women were expected prayerfully to endure the abuse of male power in the church, the wider society and the home. With respect to domestic abuse especially, wives were expected to demonstrate their submission to God through silent and prayerful suffering, attempting to change their husbands only by example.[49]
- *Children.* The 'psychohistorian' Lloyd deMause has said that the history of childhood is a nightmare from which we have only recently begun to awaken.[50] For many, Christendom represents an era of negative discipline, based on the assumption that

[48] See Clare Drury, 'Christianity' in Jean Holm and John Bowker (eds.), *Women in Religion* (London: Pinter Publishers, 1994), pp. 30–58; Rosemary Radford Ruether, 'Christianity' in Arvind Sharma (ed.), *Women in World Religions* (New York: State University of New York Press, 1987), pp. 207–34; Rosemary Radford Ruether, *Sexism and God-Talk: Toward a Feminist Theology* (Boston: Beacon Press, 1983).

[49] Nelia Beth Scovill, 'The Liberation of Women in Religious Sources', submission to the Religious Consultation on Population, Reproductive Health and Ethics.

[50] Lloyd deMause, 'The History of Child Abuse', *The Journal of Psychohistory*, 25 (3), Winter 1998. The article notes that several hundred studies in the journal have been published that provide substantial evidence to back up this claim.

babies were born full of original sin[51] and that virtue must therefore be imposed upon them.[52] It fostered the belief that children should be absolutely obedient to their parents but were by nature sinful, depraved and antisocial, so that it was necessary to 'break their wills' at a very early age, sometimes with harsh physical punishment.

- *Gays and lesbians.* Laws were introduced in Christendom that criminalised homosexual practice and at times resulted in the oppression and even death of gay and lesbian people.
- *Religious and ethnic minorities.* In Christendom there was widespread anti-Semitism and ill-treatment of people of other faiths in Britain. Christians, too, were oppressed, for there were inquisitions to root out heresy, and groups such as the Anabaptists were persecuted. Catholics and non-conformists were often accorded lower status and experienced discrimination.
- *Foreigners.* Partly because of the association of Christianity with particular territory, many people outside Christendom were labelled 'pagans' or 'heathens' and treated as inferiors and objects for conversion. Wars were waged in the name of God and whole countries and continents were ravaged.
- *The poor and the vulnerable.* The church often seemed reluctant to challenge unjust social systems in Christendom. The poor were helped, but often not enough, and other vulnerable people suffered too. Although in Christendom the church often proposed reform of prisons to alleviate their harshness,[53] it rarely advocated alternatives to prison, corporal punishment or the death penalty.

---

[51] Of course, belief in original sin does not necessarily lead to an endorsement of physical punishment. Augustine himself, though he regarded infants as sinful, was opposed to punishing them physically. He describes infants as being in a state of 'non-innocence', neither completely innocent nor completely depraved. See Marcia J. Bunge (ed.), *The Child in Christian Thought* (Grand Rapids: Eerdmans, 2001).

[52] Penelope Leach, *Children First* (London: Penguin, 1994).

[53] For example, in 1777 the evangelical John Howard reviewed British prisons and published the book *State of the Prisons*. He proposed that prisons should provide a healthy, disease-free environment and also suggested that jailers should not be allowed to charge prisoners.

- *The planet.* Amidst fears of impending environmental catastrophe, Christians are now being urged to accept some of the blame for the current global crisis by 'desacralising' Nature in Christendom.[54] It is claimed that they allowed it to be exploited without restraint.[55] Many evangelicals have come close to actually celebrating the demise of the earth, enthusiastically citing its decay as evidence that the return of Christ is very near.[56] Debates over evolution and creationism have also distracted us from caring for the planet.[57]

Political Engagement

Post-Christendom is the context for Christian radicalisation of a different kind. The passing of Christendom affords new opportunities for justice. Crucially, however, post-Christendom does not herald a universal liberation. Many people still suffer oppression, discrimination and injustice – though this, too, is the context for political radicalisation on their behalf. As the assumptions of Christendom lose their hold, so Christians appear to be discovering new political applications for their faith. Many are motivated by ideas and priorities of

- Justice
- Being 'prophetic'

---

[54] A claim made perhaps most notably by Lynn White, 'The Historical Roots of Our Ecological Crisis', *Science*, 155: 1203–07, 1967.
[55] See, for example, Francis Schaeffer, *Pollution and the Death of Man* (Wheaton: Tyndale, 1970). However this claim is disputed. See J.K. Sheldon, 'Twenty-one years after the "historical roots of our ecological crisis": How has the church responded?', *Perspectives on Science and Christian Faith*, 41: 152–58, 1989; E. Whitney, 'Lynn White, Ecotheology and History', *Environmental Ethics*, 15: 151–69, 1993; and also Alister McGrath, 'The Stewardship of the Creation: An Evangelical Affirmation' in Berry (ed.), *The Care of Creation*, pp. 86–9.
[56] Ronald J. Sider, 'Biblical Foundations for Creation Care' in Berry (ed.), *The Care of Creation.*
[57] R.J. Berry, 'Creation and the Environment', *Science and Christian Belief*, 7:21–43, 1995.

- Peacemaking
- Care for the planet
- Protection of the vulnerable
- Equality
- Stewardship
- Freedom and liberation
- The demands of the gospel

The application of such principles can be seen throughout the church and para-church groups. A few developments are particularly notable:

Defending children. In some sections of the church, there has been a re-evaluation of the importance of children,[58] who have come to be seen less as the property of their parents and more as unique human beings who are entrusted to their parents' care for a while. As such, they are increasingly accorded the dignity that is 'richly and equally deserved by every human being created in God's image.'[59] While some Christians (as we have noted) campaigned for the retention of the right to smack children, many churches – and some whole denominations – campaigned for its abolition.[60]

Care for the environment. The past few decades have seen the churches beginning to take some determined action on ecological and environmental issues. One of the biggest and most significant initiatives has been the Justice, Peace and Integrity of Creation programme (JPIC) of the World Council of Churches launched in 1983. In 1986, the Worldwide Fund for Nature issued a set of 'Assisi declarations' containing 'messages on man [*sic*] and nature from Buddhism, Christianity, Islam and Judaism'. A significant Christian recognition of the environment came from the Anglican Consultative Council in 1990, whose report *Mission in a Broken*

---

[58] Bunge (ed.), *The Child in Christian Thought.*

[59] E.M. Smith, *The New Dictionary of Christian Ethics and Pastoral Theology* (Leicester: IVP, 1995).

[60] For example, a resolution was passed in the United Reformed Church's general assembly in 1999 that the denomination should become a member of the 'Children are unbeatable!' Alliance. Anglicans and Methodists have also lent their weight to the campaigns.

World added to its definition of mission the goal of safeguarding the integrity of creation and sustaining and renewing the life of the earth. Christians were represented at the 1991 Earth Summit in Rio and books have began to appear that explore the theology of creation or, at a more popular level, offer Christians advice on how to respond to environmental problems.[61]

The theological approaches vary. Some evangelicals are concerned that confusion in the approaches of some Christians and churches (such as the 'creation spirituality' of Matthew Fox) is diminishing the 'exalted status within creation' of human beings.[62] But Christians in very great numbers are now engaging in environmental action. Groups such as Christian Ecology Link and the Evangelical Environment Network have been formed. Operation Noah, a project of the 'environmental issues network' of Churches Together in Britain and Ireland, encouraged people to sign a 'climate covenant', which was backed by major church denominations such as the Methodist Church. Other issues such as care for animals are now coming to the fore.[63]

Criminal justice. Churches are also doing a lot of work in the field of criminal justice. One major feature of the Christian response has been a focus on conditions in prisons, and calls for their reform. The Catholic Church[64] and a number of high-profile Anglican bishops[65] have spoken out, urging that fewer people

---

[61] See, for example, Tony Campolo, *How to Rescue the Earth without Worshipping Nature* (Nashville: Thomas Nelson, 1992) and Chris Seaton, *Whose Earth?* (London: Crossway, 1992). Are these books both examples of the latter concern, 'advice on how to tackle environmental problems'? I rather suspect that the second book is an example of the former concern, the theology of creation (or whatever).

[62] See Sider, 'Biblical Foundations for Creation Care'.

[63] See, for example, Linzey, *Animal Gospel*; Tony Sargent, *Animal Rights and Wrongs: A Biblical Perspective* (London: Hodder & Stoughton, 1996).

[64] 'A Place of Redemption: A Christian Approach to Punishment and Prison', The Catholic Bishops' Conference of England and Wales (Burns and Oates, 2004).

[65] For example, Peter Selby, Bishop of Worcester.

should be sent to prison and that those who are should be given opportunities for rehabilitation while inside.

To some extent, this has been a continuation of earlier moves in Christendom; but some churches and para-church organisations have gone much further and have begun to advocate radical reform of the criminal justice system itself. Some have proposed a 'relational' approach.[66] Others, such as the Churches' Criminal Justice Forum (CCRJ), have advanced the related idea of restorative justice which, based on the notion that justice is a matter of making good the damage done through crime, champions the interests of both victim and offender. Catholic bishops have stated emphatically that 'true justice must produce a positive outcome for the victim, for society and for the offender.'[67] Restorative justice has been seen as offering considerable potential to change both sentencing practice and (more ambitiously) the way in which society puts right the damage done by crime.[68]

International justice. In addition to their work toward the cancellation of international debt in the developing world, development agencies such as Christian Aid have repeatedly become involved in advocacy on behalf of Palestinians in the Occupied Territories. Others have drawn attention to the effects of sanctions against countries such as Iraq, or have taken up the cause of people suffering at the hands of regimes such as Robert Mugabe's in Zimbabwe or those in power in Sudan.[69] Many para-church groups campaign on behalf of the persecuted church around the world. Others have begun lobbying vigorously for trade justice or for affordable medicines to treat people with HIV or Aids.

Peace and war. Many bishops and other church leaders invoked the notion of 'just war' to oppose the invasion of Iraq by

---

[66] Jonathan Burnside and Nicola Baker (eds.), *Relational Justice: Repairing the Breach* (Winchester: Waterside Press, 1994).

[67] 'A Place of Redemption', Catholic Bishops' Conference.

[68] For a US perspective on restorative justice, see H. Zehr, *Changing Lenses: A New Focus for Crime and Justice* (Scottdale: Herald Press, 1990).

[69] Press release from the Methodist Church, 'Methodist Church calls for action to end Darfur violence', 3 February 2005.

Coalition forces in 2003. However, the inadequacy of the theory for post-Christendom has become evident to many, and it is being revised. Others have worked against nuclear proliferation and in peacemaking and reconciliation initiatives. A notable feature of post-Christendom has been the growing Christian opposition to war in general and to nuclear weapons in particular. The World Council of Churches has declared 'a Decade to Overcome Violence', which is being supported by many British churches.

Identification with the marginalised. For a number of years, Church Action on Poverty (CAP) has encouraged bishops and others to live on the minimum wage during Lent.[70] Bob Holman, in his book *Faith in the Poor*, has suggested that policy needs to be made by the people it is actually going to affect. CAP, Holman and others have brought together people with first-hand experience of debt and financial exclusion with policy-makers, politicians and civil servants.[71] There has been interest in 'participatory budgeting', which enables local communities to get much closer to the decision-making process behind local authority budgets.[72] Pressure groups have published proposals for delivering affordable credit and other financial services to low-income households.[73] There is increasing awareness of the processes by which people become marginalised,[74] and the voices of the poor have been heard speaking from their own experience.[75]

---

[70] For an account of how *The Guardian* journalist Polly Toynbee took up the challenge, see Toynbee, *Hard Work: Life in Low-Pay Britain* (London: Bloomsbury, 2003).

[71] See Stephen Matthews, 'Forgive Us Our Debts' (CAP, 2005).

[72] Something promoted by Church Action of Poverty. See 'Breathing Life into Democracy: The Power of Participatory Budgeting' and also 'Bringing Budgets Alive: A Practical Guide on How to Do It'.

[73] Jenny Rossiter, 'Scaling Up for Financial Inclusion', a report published by CAP on behalf of Debt on Our Doorstep.

[74] John Atherton suggests a new political economy that engages mainstream economics and interfaith economics. See Atherton, *Marginalization* (Canterbury: SCM/Canterbury Press, 2003).

[75] Kathy Galloway, 'A Scotland where Everyone Matters: A Report on Church Action on Poverty's Scottish Poverty Indicators Project', 2003.

There are many other developments we could consider, not least work on issues of racial justice, action to combat racism and extremism in society, particularly around political elections. When we take all these things together, a picture emerges of a church that is becoming increasingly politicised across a range of issues involving justice, liberation and care for the planet.

Post-Christendom is thus not simply the context for the increasing radicalisation of Christians, it is also a catalyst – if not the cause – of it. Christians are responding politically to post-Christendom for different reasons and in different ways. Some have reacted negatively, often under the influence of fear. Others have been positive, perceiving new opportunities in post-Christendom to express their faith politically, especially in demands for justice.

6

Uncritical Engagement

Almost 30 years before seventy thousand protesters encircled Birmingham to demand the cancellation of debts in the developing world, a missionary came home on a boat from India. As he drove through Dover, Peter Hill was alarmed to see a poster of a 'scantily-clad girl proffering a pint of beer' dominating the street.[1] As he looked around, he was more and more shocked by what would later be termed 'the slide into moral permissiveness' in the four years he had been away, and the abandonment of 'Christian values' that it indicated.

Hill shared his thoughts with other Christians and found that they were of like mind. They planned a national event inspired by a vision to draw attention to the 'moral pollution' in Britain. On 25 September 1971, a crowd of sixty thousand gathered in Trafalgar Square and heard proclamations to the government, the media and church leaders. A new movement, the Nationwide Festival of Light, was born.

In the last chapter, I identified two forms of Christian radicalisation within post-Christendom. The first is the negative radicalisation that Hill experienced. It stems from alarm at post-Christendom and an urgent sense that 'something must be done about it'. The second is the kind that resulted in the Jubilee 2000 Coalition – a positive view of post-Christendom that embraces the new opportunities to do justice and apply a Christian understanding in fresh ways.

[1] John Capon, *And There Was Light: The Story of the Nationwide Festival of Light* (Cambridge: Lutterworth Press, 1972).

It is rare, however, in any context that there are completely discrete and coherent motives for political engagement. Many people are driven not just by one factor but by a number – and usually a complex mixture. Fears about the end of Christendom on one hand and a desire to do justice on the other are not mutually exclusive in the minds of many Christians. For most, there is a mixture of both positive and negative feelings.

There are other complexities, too. Some who are fearful of the decline of Christendom do not fear discrimination or persecution. Some who could be considered 'liberated' in post-Christendom do not welcome it.[2] Some regret the passing of Christendom because they feel that Christendom in many respects was 'just'. Some lament the passing of some aspects of Christendom but not others. To others pursuing justice, the passing of Christendom seems unimportant.

How, then, should we assess the new radicalism? Christian political perspectives are often considered in terms of distinct traditions, such as:

• Catholic
• Evangelical/Reformed
• Baptist
• Anabaptist

Alternatively, they can be considered in terms of ideologies – for example:

• Christian Right
• Christian Democratic
• Christian Socialist

However, although these terms helpfully identify streams in Christian political thought, they are of limited use in post-Christendom when it comes to assessing the new radicalism. Trends in the church suggest a 'post-denominationalism' in which inter-church networks are increasingly important. The new

---

[2] For example, many Afro-Caribbean churches lament the 'de-Christianisation' of Britain.

radicalism has involved the mobilisation of many lay people, who often express themselves politically outside traditional church structures.

A second factor is that much of our political categorisation was formulated in Christendom and so reflects a specific location of the church in relation to the state, even during Christendom's decline. Many of these political perspectives were based on Christendom assumptions, such as a close involvement with government – often within the context of a particular political party. But things have changed drastically and much of the church's political involvement now takes place outside the immediate sphere of government.

Neither do political theology and political theory always reflect the reality of what is happening on the ground. There is a gulf between (for example) the ideology of the New Right and how governments associated with the New Right have behaved. Few Christian political groups have a considered theology of the state, and even fewer apply one consistently.

We can perhaps make more sense of things if we look closely at the groups and figures involved.

A Question of Identity

A number of Christian groups explicitly trace their origins to concern about post-Christendom. The National Viewers' and Listeners' Association[3] was founded by Mary Whitehouse in 1965 in the belief that the media had an influence on moral standards and values, that these were declining and that 'taste' and 'decency' needed to be defended.[4] The cross-party Movement for Christian Democracy (now the Centre for Christian Democracy) was launched in 1990 in response to 'the trend towards secularism'.[5]

---

[3] Now mediawatch-uk.
[4] Comprehensive archives of correspondence and the history of the NVLA can be found in the Albert Sloman Library.
[5] David Alton, *Faith in Britain* (London: Hodder and Stoughton, 1991), Introduction.

The Christian Institute and Christian Voice were both formed out of similar concerns. The Christian People's Alliance (CPA) lists amongst its goals 'respect of God's law as the basis for constitutional government and a stable society.' These can all be considered as organisations set up with the intention to influence and change culture and legislation in response to post-Christendom – or at least to stem its advance.

Many of these groups have variously been lumped together as evangelical, fundamentalist, traditional, orthodox, socially conservative or right-wing. But while these terms may suggest some characteristics of some of these groups, they do not give the whole picture:

- They are not all Protestant evangelical in character. Many include Catholics amongst their supporters.
- They are not all fundamentalist. Many have support from more open evangelicals and sometimes from liberal traditionalists.
- They are not all traditional or orthodox. Some of their members and supporters have some very unorthodox views about 'the end times' or the state of Israel.
- They are not all socially conservative. Some espouse more progressive ideas, such as care for the environment.
- They are not all located on the political right. Some position themselves at the centre and have views that would be considered by many to be left-of-centre.[6] Most would not associate themselves with one political party.

When it comes to those Christians who are radicalised in the pursuit of justice and take a more positive view of post-Christendom, there is also a good deal of complexity. It might be expected that people who are primarily motivated by justice would be liberal, left-wing or radical, but some of these groups are largely evangelical in outlook. Examples would be Speak, formed in the late nineties as a network connecting the emerging generation to campaign and pray about issues of global justice, and Micah Challenge. Many others involve collaborations of left

---

[6] For example, the Christian People's Alliance.

and right and span many denominations. Church Action on Poverty was launched as an ecumenical response to poverty in Britain. Christian CND grew from a desire to work ecumenically to persuade people that nuclear weapons are intrinsically evil.

Post-Christendom politics is thus the context for an interesting mix of traditions, ideas, feelings and perspectives that don't fit neatly into the old categories. The situation is made all the more complex by the fact that things are changing at a great pace. Many groups that would not necessarily be considered political are becoming more so by choice.[7] Others, such as UCCF, are finding that circumstances are placing them in political situations. We can observe three important trends:

Agendas are broadening. New political groups are forming all the time, but the policy agendas of individual Christians, parachurch groups and denominations are also beginning for the first time or expanding. Pro-life groups such as the Society for the Protection of Unborn Children have become interested in family policy. The Jubilee 2000 Coalition laid the groundwork for Make Poverty History, which addressed issues of HIV/Aids and trade justice. The Evangelical Alliance and Care have steadily extended the areas of public policy they are involved in, to include (for example) asylum seekers and juveniles on remand. As we noted in Chapter 4, there is a growing awareness that many issues cannot be considered in isolation. Pope John Paul II was amongst those who called for a consistent 'ethic of life' that opposed both abortion and war.[8] The Christian groupings within the main political

---

[7] In October 2005, for example, more political groups such as Care, Christian Solidarity Worldwide, the Evangelical Alliance, the Lawyers' Christian Fellowship, Premier Media Group and Transform UK (claiming to 'represent' 86 workplace organisations) were joined by the Deo Gloria Trust, the Christian Broadcasting Council, the Elim Pentecostal Church, Ichthus, the Kingsway International Christian Centre, the London School of Theology, Share Jesus International and Youth for Christ in organising protest communications over the Incitement to Religious Hatred Bill. See the press release from Premier Radio 'PM receives Premier protest post', 10 October 2005.

[8] See the encyclical *Evangelium Vitae*.

parties too have found that they need to be able to address a broad range of political issues if they are to be relevant.

Arguments are changing. There has also been a change in the arguments that many groups employ in their campaigns. Some of these have 'crossed over', so that the virtues of Christendom are extolled by those campaigning for justice and vice versa. Campaigners for the rights of asylum seekers, for example, point to a Christendom tradition of care for the vulnerable. Appeals to justice are increasingly made by groups associated with a largely negative response to post-Christendom. The Nationwide Festival of Light was relaunched as Care – a deliberate name-change to emphasise a more compassionate approach. Organisations that have been keen to defend the institution of marriage have begun to highlight differences in the benefits and tax breaks accorded to married couples and those enjoyed by single parents and cohabiting couples, focusing on the impact on children.[9]

Organisations that were born out of a reaction to the 'permissive' legislation of the sixties have begun to characterise themselves as (for example) having a 'concern for the well being of all in society but particularly for the most vulnerable and needy.'[10] Those campaigning for Sunday to remain a day of rest have argued their case in terms of justice for employees against the interests of big business. Pro-life campaigners have started to describe themselves as 'human rights groups',[11] as arguments against abortion are increasingly advanced in terms of protecting those who have no voice.

---

[9] Press release from Care, 'Families troubled by taxing times: Government figures reveal that tax credits are failing poor two-parent households', 13 April 2005.

[10] This is how Care now describes itself. Previously, it described itself as being 'salt and light' in society.

[11] Press release from the Evangelical Alliance, 'Evangelical Alliance backs new anti-abortion campaign', 26 September 2005. Although the groups are not listed on the press release archived on the organisation's website, they were listed at the end of the original press release. They were: Care, Comment on Reproductive Ethics, the Evangelical Alliance, the Guild of Catholic Doctors, the Lawyers' Christian Fellowship, Life, the ProLife Alliance and Student LifeNet.

Political habits are maturing. The diversity of political views, particularly when coupled with broadening agendas and the 'crossover' of arguments, can be seen as a sign of a growing maturity in Christian political perspectives. Briefings and other contributions to public-policy debate by Christians have become noticeably far more considered and better argued.[12] Although more reactionary groups from time to time make what many regard as ill-conceived and inflammatory statements,[13] others that have been around rather longer are starting to make more considered, more profound and more rigorous contributions. A comparison of the reactions of the institutional church to the controversial film *Monty Python's Life of Brian*[14] and *Jerry Springer – The Opera* 30 years later is revealing. Anglican bishops were not nearly as outspoken in their opposition to the latter, and when they did respond were more measured, evidently taking account of realities including the limitations of politics. As we have noted in Chapter 4, campaigning methods are also becoming more sophisticated.

Post-Christendom Divisions

It should by now be clear that Christians in post-Christendom disagree. Indeed, the divisions on individual ethical and moral

---

[12] David Alton, when a MP, observed in his book *Faith in Britain* both a widening and a maturing agenda among para-church groups. The trend can be seen to have continued since then, and that maturity is now being recognised outside the church as well. The Methodist Church and the Salvation Army, for example, won a Third Sector Award for their campaign over the government's Gambling Bill in 2005.

[13] See, for example, the press release from Premier Radio 'Christians demand broadcasting clarity', 29 September 2005, in which the radio station criticised the BBC's decision to invite Stephen Green of Christian Voice onto BBC1's programme *Question Time*. In it, Peter Kerridge of Premier said: 'From previous experience, the BBC are aware of Stephen Green's reputation for making inflammatory comments.'

[14] Robert Sellers, *Always Look on the Bright Side of Life: The Inside Story of Handmade Films* (London: Metro, 2003).

issues may never have been so many and so wide. The fact that Christians are involved in politics doesn't mean that they take the same ethical positions. Political debates often find Christians lining up against each other on opposing sides – perhaps most obviously in the House of Commons, where Christians belong to different parties, and to different Christian groupings within those parties. The emergence of an explicitly 'Christian' party, the Christian People's Alliance, introduced still more visible divisions during election campaigns. However, there are also clear disagreements between different denominations and para-church groups. These are most obvious, perhaps, when Christians find themselves on diametrically opposed sides over proposed changes to the law – for example, on:

- Smacking.
- The age of consent for homosexual sex.
- Civil partnerships.
- The repeal of Section 28 of the Local Government Act.
- Euthanasia.
- Religious hatred.[15]

But they have also been split over a range of political issues that do not directly involve legislation, from the use of markets to the establishment of the Church of England to the question of whether to invade Iraq.[16]

Political division between Christians is in many respects nothing new – during the English Civil War, for example, there were sharp political disagreements over religion. But now the differences are perhaps of a different sort. Whereas previously they were often between powerful elites or those who had power and those who had none – the institutional church, for example and dissenters – now, as the whole church moves away from

---

[15] Supporters of the Incitement to Religious Hatred Bill included Catholic and Anglican bishops and the Methodist Church. Opponents included the Evangelical Alliance, the Christian People's Alliance, the Lawyers' Christian Fellowship and other para-church groups.

[16] Although many Anglican bishops opposed the invasion of Iraq, others supported it.

government, the divisions are far more complex, cutting across denominations, traditions, class, race, gender, party allegiance and theology.

Some of them concern the values and ethics Christians subscribe to. For example, to continue with examples I cited earlier, some Christians see the smacking of children as something perfectly acceptable, even if as a last resort; others see it invariably as violence. Some regard homosexual sex as sinful; others see it as something quite proper within a loving and committed relationship. For many, the waging of war is always wrong, because it involves the taking of life; for others, it is a legitimate instrument for a government to use, though only if it cannot be avoided.

Other divisions arise between Christians (who may or may not share the same values and ethics) as they disagree about the consequences of proposed courses of action, and the limits of governments and the law. For example, some Christians feel that prostitution is wrong but don't automatically conclude that it should be criminalised. Some may not want to encourage cohabitation but feel nevertheless that justice demands that the law should protect and provide for cohabiting couples. The reasoning behind the political positions that many Christians take is often complex.

One of the most complex areas of division is economics, and specifically how to use markets and how to tackle poverty. As Christendom has declined, so at least three major views of economics have been current amongst Christians. The teaching of the church was originally characterised by a 'deeply ingrained scepticism'[17] towards capitalism. The outcome of market forces needed to be 'scrutinised and if necessary corrected in the name of natural law, social justice, human rights and the common good.'[18] A harder line was taken by Christian Socialists. The church had

---

[17] Griffiths, 'The Culture of the Market' in Hay and Kreider (eds.), *Christianity and the Culture of Economics*, p. 17.

[18] Clifford Longley, 'Structures of Sin and the Free Market: John Paul II on Capitalism' in Paul Vallely (ed.), *The New Politics: Catholic Social Teaching for the 21st Century* (London: SCM, 1998).

suggested that 'no one can be at the same time a Catholic and a Socialist,'[19] but some Christian Socialists attempted to show that the ideas of Marx and Engels were not so very different from Christian ideas. However a third perspective was also in evidence, which took the most positive view of markets. David Hume and Adam Smith had suggested that free trade encouraged such virtues as industry, frugality and probity, and even those who saw markets as essentially neutral felt that the right values could guide them towards the common good.

With Socialism apparently discredited following the demise of Soviet Communism, much discussion has revolved around the other two viewpoints. Some see the market as no more than a mechanism for allocating resources, and suggest that its 'decisions' reflect the values that are brought to it by its participants. Others argue that, far from being a neutral thing, the market has developed its own values – which they usually see as detrimental, and sometimes destructive.[20]

The latter view, which emphasises the negative effects of the market, was evident in the 1985 report 'Faith in the City',[21] which was published by the Archbishop of Canterbury's Commission on Urban Priority Areas. Its commission by Robert Runcie was prompted by concern over what was happening to communities on council housing estates in Britain's inner cities. It played a crucial role in raising awareness of the gaps that were growing in our society, gaps that had become painfully obvious in the riots of 1981 and 1985 in Brixton (London), Handsworth (Birmingham) and Toxteth (Liverpool). In 1990, there was a follow-up, titled 'Living Faith in the City'.[22]

But more sympathetic views of the market were also forthcoming, though some of these still regarded the driving force of

---

[19] *Quadragesimo Anno.*

[20] For a discussion of these two perspectives, see Hay and Kreider (eds.), *Christianity and the Culture of Economics.*

[21] 'Faith in the City: A Call to Action by Church and Nation'.

[22] 'Living Faith in the City: A Progress Report by the Archbishop of Canterbury's Advisory Group on Urban Priority Areas' (London: General Synod of the Church of England, 1990).

capitalism as 'covetousness'.[23] The fall of Communism signalled a major shift to the far more positive view of markets from Christians and the churches, who now recognised potential in profit, private property and business.[24] The emphasis of the mainstream churches was now on promoting more humane forms of capitalism and keeping markets in their 'rightful place'.

'The Common Good', published by the Catholic bishops of England and Wales in 1996, has been credited with establishing the principle that market forces should be society's servants, not its masters. (A similar report was issued by Catholic bishops in the US.[25]) 'Unemployment and the Future of Work', published by the Council of Churches for Britain and Ireland,[26] challenged the idea that unemployment and the costs associated with it were inevitable. Both studies, however, recognised the role of markets in wealth creation.

However, whereas Runcie had spoken of an 'excessive preoccupation with prosperity',[27] by 2005 the churches' principal focus had become how to utilise it. Brian Griffiths, amongst others, has called for a theology of wealth creation,[28] and the church has obliged. 'Prosperity with a Purpose' is regarded as the most emphatic endorsement of free-market economics ever given by the church.

Seeking the Common Ground

Nonetheless, the reality, and often complexity, of such divisions has not prevented Christians from seeking to unite themselves

---

[23] Lesslie Newbigin, *Foolishness to the Greeks* (London: SPCK, 1986), p. 113.

[24] Richard Harries, *Is There a Gospel for the Rich?* (London: Mowbray, 1992), p. 72.

[25] 'Economic Justice for All: Catholic Social Teaching and the US Economy'.

[26] The precursor of Churches Together in Britain and Ireland.

[27] Robert Runcie, interviewed on *Panorama*, cited by F. Mount in the *Daily Telegraph*, 1 April 1988, and in a speech to the Global Survival Conference in Oxford, reported in the *Daily Telegraph*, 12 April 1988.

[28] See Griffiths, 'The Culture of the Market' in Hay and Kreider (eds.), *Christianity and the Culture of Economics*, p. 23.

politically in post-Christendom. Some argue that, whilst they are clearly going to disagree about complex issues of economics, Christians should be able to reach a consensus on key 'moral' issues such as euthanasia, abortion and homosexual practice. Others have gone further and suggested that Christians should unite behind a particular political party. So far, such calls have failed. Huge divisions within churches themselves over ethical issues and their appropriate political expression make it unlikely that they will succeed in the near future.

The most successful attempt in post-Christendom to unite Christians of diverse backgrounds around a political cause related in fact to an economic issue – that of developing-world debt. Such campaigns might have been associated with Christians of a more liberal persuasion, but in a major survey of political opinion in the run-up to the 2005 general election[29] an over-whelming majority of evangelicals attending the Spring Harvest festivals signalled their desire to see politicians take action to end global poverty. Of the 2,000 Christians polled by the Evangelical Alliance, 60 per cent said it was the political issue most on their minds. This sample represents only a small section of the church but it nonetheless suggests a degree of unity rarely achieved by Christians in any walk of life. It is notable, too, that few, if any, Christian campaign groups ever spoke out against either the Jubilee 2000 Coalition or the Make Poverty History campaign, while most of the major Christian denominations got behind both initiatives.

British Christians generally refuse to join in one grand political coalition, nevertheless political activity has become a focus for a degree of unity on a smaller scale too – for example, around smaller campaigns such as that against the Incitement to Religious Hatred Bill. As we have already noted, many camp-aigning groups have been set up on an ecumenical basis. Protestants have found common cause with Catholics over the perceived marginalisation of Christians and the Christian faith. Different denominations have come together to make joint state-ments against political extremism and to hold local hustings at

---

[29] Press release from the Evangelical Alliance, 7 April 2005.

election-time. In fact, given the diversity within the church of theology, doctrine and denominational allegiance, politics is perhaps remarkable in its ability to unite, as well as divide, Christians and transcend their differences.

We can also observe a consensus amongst Christians about a number of key political propositions, in particular that the church should use the political system to achieve its political goals.

Endorsement of the political system. Groups such as the Evangelical Alliance and the Faithworks campaign have encouraged and campaigned for trust in the political system and respect for politicians.[30] 'Of the 650 Members of Parliament, the vast majority are hardworking and professional people committed to the common good,' wrote Joel Edwards, general director of the EA, in the foreword to Steve Chalke's book *Trust: A Radical Manifesto.*[31]

An emphasis on voting. Rather than 'Would Jesus vote?', the question is increasingly asked: 'How would Jesus vote?'[32] At the 2005 general election, numerous agencies encouraged Christians to think carefully how they were going to vote.[33] Many Christians regard voting as an important way to bring influence to bear – maybe to get more Christians elected, and certainly to ensure that extremists and other undesirables do not gain political power.[34]

Involvement in party politics. This is seen as both a legitimate and a desirable means of influence. Many groups have implied

[30] Press release from the Evangelical Alliance, 'Evangelical Alliance back Prime Minister's call for more respect: Champions of Respect Awards to highlight young role models of respect', 16 May 2005.

[31] Steve Chalke with Anthony Watkis, *Trust: A Radical Manifesto* (Milton Keynes: Authentic Media, 2004).

[32] Ram Gidoomal and David Porter, *How Would Jesus Vote? What to Look for in Your National Leaders* (Oxford: Monarch, 2001).

[33] For example, the Evangelical Alliance, Churches Together in Britain and Ireland, Care and the Roman Catholic, Anglican and Methodist Churches.

[34] Statements to this effect have been forthcoming from the Methodist Church, the URC, the Church of England and the Catholic Bishops' Conference of England and Wales amongst others.

that Christians who don't get involved in party politics are part of the problem. 'There are unparalleled opportunities in Britain's political parties for good people to stand up for social justice and personal responsibility,' said one group, adding: 'But too many Christians are complaining from the sidelines about the sorry state of politics. Are you a whinger or are you ready to play a part in being the solution?'[35] Others have produced information packs explaining how to join the major political parties and have sent all their supporters membership forms for these parties in the hope that they will join one. One congregation even generated headlines in the national press after they infiltrated a local party en masse and provoked the 'anti-sleaze' campaigner Martin Bell to stand in their constituency as an independent candidate.[36]

The numbers game. Campaign groups across the board have also appealed to the authority of numbers and 'the silent majority'. The Christian Institute denounced the decision of the Liberal Democrat party conference to support civil partnerships and adoption rights for homosexuals as 'a vote loser'.[37] The same group pointed out that there was strong support for Section 28 amongst Labour voters in the Prime Minister's own constituency of Sedgefield.[38] Targeting 'marginal' constituencies is another tactic employed by many Christian groups, that want to get an issue on the agenda, in the hope that the political parties will note the number of Christians in a constituency who might make the difference in an election.

Censorship and control. One particular tactic used by some Christians has been to try to suppress things that are seen as threatening Christian values or the Christian faith. In the

---

[35] The Conservative Christian Fellowship, under 'Our beliefs' in a section entitled 'We believe in political involvement.'

[36] For an example, see 'Bell prepares to stand against evangelical Conservatives', *The Guardian*, 8 December 2000.

[37] Press release from the Christian Institute, 'Christian group attacks Lib Dem vote for gay marriage and adoption: Gay marriage and homosexual adoption rights – a sure vote loser', 18 August 2000.

[38] Press release from the Christian Institute, 'System 3 Poll on Section 28: Sedgefield backs the Clause', 8 March 2000.

seventies, *Monty Python's Life of Brian* suffered a degree of censorship after pressure from Christians persuaded local authorities to use their powers to prevent it being shown.[39] Censorship has also been urged by Christians who are campaigning for justice. A thorny question at election-time has been whether to allow political parties such as the British National Party a platform. Many hustings are held in local churches and so it is an issue that churches have been forced to face. In the run-up to the 1997 general election, the Catholic Church called for organisations such as the BNP to be 'further restricted by electoral law'.[40] The United Reformed Church also declared that, whilst it accepted that such parties were entitled to operate within the democratic process, it was 'vital that they do not become accepted as part of normal political life'.[41] In the end, the decision was usually left to the local church – but it is known that a number of churches did not invite BNP candidates to their hustings.[42] Certainly the BNP felt that at least one denomination had instructed its congregations not to do so.[43]

Acceptance of government funding. Many Christian organisations involved in lobbying activities also have charitable status, and sometimes the line between their political and their charitable activities is blurred. For example, appeals for money are sometimes related to a political issue and yet supporters respond by donating through Gift Aid, which allows the recipient to reclaim tax from the government.

There have been a number of complaints involving allegations that charitable money has been used for political purposes. The Christian Institute was reported to the Charity Commission for using money raised for charitable purposes to finance a campaign

---

[39] Sellers, *Always Look on the Bright Side of Life*.
[40] Statement on pre-election broadcasts from the Roman Catholic Church, 18 April 1997.
[41] Statement from the URC Mission Council, January 2004.
[42] For an example, see 'Church snubs BNP candidate in election talks', *Heywood Advertiser*, 27 April 2005.
[43] See the news story on the BNP website 'Methodist Church says "no" to free speech', 21 March 2005.

to stop same-sex couples adopting children,[44] and the Christian MP Ben Bradshaw asked the commission to investigate Care's political activities, and in particular its internship scheme.[45]

Some campaigning groups have also received more direct government funding for their work. Care obtained significant Home Office funding for its remand fostering scheme, and Oasis and Faithworks have secured substantial funding to build city academies. Indeed, most Christian groups, whether they are political in nature or not, are happy to accept funding from government if they can get it, and would regard it as a wise and good thing to do. Some have actually invested resources in helping Christians to obtain it. Faithworks has run PR campaigns to make central and local government more sympathetic to churches in their funding decisions, and also ran a campaign to equip and inspire churches to gain more statutory funding.

Knowing Your Enemy

It is an interesting paradox that whilst Christians are fairly positive about the political system, and happy to take money from it, they are often quite hostile towards government. Those who take a negative view of post-Christendom often argue that certain institutions such as marriage are ordained by God and that the duty of government is to help to protect them – but instead it has at best done nothing, and at worst it has led the assault against them.[46] Those who take a positive view of post-Christendom often find that government doesn't deliver the justice they demand – for example, in its treatment of asylum seekers. Meanwhile, Christian politicians, whether in office or not, for their part often find that many in the churches do not understand their

---

[44] Amelia Hill, 'Gays hit back at charity over right to adopt', *The Guardian*, 29 December 2002.

[45] Kamal Ahmed, 'Onward Christian lobbyists', *The Observer*, 30 July 2000.

[46] See, for example, the press release from the Christian Institute 'Family Law Bill: A fundamental attack on marriage', 10 January 1996.

work, and they feel judged and pressured by para-church groups who want to impose their own agendas.[47]

Christians in and around the House of Commons have done their best to build bridges with the churches. The Conservative Christian Fellowship led an initiative called 'Listening to Britain's Churches' during William Hague's leadership of the Conservative Party. The Christian Socialist Movement undertook a similar exercise, but extended it to include other faith communities. Nonetheless, many Christians see government increasingly as an enemy, to be harried, fought and sometimes defeated.

But it is not only government that is seen in these terms. Other groups and institutions, too, are identified as campaigners against whom political battles must be fought. Christians concerned with justice have targeted 'consumerism', big business, the arms industry and globalisation, and international institutions such as the World Trade Organisation. Others who take a more negative view of post-Christendom often see 'the gay lobby', 'secularists' or 'humanists' as the enemy.

But what is perhaps most surprising is that for some the enemy is the church itself. How do we account for the fact that so many groups have formed outside traditional church structures? For many, the reason is political disillusionment with the institutional church. They feel that it has let them down, either because it hasn't taken the positions Christians wanted it to take or because it hasn't done enough to promote them. This is perhaps particularly true for those who have been radicalised by a more negative view of post-Christendom. Almost by definition, those who feel discriminated against, oppressed and even persecuted feel that they have few advocates to speak on their behalf.

Now that it is on the margins of our society, the church no longer has the same kind of influence it had when it was at the centre. Whereas in the past the institutional church could be relied on to deliver what Christians wanted politically, this is no longer the

---

[47] Press release from the Evangelical Alliance, 'MPs need our prayers not criticism: A call from Liberal Democrat Shadow Health Secretary to churches', 23 June 2005.

case. Accordingly, people have formed groups to campaign for changes in the law in accordance with their particular perspective; and these have often involved the laity, to find in greater numbers the influence the institutional church has lost.

When the Bishop of Oxford, Richard Harries, urged Parliament to lower the age of homosexual consent to 16 and to scrap the law that banned the promotion of homosexuality in schools, the Christian Institute attacked him and said he had been misled by gay-rights pressure groups.[48] The then Bishop of Blackburn Alan Chesters was similarly criticised for supporting the repeal of Section 28 of the Local Government Act, which prevented the 'promotion' of homosexuality by local authorities.[49] Other churches have been attacked as 'naive' for backing measures to outlaw religious hatred. In 1977, having failed to mobilise church leaders, Mary Whitehouse prosecuted *Gay News* herself for blasphemy when it published James Kirkup's poem 'The Love that Dares to Speak Its Name', which explored the feelings of a Roman centurion as he imagined having sex with Jesus on the cross.

But others whose radicalisation has been more positive have also been willing to challenge the church. Indeed, sometimes they have made it the target of political action. As already mentioned, the Campaign Against Arms Trade's Christian Network was unhappy with the church's stand on peace-and-justice issues and mobilised against it, running a 'clean investment' campaign aimed at persuading the Church of England to sell its shareholdings in arms companies. The Lesbian and Gay Christian Movement, which was previously concerned solely with equality within the church, has increasingly turned its attention to the way the church operates politically. It has declared that faith schools should not be allowed by law to harass or discriminate against pupils on grounds of their beliefs,[50] and has also

---

[48] Press release from the Christian Institute, 'Bishop wrong to back sodomy laws', 5 November 1997.

[49] Press release from the Christian Institute, 'Section 28 debate: Bishop's amendment allows promotion of homosexuality', 17 February 2000.

[50] Press release from the LGCM, 'LGCM calls for amendments to government equality', 14 June 2005.

campaigned for equality outside the church – for example, for civil partnerships.[51]

Conclusion

In post-Christendom, the church's political influence is no longer the preserve of the clergy or church leaders. Christians take many different positions on political issues. Political engagement creates division in the church, but also has the capacity to unite Christians in a way that overcomes doctrinal and denominational differences. And where there is disagreement over the specific positions Christians take, there is widespread agreement about the methods of engagement.

However, much of this political engagement is undertaken uncritically. The argument is often heard that in a democratic system the church, or Christians, have just as much right to engage as everyone else. Contemporary Christian political approaches are characterised by a certain pragmatism, and even those who campaign in the name of justice are prepared to use what others might regard as unjust institutions to get what they want.

Christians have called for higher standards in public life,[52] they have campaigned for reform of voting systems, they have even challenged the legality of the government's refusal to allow people to opt out of paying taxes to fund military operations and give the money instead to other causes.[53] Nonetheless, often the methods they employ involve an uncritical use of the very system they are seeking to change.

---

[51] Press releases from the LGCM: 'Civil Partnership Bill – Lords give final approval', 17 November 2004; 'Lords try to wreck Civil Partnership Bill', 24 June 2004; 'Civil partnerships – good, but not good enough', 20 March 2004.

[52] Patrick Dixon, *The Truth about Westminster: Can We Change the Heart of British Politics?* (London: Kingsway, 1996).

[53] Richard Norton-Taylor, 'Judge rejects peace tax plea', *The Guardian*, 26 July 2005.

7

Signs of Contradiction

In George Orwell's *Animal Farm*, the revolutionaries' Seven Commandments are eventually reduced to just one: 'All animals are equal, but some animals are more equal than others.'[1]

In the last chapter, we saw how the church is engaging politically and flexing its muscle. It is taking most of the political opportunities it can find, defending old methods of engagement and creating new ones. But it is doing so quite uncritically. In the main, it accepts the values of the political system and is happy to engage in it in the same way that everyone else does.

But as it emerges from Christendom – a context in which it wielded power and influence – the church does not automatically begin from the same point as everyone else. It brings with it baggage from another era. Christendom may have passed but its ecclesiastical and social vestiges remain,[2] and this has an impact both on how the church engages politically and on how others interpret its political activity.

The church may be fragmented and Christians may hold different political beliefs and positions, but the outside world does not easily make such distinctions and often considers Christians as a single entity. The 'post-denominationalism' of the post-Christendom church in general, and the advent of para-church campaigning groups in particular, further confuses the picture. Our uncritical engagement in the political system can lead to a

---
[1] *Animal Farm*, chapter 10.
[2] See Murray, *Post-Christendom*, pp.189–93 for a list of these.

number of difficulties and apparent contradictions, especially when it comes to the church's political witness.

Establishment

The most obvious difficulties arise as a result of the Church of England's established status. The Reformation 'prised open the historic Christendom vision of a religio-political unity.'[3] Henry VIII's break with Rome involved the creation of his own church. Over the next four centuries, it has been argued, five phases of establishment followed.[4] The relationship between church and state has been far from static, and the ties between them have been loosening; but at the beginning of the 21st century there remain several features of establishment that have a direct bearing on the church's political engagement and witness.[5]

It is important not to overstate the significance of establishment, and important also to recognise that it has often been 'facilitative of creating openings for the wider participation of religious minorities in civic and political life.'[6] Arguments against establishment made by Christians tend to focus on the ways it constrains the church,[7] but others have pointed out that it also affords the church a number of political advantages. The case is also mounted that disestablishment may lead to a further separation of religion and politics.

The political consequence of establishment that is most often cited is the allocation to bishops of 26 seats in the upper chamber of Parliament, the House of Lords. While many attend on a rota

---

[3] Paul Weller, *Time for a Change: Reconfiguring Religion, State and Society*, p. 22.

[4] Colin Buchanan, *Cut the Connection: Disestablishment and the Church of England* (London: Darton Longman Todd, 1994).

[5] Weller, *Time for a Change*; Theo Hobson, *Against Establishment: An Anglican Polemic* (London: Darton Longman Todd, 2004).

[6] Weller, *Time for a Change*, p. 183.

[7] See, for example, Buchanan, *Cut the Connection* and Kenneth Leech (ed.), *Setting the Church of England Free: the Case for Disestablishment* (The Jubilee Group, 2001).

basis and the bishops are therefore rarely present in any great numbers, many of them do sign amendments to bills, speak in debates and sit on committees. They also have a degree of access, both formal and informal, to government and to other parliamentarians. Although the extent of their influence is a matter of debate, few would argue that they have none at all.

However, the mere fact that they have seats in the Lords simply because they hold high rank in the Church of England raises significant questions of justice. A charge of hypocrisy can be levelled at a church that claims to speak up for the poor and the marginalised but yet is happy to hold on to a privileged position of power and influence that some would say is undeserved. Although no one at present is elected to the House of Lords by a national ballot, it can still seem a contradiction to extol the virtues of democracy on the one hand, while enjoying the benefits of a fundamentally undemocratic arrangement on the other.

Another feature of establishment is the status of the Monarch as the 'supreme governor' of the Church of England. Although this is not obviously political, given the symbolic role of the King or Queen, it nevertheless has important political implications. The circumstances of the marriage of Prince Charles and Camilla Parker Bowles highlighted the church's somewhat strange and uneasy relationship with the Crown, as it found itself in the anomalous position of having as its future governor and 'defender of the faith' a man it could not allow to remarry or to say the liturgy he would one day pledge to uphold at his coronation. It made the church look somewhat quaint, and it also made it look harsh. The public found it hard to understand how the church could preach about grace, compassion and forgiveness but still refuse to marry its own future governor.

The Church of England has traditionally employed a curious dualism to justify the fact that its governor is a man or woman chosen not for their qualities of Christian leadership but by virtue of the family they are born into. The argument is that the *legal* status of the Monarch is a different matter from the *spiritual* authority the bishops exercise. But such a distinction no longer seems so convincing in post-Christendom, especially when so many Christians are suggesting that the sacred and the secular, faith and politics, are inextricably linked.

Within the church, too, establishment raises questions of equality. The alliance of church and state makes it look as if some Christians and some types of Christianity are more important than others. It accentuates political divisions within the wider church over issues of funding and influence where other denominations and groups feel disadvantaged and have to work harder to make their political voices heard. It may also accentuate divisions within the Church of England itself. Rows over whether female clergy should be permitted to become bishops, for example, dominate the news agenda in a way they might otherwise not, leading to accusations of injustice and hypocrisy.

The status of establishment also encourages the belief that Christianity is about power, just as other Christians are emphasising the churches' identification with the powerless. There is a potential cost for the church as a political community, too. It accustoms Christians to trust in earthly power rather than in God's disarming strength displayed in Jesus. And whilst some in the church are calling for radical reforms, establishment also to some extent allies the church with the status quo. The Crown is an institution that exists to preserve an order based on eugenic privilege, and the involvement of clergy at major political events reinforces this. The Monarch is crowned in Westminster Abbey, and many senior Anglicans take part in the ritual.

For those Christians who believe that the message of the gospel is that God's grace and forgiveness are available to all, whatever their status, and combines with justice a special regard for the poor and vulnerable, the power and privilege of establishment are an apparent contradiction.

Fairness

This privilege is all the more problematic whenever the church calls for a level playing field.[8] If it is going to campaign for equal

---

[8] Chalke, *Trust*, p. 44.

treatment, either for itself or for other groups, it will have to address the situations in which it has clear advantages over others. It can't have it both ways.

There are at least four major issues on which some in the church feel threatened but which they will have to address if they want the church's calls for fairness to be taken seriously:

- Blasphemy law
- Church schools
- Broadcasting
- Taxation and funding

Blasphemy law

In 2004–5, Christians became greatly exercised about the government's Racial and Religious Hatred Bill. Afraid that their freedom to evangelise would be compromised if it became law, they were vocal in their opposition. There were mass lobbies of Parliament and demonstrations on the streets, letter-writing campaigns and petitions. Broad alliances were formed to fight the bill.

If we look back over the preceding decade, however, we shall see that the bill did not simply appear from nowhere. Its emergence can really be understood only when we examine the church's approach to one of the vestiges of Christendom: the law against blasphemy.

The legal concept of blasphemy goes back centuries to a time when challenging or insulting the Christian faith was thought to threaten the very fabric of society. The present law defends only Christianity and a judgment in 1838 restricted it further to protect only 'the tenets and beliefs of the Church of England'. When some British Muslims called for the law to be enforced after the publication of Salman Rushdie's controversial novel *The Satanic Verses*, it proved impossible, and the failure to bring a prosecution demonstrated for many the lack of protection that the law affords to other faiths.[9]

---

[9] An observation made by, amongst others, the Churches' Commission for Racial Justice in 'Religious Discrimination: A Christian Response' (Church House Publishing, 2001).

In fact, the law against blasphemy was rarely invoked, even by Christians,[10] and it has often been condemned as outmoded[11] (though as recently as February 2006 Stewart Lee, director of *Jerry Springer – The Opera*, said that threats of prosecution by Christian groups had frightened a third of possible venues off a proposed tour).[12] In the context of an increasingly pluralist society, the government initiated moves to review the law, and the calls for its replacement increased as followers of other faiths asked for protection against religious hatred – something for which Christians felt little need.

However, many Christian groups opposed the repeal of the law from the start. They also objected to its extension to cover other religions, and also to the creation of a new offence of 'incitement to religious hatred' that might offer protection for all religions.[13] Nor did they suggest any alternative to provide the shield that representatives of other religions were asking for, particularly in the context of the backlash against Muslims following certain terrorist atrocities. Many Christians suggested that existing laws were adequate to protect them.

Those who were fearful of post-Christendom argued that the law on blasphemy helped to buttress Britain's 'Christian constitution'. Retaining it would be a symbolic reminder of the 'Christian basis to UK law'. It was suggested that the law bore witness to the 'long-standing importance' of the Judaeo-Christian laws and

---

[10] The last man to be sent to prison for blasphemy was John William Gott, who in 1922 was sentenced to nine months' hard labour for comparing Jesus to a circus clown. In Scotland, there has not been a public prosecution since 1843.

[11] As far back as 1949, in a speech on freedom under the law, Lord Denning said: 'The offence of blasphemy is now a dead letter.'

[12] Stewart Lee , 'Christian Voice is outside, praying for our souls...', *The Guardian*, 15 February 2006.

[13] Evidence from the Evangelical Alliance to the House of Lords Select Committee on Religious Offences in England and Wales, 2002–3. See also the submissions from the Christian People's Alliance, Christian Voice, Christian Watch, *Evangelicals Now*, Jubilee Campaign and the Maranatha Community to the same select committee.

customs that underpinned democracy and the social and moral values that we shared in Britain's open society. Repeal would be interpreted as an official declaration that, after some 1,500 years, Britain was 'no longer a Christian nation', and it would also raise wider problems relating to the status of the established church. The state ignored both the power of religious commitment and its 'heritage of Christian values' at its peril.[14]

What was striking about the way this case was put, even before any detailed proposals were forthcoming from the government, was the absence of any arguments about justice. The primary concern of many Christian groups was the preservation of Britain's 'Christian heritage' – and that didn't seem to include concern for equality or protection for the vulnerable.

But there was disagreement between the churches. Not all Christians took this position. The Catholic, Methodist and (perhaps most remarkable, given its established status) Anglican Churches proposed that the government should introduce a new law against incitement to religious hatred and should repeal the law against blasphemy.[15] Laws protecting only one faith and indeed one church, were now recognised as an anomaly.[16] It was suggested that this would send a clear signal that measures to prevent incitement to religious hatred was not about shielding religion from criticism, vilification or mockery but about defending people from real harm done in the name of religion.[17]

---

[14] See the submissions from the Christian People's Alliance, Christian Voice, Christian Watch, *Evangelicals Now*, Jubilee Campaign and the Maranatha Community to the House of Lords Select Committee on Religious Offences in England and Wales, 2002–3, made on 24 July 2002.

[15] See submissions to the House of Lords Select Committee on Religious Offences in England and Wales, 2002–3 from the Archbishops' Council of the Church of England, the Catholic Bishops' Conference of England and Wales and the Methodist Church.

[16] Speech by the Bishop of Portsmouth, Dr Kenneth Stevenson, in the House of Lords, *Hansard*, HL, 14 March 2005, col. 1108.

[17] See 'Bishop calls for repeal of Blasphemy Law', *Church of England Newspaper*, 18 March 2005.

Church schools

One quarter of all primary schools and one in twenty secondary schools in England are Church of England schools. In 2001 the contribution of faith schools was welcomed by the government, which proposed the creation of many more.[18] This simple fact brought into question claims made around the same time that the church was being discriminated against in matters of public funding. One hundred per cent of the running costs and most of the capital (building) costs of voluntary-aided, faith-based schools are paid for with taxpayers' money.

Nonetheless, there were calls from some Christian quarters for an end to discrimination, and these sounded particularly hypocritical to some people given that many voluntary-aided, faith-based schools (of all religions) operate their own discriminatory policies – for example, having control of their own religious education and worship. Many church schools have also long discriminated in favour of church-goers through their admissions policies. Often, despite being publicly funded, they openly – and legally – apply admissions criteria that favour children who attend churches that are linked to them. This suits both the schools, which want to maintain their Christian ethos, and the clergy, who want more people to attend their churches. Whenever it has been suggested that this discrimination should end, Christians have fiercely objected.

Many Church of England schools also discriminate in favour of their own religion when employing teachers, and advertise for head teachers of Christian faith only.

Nor are these rights simply a legacy of Christendom that the church is willing to take or leave. They have been consistently defended, in particular by the Church of England. Rights to discriminate in employment were only recently won. For example, the Evangelical Alliance, the Christian Schools' Trust and Care intervened in a court case mounted by seven leading trades unions which claimed that the government's 2003 Employment Equality (Sexual Orientation) Regulations were legally flawed because

---

[18] Government 2001 green paper, 'Schools Building on Success'.

exemptions for religious organisations would in effect allow discrimination. The Christian groups argued that Christian organisations had the right to discriminate against gay and lesbian people and to formulate and apply their own policies regarding their employment as clergy or as teachers in faith-based schools.[19]

The argument that is often made to justify the massive government funding of church schools is that they deliver better results than others.[20] However, the discrimination in these schools' admissions policies appears to undermine the line that 'faith works.' In the words of Ofsted: 'Selection, even on religious grounds, is likely to attract well-behaved children from stable backgrounds.'[21] As the British Humanist Association puts it, church schools 'take less than their share of deprived children and more than their share of the children of ambitious and choosy parents.'[22] This has been backed up by research that suggests that church primary schools in England are less likely than local authority schools to accept children from poorer homes.[23] Better results are a foregone conclusion given the admissions criteria that many church schools apply.

Broadcasting

Although Christians have claimed that religion is being marginalised in broadcasting, that is not a conclusion shared by many people – including the BBC's director general, Mark Thompson, himself a Christian. Speaking to the Churches' Media Council in 2005, he suggested that in fact religion was 'front- and centre-stage'.

---

[19] 'Evangelicals win discrimination court battle', Ekklesia News (www.ekklesia.co.uk/content/news/news.shtml), 28 April 2004.
[20] The green paper 'Schools Building on Success' said: 'They have a good record of delivering a high quality of education.'
[21] Quoted in *The Times Educational Supplement*, 16 February 2001.
[22] 'Faith Schools – Why Not?', an article on the website of the British Humanist Association (www.humanism.org.uk).
[23] '"Richer pupils" at church schools', BBC Online, 13 February 2006.

Indeed, religion pops up all over the schedules, from drama and comedy to reality TV.[24] There are fly-on-the-wall documentaries such as *Seaside Parish*, Tom Wright's explorations of the historical Jesus and the Resurrection and 'Thought for the Day' on Radio 4's *Today* programme, alongside interviews of Christians broadcast every week on *Songs of Praise*. Christians may not be able to use public-service broadcasting to evangelise or proselytise, but in 2001 ITV broadcast a ten-part series about the Alpha course. The news programmes often report statements made by bishops and regularly ask church leaders and representatives of para-church groups for comment on important moral, ethical and political issues.

But as Thompson has hinted, it is the obsession of some Christians with a particular share of the schedules that has confused the issue. The category of religious broadcasting has become a distraction. Rather than thinking of Christianity as something that should inform every area of life, and rather than concentrating on producing material that is relevant to the general public, Christians have focused on a narrow area of broadcasting and put all their efforts into defending 'their' share of the available airtime. In the words of Ofcom: 'Given the moral, ethical and philosophical elements of religion that give it a broad relevance to many issues explored on television, there have been few religious programmes which demonstrate or exploit that relevance to topical Factual [*sic*] issues to successfully bid for mid-evening slots.'[25] What some sections of the church perceive as discrimination is something they have brought upon themselves.

There is another sense in which this is true: many Christian groups feel they are being discriminated against in the allocation of broadcasting licences, but what is often overlooked is that the churches themselves helped to create the conditions for this. During the passage of the 1990 Broadcasting Bill, mainstream

---

[24] A point made by Mark Thompson in his speech to the Churches' Media Council, on 6 June 2005.

[25] Ofcom documents supporting a consultation on religious programming, 21 April 2004.

churches[26] actually opposed allowing religious groups to own national broadcast licences. Not only were they fearful of tele-evangelists and cults, they were also concerned that they would be squeezed off the main channels, and accordingly lobbied to prevent religious broadcasters from appealing for funds and proselytising on air.

The 1996 Broadcasting Act (which was designed to take account of the emergence of digital broadcasting) was worded in such a way that it meant, inadvertently, that religious bodies were automatically excluded from applying for the new licences for digital local radio. The government recognised this anomaly and promised to remove the restriction. However, some Christians wanted far more than that. The Christian broadcasting lobby came together to form the Centre for Justice and Liberty (CJ&L), which campaigned vigorously for the total removal of all restrictions and disqualifications of religious organisations and individuals from owning a licence to broadcast.

The government said it wished to remove as many restrictions as possible on ownership but it didn't think it fair that one religious group might own one of the scarce national licences, for Channel 3 or Channel 5 on television or one of the three commercial radio stations. It made it clear that the remaining restrictions would be lifted when more channels were available.

Those who were campaigning for the total removal of the restrictions and disqualifications did so on grounds of principle – they wished to see an end to all discrimination against Christian groups – and cited the European Convention on Human Rights as well as competition and other law. However, at the time no Christian broadcaster or church actually aspired to own a licence.

But it has been the penchant of Christians to label themselves 'religious' and put themselves in a box that has been the problem. It has always been possible for individual Christians, involved in Christian activities, to be directors and shareholders of a broadcast station, and there was never any bar to Christians forming a company that was *not* labelled 'religious' and competing for a

---

[26] Including the Anglican, Catholic, Methodist and United Reformed Churches and the Church of Ireland.

licence with innovative and creative programming that expressed Christian values. Religious bodies have also always been able to form production companies and make their own programmes to offer to broadcasters. To many observers, therefore, claims of discrimination seemed rather far-fetched.

Taxation and funding

Another legacy of Christendom is that the advancement of religion qualifies for tax relief, which means that Christian evangelistic activities are tax-exempt. This has now been extended to other religions. But the distinctions between evangelism, social care and political activity are increasingly blurred. This means, for example, that Christian radio stations have been able to claim tax relief on much of their work while campaigning on a range of political issues. As noted in the last chapter, many Christian campaign groups have charitable trusts attached to them and it is not always clear which of their funds are being used for charitable and which for political purposes. Some appeal to their supporters for funds to support political campaigning and inform them that they can Gift Aid their donations. And when it was suggested that tax relief should be restricted to organisations that did 'good works', Christians were urged to write to the Cabinet Office in protest.[27]

Charitable status also means that Christian groups can apply more easily for other forms of funding, such as money raised through the National Lottery. Ironically, an earlier national lottery had been abolished in 1826, after campaigns involving Christians. When a Conservative government reintroduced it on 21 October 1993, it met – not surprisingly – with renewed opposition from churches and church groups across the denominational divides,[28] who formed a huge and holy alliance that put up a valiant fight.

---

[27] 'Christian groups may lose tax breaks', *Evangelicals Now*, December 2001.

[28] Press release from the Christian Institute, 'Abolish the Lottery', 10 September 1996; also 'The National Lottery: A Critique of State Sponsored Gambling', published by the Christian Institute in 1996.

The battle was finally lost – and only a few years later many churches were receiving Lottery funding.[29] The quick change was at one level understandable. Ageing denominations with creaking infrastructure need all the help they can get,[30] and Christians who want to play a full part in community projects seem to have little choice but to avail themselves of such sources of funding. The Evangelical Alliance observed that its members, whether churches, para-church groups or faith-based community groups, constantly found themselves directed towards Lottery funding to finance their activities, and those that refused such funding were being seriously hampered when it came to providing 'vital services' in the community.[31]

Nonetheless, the church appears to have compromised its witness, and in a very short space of time. Its complete and determined opposition has collapsed into routine involvement in actions that appear implicitly to endorse what it only very recently regarded as an institutionalised evil that hurts the most vulnerable.

Some sections of the church still hold out resolutely, especially in Northern Ireland,[32] but the acceptance of Lottery money by

---

[29] The Methodist Church decided in 1999, a year after the Lottery Act, to allow individual Methodist churches to consider applying for Lottery funding.

[30] See, for example, the press release from the English Heritage Lottery Fund '£17.5 million blessing for more than 150 religious buildings', 1 March 2005; also the memorandum submitted by the Church of England's Church Heritage Forum in November 1998 to the House of Commons Select Committee on Culture, Media and Sport, which states: 'The Heritage Lottery Fund has had a significant impact on church buildings even in the relatively short time since its foundation.'

[31] See, for example, the Evangelical Alliance's submission to the review of Lottery funding by the Department for Culture, Media and Sport's National Lottery distribution and communities division in October 2002.

[32] 'Lottery Funds and Religious Groups: A study into the accessing of Lottery monies by religious groups and the impact on groups with religious objections to applying for Lottery funding', Macaulay Associates and Vision Management Services, October 2002.

others undermines their stand and compromises the witness of other Christians who are campaigning against not only further developments in the Lottery but also new measures such as the 2004 Gambling Bill.

Campaigning Contradictions

Other contradictions are apparent when we set Christian claims of discrimination and marginalisation against the reality of their political activity. While some in the church have lamented their lack of political influence, outside the church there has been growing concern that Christians have too much influence.[33] Bearing in mind how few people in Britain go to church, the number of MPs associated with the Christian Socialist Movement, the Conservative Christian Fellowship and the Liberal Democrat Christian Forum gives the lie to suggestions that Christians have little political influence. Besides the bishops who sit in the House of Lords, many former leaders of Christian denominations are given life peerages.[34] At one time recently, the Prime Minister and the leaders of the two main opposition parties all professed Christian faith. The last two leaders of the Labour Party[35] and three of the last six leaders of the Conservative Party[36] have professed Christian faith. At the 2005 general election, the leaders of all three of the principal parties went out of their way to address Christians.[37] It has even been asserted that Catholic votes secured Labour's third term.[38] In 2003, religious groups were granted an enhanced role in the development of government policy through the setting-up of a new 'faith community liaison group', which included the Evangelical Alliance amongst others.

---

[33] See Polly Toynbee, 'The Bishops have no right to restrict our right to die', *The Guardian*, 14 October 2005.
[34] See Toynbee, 'The Bishops have no right to restrict our right to die'.
[35] John Smith and Tony Blair.
[36] Margaret Thatcher, William Hague and Iain Duncan Smith.
[37] In lectures organised by Faithworks.
[38] Robert Worcester (of Mori) and Roger Mortimer, 'Catholics secured Labour's third term', *The Tablet*, 21 May 2005.

Complaints of marginalisation also seem to be at variance with the claims that many Christian groups make about the numbers they represent. When the church wants to wield political clout, it often resorts to petitions to demonstrate how many people support the positions it is taking. At other times, when they want to justify their influence, Christians draw attention to statistics from the census that show that over 70 per cent of the population believe in God or identify themselves as Christian.[39]

Such large figures might suggest to many people that the church could use its powerful position to show care for other religions, but this often is not the case. While rejecting the charge that they are oversensitive about 'blasphemous' portrayals of God and Jesus, some Christians have at the same time suggested in evidence to government that followers of other faiths need to be less sensitive about public criticism of them.[40] There have been calls for 'the re-privileging of certain religious [that is, Christian] traditions and, if necessary, the public exclusion of others.'[41]

It also appears that double standards are applied to questions of censorship. When Sikhs in Birmingham protested against a play they felt was offensive, evangelicals declared that the 'correct response to provocation should not be coercive censorship. In this country we have the freedom to express ideas, many of them controversial, which is a precious liberty that should be preserved.'[42]

What of claims that other faith communities get better treatment than Christians? Muslims would certainly beg to differ.

---

[39] In arguing that policy makers should acknowledge Christianity, the Evangelical Alliance said: 'The Christian faith has shaped Europe for the past 1,500 years. At the last census 71% of the population said they had at least a nominal commitment to the Christian faith and 11% attend church at some point in the year' ('Religious Discrimination', *PQ*, September 2003).

[40] The Evangelical Alliance told a House of Commons select committee that Muslims should be 'less sensitive' about public criticism of their faith.

[41] David Holloway, 'The Crown and the Courts', 1996 (www.christian.org.uk/html-publications/courts.htm).

[42] Press release from the Evangelical Alliance, 'Evangelical Alliance rejects violent censorship', 23 December 2004.

Muslim organisations have consistently reported higher levels of discrimination than most other religious groups, in education, employment, housing, law and order and local government services.[43] They point out the constant negative stereotyping of Muslims in TV dramas such as *24*, the drama series shown on both the BBC and Sky.[44] Hindu and Sikh organisations have also drawn attention to high levels of unfair treatment.[45] When the Asian comedy programme *Goodness Gracious Me* was commissioned, the BBC received letters from Muslim, Sikh and Hindu religious leaders, each complaining about the treatment of their faith and each certain that it wouldn't dare to make similar jokes about other religions.[46]

Christian organisations have certainly been much less likely to report unfair treatment than Muslims, Sikhs or Hindus.[47] This does not necessarily mean that Christians are not treated so unfairly, but those who *have* felt discriminated against have been concerned primarily about the media's indifference and ignorance. Few have complained of aggression or violence. This is in marked contrast to Muslim, Sikh and Hindu respondents, who have reported hostility, verbal and physical abuse and damage to property.[48]

Finally, we should also bear in mind that most other faith communities are in fact more vulnerable and more marginalised than

---

[43] Paul Weller, A. Feldman, K. Purdham et al., 'Religious Discrimination in England and Wales' in Jamel Malik (ed.), *Muslims in Europe: From the Margin to the Centre* (Frankfurt: Verlag, 2004).

[44] Jamie Doward, 'Muslim anger at terror plot in TV drama', *The Observer*, 30 January 2005.

[45] Weller, Feldman, Purdham et al., 'Religious Discrimination in England and Wales'.

[46] Mark Thompson, 'Why I stand by my decision to broadcast *Jerry Springer – The Opera*', *The Times*, 8 March 2005. www. timesonline.co.uk/article/0,,1072-1515832,00.html

[47] Weller, Feldman, Purdham et al., 'Religious Discrimination in England and Wales'.

[48] Weller, Feldman, Purdham et al., 'Religious Discrimination in England and Wales'.

Christians. If we believe that society should especially protect the weak, we must conclude that it would be no bad thing if they did indeed get special treatment.

When it suits us, however, it seems that Christians are prepared to make common cause with others we would normally repudiate. Political expediency led Christians opposed to the Racial and Religious Hatred Bill to ally themselves with secularists and humanists they had previously attacked. Indeed, some of their new partners-in-arms were comedians who wanted to retain the right to ridicule the church – something that Christians had earlier campaigned against.

Of course, there are many other paradoxes and contradictions we could explore. Often Christian political action involves campaigning for new laws that would criminalise certain groups and behaviours. Christians have advocated harsher penalties for drug possession,[49] gun control and homosexual activity for those under 21 years of age. Even those who campaign for human rights and justice still seem keen to call for tougher sentences for transgressors. Some Christians might argue that such things stand in opposition to the gospel of forgiveness and freedom we are called to proclaim. From such a perspective, many political campaigns can be considered contradictory. It is certainly hard to see how such calls can be reconciled with the commitment to find alternatives to prison that other Christians are exploring.

One overarching contradiction is this, that amidst so many charges of hypocrisy the church is running PR campaigns to restore trust. This begs the question: Should the church be urging us to trust it, or should it get its own house in order first to win our trust again?

---

[49] Press release from the Christian Institute, 'As David Blunkett prepares to make a Commons statement this week: Government to cut sentences for drug dealers', 8 July 2002; see also the press release from the Christian Institute 'Christian group publishes briefing against plans to soften the law on cannabis: Sentences for dope dealers to be slashed', 28 June 2002.

Persecution

When we talk of 'persecution', we ought to note some important differences between the contemporary experience of the church in Britain and that of the early church, or indeed of marginalised groups in Christendom.

- In pre-Christendom and Christendom, persecution often led to torture and death. In post-Christendom, this is not so.
- In pre-Christendom, persecution was a response to the perception that Christians were subverting the social and political order. In post-Christendom, it more often results because Christians want to defend them.
- In pre-Christendom, Christians were persecuted because they refused to participate in activities that the government demanded. In post-Christendom, Christians feel persecuted because they are no longer able to impose things on others.
- In pre-Christendom, persecution was something to be 'rejoiced in'. In post-Christendom, it is something to be fought, by legal action, campaigning and legislation.
- In pre-Christendom, persecution was unmistakable. In post-Christendom, many Christians would dispute that it was persecution.
- In pre-Christendom, Christians had little in the way of privilege. In post-Christendom, it is a loss of privilege that Christians often perceive as persecution.
- In pre-Christendom, persecution was often an opportunity to address those in power. In post-Christendom, it is an inability to address those in power that Christians often perceive as persecution. They feel they are being victimised because they no longer have a voice.
- In pre-Christendom, persecution was a consequence of refusing to take part in government. In post-Christendom, it is exclusion from government, or denial of government funding, that Christians often perceive as persecution.

Finally, we may observe that in post-Christendom many of the charges of 'persecution' that Christians make against others – of prejudice or injustice that causes offence and distress – can just as reasonably be made against them.

None of this is to deny that Christians today feel that they are being persecuted. But we ought to note important differences in what 'persecution' once entailed and what it entails now – and to note, too, that the need to use the state to shield Christians from discrimination and abuse is perhaps far less pressing now than it was when the foundations of Christendom were being laid.

Conclusion

Archbishop William Temple suggested that the church is 'the only organisation that exists primarily for the sake of those who are not its members.' This is not necessarily how it is perceived by those outside it when it comes to its political activity and witness. One crucial point underlies all the above. When the church engages in politics uncritically, it can appear to be little more than a self-interested pressure group, defending and advancing its rights and interests wherever it can.

This perception, of course, may divert attention from some bold stands for justice that the church is making. Christians have campaigned on issues of debt forgiveness and trade justice and have spoken up on behalf of the vulnerable around the world, not least in Darfur, Guantanamo Bay and Zimbabwe. But this selfless message of compassion and justice is compromised by their own behaviour closer to home. As a result, even those organisations that campaign for an end to the persecution of Christians around the world are vulnerable to the charge that they are simply defending their own, with little regard for others.

Sometimes, statements of self-interest are explicit. The Archbishops' Council's 2001 report 'The Way Ahead: Church of England Schools in the New Millennium' 'confirmed the crucial importance of the church schools to the whole mission of the Church to children and young people, and indeed to the long-term well-being of the Church of England.'

On the one hand, sections of the church are calling for a level playing field,[50] especially when it comes to their applications for government funding and calls for equal treatment before the law. On the other hand, often it is the same people who are hanging on to the privileges the church enjoyed in a bygone age – or, in some cases, actually demanding new privileges and protections.

Even those who have no wish to try to regain the privileges of Christendom often fail to assess properly their political engagement and the tactics they use, and so exercise influence and power uncritically. 'The system is there, so why not use it?' the argument runs. Old habits die hard, too. The church has been used to a 'governing' role in the past, and often this means that the methods of engagement it adopts smack of Christendom.

As a result, the church often sends out mixed messages in its political witness to the society around it. On the one hand, it seems to be standing for justice, equality and integrity, for the poor and the vulnerable. On the other hand, many of the tactics it uses appear unjust, unequal and hypocritical. Also, the outside world often lumps all 'Christians' together. There may be difference and diversity within the church, but these are seldom taken into account by others, and this is another reason why the church appears to be sending out mixed messages.

---

[50] Chalke, *Trust.*

8

The New Deal

Our message to local and national government is this: Treat us fairly and you can rely on us to deliver good results. Partner with us and we rise to the challenge. Fund our work and we will not let you down. Celebrate, endorse and support our diversity and offer us equality. Judge us on our merits. Not on our beliefs.

Steve Chalke[1]

People talk a great deal about the decline of religion and the churches in our national life. But in terms of social action and commitment, community by community, it is your revival and adaptation which are striking ... I would like to see you play a bigger, not a lesser, role in the future. I say this because of the visible, tangible difference you are making for the better in our society for so many people. That is the proof of your faith in action in the service of others.

Tony Blair[2]

In the last chapter, we noted a number of evident contradictions. These are not simply epiphenomena. They are being entrenched in a new relationship that is developing between Christians and government. As Christendom disappears, it is not leaving a void behind it. New arrangements are coming into place. Sections of the church are becoming clearer in their demands from government, and the government, too, is realising the

---

[1] Chalke, *Trust*, p. 44.
[2] Tony Blair's address to Faithworks during the 2005 general election campaign.

advantages that can be had from Christianity in post-Christendom.

Under the Edict of Milan, the church won various protections from persecution. It gained equal rights, where previously it had felt vulnerable and oppressed. Later emperors extended its privileges. They often acted as its patron. The Empire, too, seemed to benefit from these developments. A new religion was in the ascendancy that would help it to achieve its goals.

As Christendom changed, so the relationship between church and state changed too. However, the basic concerns of political leaders – for example, to legitimise their rule, create a stable order and deliver their policy objectives – remained the same. It should be no surprise that in post-Christendom, too, church and state have been finding that the other still has its uses.

Observers have identified an emerging 'multi-faith Constantinianism',[3] or 'multi-faith establishment',[4] that involves partnerships with government at local, regional and national levels.[5] Its features include:

• Strategic partnerships, promoted by government in many different ways that seek to involve religious groups.
• The formation of local inter-faith councils.
• The creation of 'faith forums'.
• The formation of a Home Office faith communities unit.
• The appointment of a faith 'envoy' for the Prime Minister.
• A range of reviews, guidance and reports addressing such partnerships.[6]

---

[3] Weller, *Time for a Change*, p. 208.

[4] Luke Bretherton, 'A New Establishment? Theological Politics and the Emerging Shape of Church-State Relations' in *Political Theology* 6 (2006).

[5] Weller, *Time for a Change*, pp. 199–204.

[6] For example: 'Guidance on Community Cohesion' (Local Government Association, 2002), which was produced in association with the Home Office, the Commission for Racial Equality and the Inter Faith Network for the UK; 'Religious Literacy: A Practical Guide to the Region's Faith Communities' (Yorkshire and Humber Assembly, 2002);

But the 'new deal' between churches and government may, in fact, be much more extensive. The best way to examine it is first to look at some of the difficulties that church and state face.

The Problems that Government Faces

As the new century gets underway, the government is confronting serious difficulties in a number of areas:

- *Authority.* The number of people voting at general elections is in serious decline. Just one in five voters elected the government in 2005. In a system where governments ultimately depend on the authority of a democratic mandate to carry out their political programmes, this is seen as a crisis in authority and a threat to the legitimacy of the system itself.[7] This is all the more true as large sections of the population express their political feelings in other ways, through demonstrations, campaign, protests, strikes and direct actions.
- *Morality.* The 'Back to Basics' scandals of the 1990s and subsequent allegations of 'sleaze' have contributed to a negative view of politics and politicians that has been accentuated by declining turnouts at elections. Governments are therefore looking beyond democratic mandates for the moral authority to

---

[6] (*Continued*) 'Working Together: Co-operation between Government and Faith Communities – Recommendations of the Steering Group Reviewing Patterns of Engagement between Government and Faith Communities in England' (Faith Communities Unit, Home Office, February 2004); J. Lewis and E. Randolph-Horn, 'Faiths, Hope and Participation: Celebrating Faith Groups' Role in Neighbourhood Renewal' (London: New Economics Foundation and Church Urban Fund, 2001); 'Partnership for the Common Good: Inter Faith Infrastructures and Local Government' (Inter Faith Network for the UK, 2003).

[7] Geoff Hoon, for example, has suggested that it threatens 'the long-term legitimacy of our political system' (in an untitled speech delivered at 'The End of the Affair? Mending the Relationship between the Citizen and Westminster', a debate hosted by the Institute for Public Policy Research, 4 June 2005).

govern, and are increasingly appealing to 'values'. Actions such as the air strikes against Yugoslavia in 1999,[8] the invasion of Iraq in 2003[9] and the ban on tobacco advertising in sport,[10] as well as tax rises and welfare spending, have been justified by political leaders as 'the right thing to do'.[11]

- *Ideas.* In 1962, Daniel Bell famously heralded 'the end of ideology'.[12] With the end of the old conflict between capitalism and communism that used to dominate mainstream political debate, a new consensus has emerged on many issues, and political parties are struggling to find 'clear water'. Politics appears to be characterised by muddling-through – often referred to as 'pragmatism' or 'managerialism'.[13]

- *Diversity.* The diversity of religious values in Britain also appears to be presenting major problems for government. One is how to foster or create social cohesion while respecting religious diversity. The end of Soviet Communism and the loosening of the grip of ideology led to a resurgence of traditional ethnic and religious conflicts, both in the many regions of the former Soviet bloc and elsewhere.[14] Immigration has contributed to difficulties in Britain. Calls for more faith-based schools have often met resistance, with the Commission for Racial

---

[8] See Tony Blair's television address to the nation on 26 March 1999.

[9] See, for example, Tony Blair's opening statement to the House of Commons in the debate on Iraq, *Hansard*, HC, 18 March 2003, cols. 761–912.

[10] Speech delivered by Tony Blair at Labour's local government, women's and youth conferences , SECC, Glasgow, 15 February 2003.

[11] See Ted Honderich, 'Mr Blair as moralist', *The Independent on Sunday*, 16 March 2003.

[12] In *The End of Ideology* – named by *The Times Literary Supplement* as one of the 100 most influential books since 1945 – Bell argued that the older humanistic ideologies of the 19th and early 20th centuries were exhausted and that new, parochial ideologies would arise in their stead.

[13] Willard Enteman, *Managerialism: The Emergence of a New Ideology* (University of Wisconsin Press, 1993).

[14] An observation made by Bell in a new introduction to the 2000 edition of *The End of Ideology*.

Equality warning of 'segregation'.[15] Religious communities have been offended by publications, broadcasts and plays. In France as in Britain, there has been controversy over religious clothing, and ethnic and religious violence erupted in towns in the north of England in the summer of 2002. Terrorist threats also appear to be inspired by extreme versions of various religious ideas. The chair of the Commission for Racial Equality, which was founded to promote 'multiculturalism', has even caused a stir by suggesting that the idea was dead.

- *Delivery.* Government is facing real difficulties about how to deliver welfare, security and health care. An ageing population threatens a crisis in pensions and the NHS. The prison population continues to grow, and so does the welfare bill. In an age when the involvement of the private sector and voluntary agencies is the fashion, government is looking for partners who will be effective in delivering what it has undertaken to provide.

The Problems the Church Faces

It is not only government, however, that is having problems. The church, too, is facing a small crisis in post-Christendom:

- *Liquidity.* While churches are keen to pursue social programmes, they have less and less money of their own money to spend. Many denominations are facing issues of viability.[16] Churches need funds to finance both their social projects and their ageing infrastructure.
- *Vulnerability.* Many in the church feel threatened. Some feel discriminated against, others even persecuted, and also unsure that they can do anything about it. Old assumptions are being challenged. Churches no longer feel quite so at home in our society.

---

[15] In a speech entitled 'After 7/7: sleepwalking to segregation', Trevor Phillips, chair of the Commission for Racial Equality, suggested, 'We are a society which, almost without noticing it, is becoming more divided by race and religion' (22 September 2005).

[16] See Murray, *Post-Christendom.*

- *Authority.* Christians feel that their influence in society is waning. They no longer have the same power and privileges, or the same weight of numbers. The church's moral authority appears to have diminished. They see injustice and want to be a force for good, but are not sure how much they can achieve.
- *Credibility.* Rows about homosexuality and women bishops and scandals about child abuse are the kind of things that make headlines. Many people see the churches as reactionary, out-of-date and obsolete. Increasingly in post-Christendom the church's ideas and points of view have to fight for attention and no longer get it simply because it is the church that is saying them.
- *Identity.* The church is struggling to make a distinctive contribution to society. It is often lumped together with others under the heading of 'religion', 'the voluntary sector' or 'faith-based welfare', and seems to have lost its unique place in society.

In the face of these difficulties, both church and government are recognising what the other can do for them.

What the Church is Doing for Government

It's clear that by encouraging its members to vote and to join political parties the church is providing a much needed boost to the political system. Churches are among the leading hosts of hustings at election time,[17] and are helping in other ways to promote faith in the political system. They still play an important and varied role in local civic life, and many Christians are active locally. Nationally, the churches have run campaigns to restore trust in government.

Churches supply an important connection to civil society. The government minister Stephen Timms is among those who have suggested that Christianity is providing 'vitally important' new

---

[17] See the press release from Churches Together in Britain and Ireland 'Christians lead the fight against voter apathy', 5 May 2005, which stated that 300 churches held hustings in the two weeks before the 2005 general election.

linkages to groups and communities.[18] In the run-up to the 2001 general election, the Christian Socialist Movement (of which he is a member) engaged in a series of dialogues with leaders of the main Christian denominations and major faiths and published a compendium of their views about what the next government should do.[19] This was greeted as 'a good example of working at links with organisations beyond the normal reach of the Labour Party'. The Conservative Christian Fellowship likewise was involved in the Conservative Party's efforts to reconnect with the electorate after its crushing election defeat in 1997, conducting the exercise 'Listening to Britain's Churches'. There is an obvious advantage for political parties in courting the 5–10 per cent of the population that attend church regularly; and, whether or not they can actually swing the vote at election time, the churches are seen to have 'opened doors to a much wider constituency'.[20]

Christianity may also have furnished government with a new terminology that has enabled it to communicate new policies successfully without waking memories of past political disputes and mistakes.[21] This is one of three 'vital contributions' that Timms claimed the church has made to the success of New Labour, both initially at the ballot box and then subsequently in government.[22] But it is not only New Labour that has employed religious language: Margaret Thatcher famously quoted Francis of Assisi on her arrival in Downing Street in 1979. In fact, all the main party leaders have seemed keen to be associated with the church in recent elections.

There are a number of individual policy ideas that the church or Christians have given the government. Gordon Brown has

---

[18] 'The Christian contribution to New Labour', speech delivered in Sarpsborg, Norway, 28 September 2002.

[19] Published under the title 'Faith in Politics', it included speeches delivered by Tony Blair, Bob Geldof, Indarjit Singh and Jim Wallis at a day conference in Westminster responding to the report from 17 national faith-community leaders (CSM, 2001).

[20] Timms, 'The Christian contribution to New Labour'.

[21] Timms, 'The Christian contribution to New Labour'.

[22] Namely, 'leadership', 'language' and 'linkages'.

talked of the Christian influence on his efforts to cancel debt in the developing world.[23] The Home Office is exploring Christian ideas of restorative justice. At a time when the government is increasingly basing its authority and its arguments on an appeal to morality, it certainly helps to have the church on side. The opposition to the invasion of Iraq showed how much trouble the church can cause when the government line is challenged on moral grounds.[24] Although its credibility is now questioned, many people still look to the church for moral guidance and some still regard it as a moral guardian of the nation.

However, it may be in the area of cohesion that the church is proving most useful. Tony Blair has been developing the theme of a new community founded on a shared moral vision,[25] and this appears to come straight from his own religious convictions. It is clear that the government recognises that religion can unite as well as divide a nation[26] and that it sees the church as a potential source of shared values in a plural society at a time when conflicting values threaten to undermine the social order. Although the number of people who go to church is quite small, those who consider themselves 'Christian' in a cultural sense still form a majority (as Christian groups often remind the government).

Blair in particular seems to have adopted a threefold approach:[27]

• Identify the unchanging essence of so-called traditional values.
• Analyse the changed context (a modern global economy).
• Apply the ideas in the particular context.

The government appears to be trying to appeal to a moral sense ingrained in the heritage of this country – much of which is the

---

[23] See Ben Russell, 'Brown launches plan to ease Third World debt', *The Independent*, 14 January 2005.
[24] Members of the government attempted to use ideas of 'just war' to justify the invasion.
[25] Mark Chapman, *Blair's Britain: A Christian Critique* (London: Darton Longman Todd, 2005).
[26] See, for example, 'Social Capital: A Discussion Paper' (Cabinet Office Performance and Innovation Unit, 2002).
[27] Chapman, *Blair's Britain*, p. 18.

heritage of Christendom – and one obvious and crucial way to do this is through the churches. Church leaders for their part seem to be happy to help.[28]

Blair concluded a speech in Tübingen with a reference to Hans Küng's 'global ethic'. As the world continues to shrink to a 'global village', a universalist ethic of peace and understanding becomes ever more necessary. In this, the various faiths play their role by ensuring that these values are upheld. Religion, said Blair, 'becomes an ally in the international search for harmony and co-operation: commonalities rather than differences between religions become the source of the new global ethic.'[29] Religious education, in particular, is identified as something that will play a key part in promoting social cohesion. Professor Gates, head of the RE Council of England and Wales, has observed that the Home Office is realising the value of RE in relation to social cohesion.[30]

It should be no surprise, therefore, that, as in Christendom, the powers-that-be continue to see moderate and orthodox religion as something to be encouraged. This is evidenced in the government's approach to charity law. Despite pressure to abolish tax relief for the 'advancement of religion', the government has continued to approve it.

Another crucial reason why the government is so keen to work closely with churches is its belief that they can deliver 'social capital',[31] which has been defined as the networks, norms, relationships, values and informal sanctions that shape the quantity and co-operative quality of a society's interactions. If 'human capital' relates to the properties of individuals, social capital refers to connections among individuals – social networks and the norms of reciprocity and trustworthiness that arise from them. Social

---

[28] Rowan Williams, for example, has closely compared ideas of the public interest or the public good with ideas of the common good. See 'The media: public interest and common good', lecture delivered at Lambeth Palace, 15 June 2005.
[29] Quoted in Chapman, *Blair's Britain*, p. 20.
[30] 'Religious studies: entering a new golden age', *Church of England Newspaper*, 30 September 2005.
[31] Bretherton, 'A New Establishment?'

capital, it is suggested, can contribute to a range of economic and social benefits, including increased GDP, more efficient functioning of labour markets, higher educational attainment, lower levels of crime, better health and more effective institutions of government.

Social capital is closely related to what some have called 'civic virtue'. It is seen as most potent when embedded in a network of reciprocal social relations, such as the church provides. A society of many virtuous but isolated individuals is not necessarily rich in social capital.[32]

The Benefits for the Church

It is easy to see why the arrangements of the new deal also suit many in the church:

- *Delivering funding*. As a partner with the state, commissioned to deliver what the government has undertaken to provide, the church gets access to much needed funding.
- *Delivering protection*. The church has the opportunity both to secure more equal treatment (where it believes it is discriminated against) and legal protection (where it feels vulnerable) and to preserve its old privileges.
- *Delivering influence*. The government is talking a language that sounds familiar to churches. It also seems to be listening to what they have to say and responding to their concerns.
- *Delivering credibility*. The receipt of government funding enhances the church's credibility. It is able, too, to demonstrate that its faith 'works', which is a way to bear witness to the wider society that Christianity, far from being ridiculous, is important.
- *Delivering identity*. The church is able to develop an identity as a welfare provider whose faith clearly has practical applications and is relevant to the world around it.

---

[32] Robert Putnam, *Bowling Alone: The Collapse and Revival of American Community* (New York: Simon & Schuster, 2000), p. 19.

As Christendom developed, Augustine had suggested that 'the City of God' and 'the City of Man' had little in common but they did share an interest: they shared a desire for peace and the maintenance of the social order. Now, once again, the interests of the church and the state coincide. The problem is that this means that the church is renegotiating its position on the basis of its own interests rather than (for example) those of vulnerable or marginalised people.

Some will argue that the interests of the church are the same as those of the vulnerable and marginalised; but history shows that that is not always the case. There are a number of crucial questions, therefore, that we have to ask.

A Question of Trust

According to one activist, 'the challenge of the moment set before us all – from government to church, media to business leaders and ordinary individuals to royal family – is simply this: consistently to adopt behaviours that rebuild trust. Or, if we will not, to watch as our society slowly disintegrates.'[33]

As with most new deals, the one between the church and the government hinges on one important element: trust. In a position of relative and increasing impotence, the church in particular needs to be able to trust the government. And the government, too, needs people to be trusting. For it, 'social capital can be measured using a range of indicators but the most commonly used measure is trust in other people.'[34] Lack of trust disables political institutions. It leads to withdrawal, a refusal to participate and engage – especially in the democratic system.[35]

We have already noted that a number of Christian groups are running campaigns and initiatives to restore trust, in the political system, social institutions, government and the church. Sometimes these are accompanied by initiatives to restore other values,

---

[33] Chalke, *Trust*, p. 4.
[34] 'Social Capital'
[35] See Chalke, *Trust*, pp. 8–10.

such as respect. They sit well with the government's emphasis on creating new community around shared values. The mere fact that Christians are focusing on this area can be seen as an indicator of how committed the church is to the new deal with government.[36]

Nonetheless, this approach entails a number of risks for the church:

It risks betrayal. The trust that the churches are placing in government could be misplaced. They could be let down. They could be betrayed. People who don't have such a positive view of the role of religion could bring pressure to bear on the government. Governments can change. Parties can change. Policies can change. Events as yet unforeseen could alter circumstances significantly. In Christendom, governments often betrayed the church (just as the church often betrayed governments).

It risks perpetuating injustice. An emphasis on trust may mean failing to point to faults and injustices in government or other institutions – or the church. As the Archbishop of Canterbury has pointed out, institutions need to be open and accountable if they want to enjoy the trust of the wider population.[37] But often they also need to be challenged in order to bring about change. Too great a stress on trust can mean that there is little incentive for the reform of public life, the raising of standards for those in public office and the strengthening of systems that ensure transparency and accountability.

It risks privatisation. An emphasis on trust can easily become a matter of changing private attitudes and personal ethics. Such an approach risks being relegated to the private realm, with little to say about challenging structural sin.

It risks a clash with Christian beliefs about 'the powers'. Biblical accounts of power and authority are often negative,[38] and

---

[36] Press release from the Evangelical Alliance, 'The Evangelical Alliance back Prime Minister's call for more respect', 16 May 2005.

[37] Rowan Williams, John Mere's Commemoration Sermon at St Benet's Church, Cambridge, 20 April 2004.

[38] From Samuel's warnings against choosing a king in 2 Samuel through to the portrayal of the Roman Empire in the Book of Revelation.

many in the church subscribe to a theology that sees behind states and governments 'powers' with which Christians are called to wrestle.

The churches' campaigns to promote trust stress that it goes both ways and encourage government and the wider society in their turn to trust the church. But there are questions we need to ask about the way some Christians are presenting trust as the right relationship between church and government. It has been suggested[39] that the more government and others trust the churches, the more they will:

- Actively seek the churches' advice.
- Be inclined to accept and act on the churches' recommendations.
- Treat the churches as they would wish to be treated.
- Respect the churches.
- Give churches the benefit of the doubt.
- Forgive the churches when they make mistakes.
- Protect the churches when they need protection.
- Warn the churches of dangers they can avoid.
- Feel comfortable with the churches.
- Make the churches feel comfortable with them.
- Work to reduce the amount of bureaucracy involved in their interactions with the churches.
- Fund the work of the churches.

A great deal is being invested in the churches' trust of government, and its advocates justify it in terms of the benefits it may deliver to Christians. For them, trust is crucial to gaining influence ('actively seek our advice, be inclined to accept and act on our recommendations, respect us'), security ('protect us when we need protection, warn us of dangers, respect us') and funding. The attraction of this approach is obvious at a time when the church feels under-resourced and vulnerable, and powerless to influence government.

But a great deal also depends on Christians trusting one another, and that, too, is a risky assumption at a time when the

---

[39] Chalke, *Trust*, p. 14.

church appears quite divided. One of the commonest reasons given to justify Christian appeals for trust is that they can work more closely together and thus be more influential. Certainly, greater unity and co-operation would give a clear message to statutory funders. 'If all denominations, networks, streams and agencies were to approach the government with one voice and a clear strategy on issues, then it would be impossible for them to ignore what we had to say and exclude us in the future.'[40]

But it may be that the new deal between church and government is the problem in this regard and not the solution. The new deal means that faith-based groups – and indeed churches – are competing with one another for scarce government funding. As a succession of reports have shown, it is often the established church that receives funding, in preference to other Christian (and, for that matter, other faith-based) groups. Nor does history inspire confidence. We saw in Chapter 3 how as pre-Christendom gave way to Christendom new opportunities arose for the state to divide and rule the church. As Constantine patronised the church, disputes and rivalries broke out. In post-Christendom, churches are already divided – and these divisions may only be exacerbated by the new deal.

A Question of Distinctiveness

What is it that makes the church distinctive in the new deal between church and government? Part of the deal is to show more effectively that faith 'works'. However, we need to ask some questions about the basis of this political witness.

We have already observed a move toward managerialism – the prioritisation of efficiency and pragmatism in the political system. Rather than the church witnessing to government, the new deal may encourage the opposite, as the church itself embraces such ideas rather than pioneering a distinctive approach in the delivery of social welfare. It is frequently said that churches are inefficient

---

[40] 'United We Stand: Building Trust', (London: Evangelical Alliance, 2005).

when they apply for government funding: they haven't done their homework and often their activities overlap. One of the answers offered is that churches need to be more professional. They need to speak with one voice. In response, government is urged to 'celebrate' faith, because it 'adds value'.

There are two areas in which, we are often told, the faith of the church makes it 'work' better than others:[41]

- *Motivation.* Christian projects work better because they are better motivated.
- *Professionalism.* The church's standards of delivery are higher.

The question the churches need to ask themselves is whether they want their distinctiveness to be based on such things, rather than (for example) their radical stand for justice. When they accept government funding they run the risk of accepting the government's policy goals and targets rather than having their own. They run the risk of blunting their more radical edge. Politicians are quite happy with a church that serves its local community diligently.[42] They are less happy with a church that challenges them.

The Faithworks charter focuses on plans, mission, strategy and management style. It certainly hauls the church into the 21st century: it challenges some of its bigotry over sexual orientation and the coercion of belief and promotes inclusivity. These things are all important. What it doesn't cover, however, is (for example) making sacrifices to keep people on in projects that are struggling financially. It also makes a commitment to working 'within the law'.

In many respects, the new deal can be seen to display the characteristics of 'functionalism',[43] a way of thinking that ascribes value to a practice or institution according to the contribution it

---

[41] See Chalke, *Trust*, pp. 40–41.

[42] In March 2001, speaking at CSM's 'Faith in Politics' conference, Tony Blair recognised the role of faith in community action. He said: 'You serve your community because of your faith, not in isolation from it – a point that government, central and local, must always appreciate.'

[43] An idea pioneered by Auguste Comte and taken up by Emile Durkheim and Talcott Parsons.

makes to the functioning of society as a whole. In the case of the new deal, the church is delivering social capital and social cohesion. When they argue that the government should fund church projects, Christians are asking it to value them because they can deliver better than anyone else what the government has undertaken to provide.

But for some Christians this is not the authority the church should be appealing to. Certainly, the new relationship with government gives churches a new authority, but this is based on their ability to deliver. And what is counted as 'delivery', and what 'works', is defined not by the church but by the government, in accordance with its agenda, strategy and policy goals. The church's authority is still defined by its relationship to government just as it was in Christendom. Moreover, the boundaries between church and state become less and less distinct, just as in Christendom. As the church becomes an agent of the state – albeit a voluntary agent – it becomes in many respects a civil servant.

In Christendom, the idea of the Evangel – the good news as a political statement – was not always comfortable for government to hear. So, evangelism was privatised and became a matter of proclamation, and the political consequences of its challenge to power were played down. Later, Christians made a distinction – within evangelicalism in particular – between faith and works, evangelism and social action. The new deal perpetuates that distinction, but by linking the two rather than seeing them as one and the same. Christians sometimes make the case for social reform in terms of its connection to evangelism. The credibility of the gospel message depends on the reputation of the church, they argue: evangelism will yield 'lasting fruit' when it is credible and attractive to outsiders.[44]

But for many, this is still a privatisation of the gospel and the move towards a new managerialism and professionalism may be at the expense of discipleship. It seems to leave little room for any radical stand, and little room, too, for any glorious extravagance. What about grace, abundance, forgiveness, foolishness? These

---

[44] Schluter and Ashcroft (eds.), *Jubilee Manifesto*, p. 26.

ideas don't fit comfortably within a culture that demands efficiency. The new deal brings with it a potentially narrow and short-sighted agenda that leaves little room for other goals and possibilities.

A Question of Funding

There are many other questions that arise from accepting funding from the state. In one respect, the new deal is uncharted territory for the church, because really it is only able to deliver welfare in the modern sense of the word because the role of the state is changing and so is the nature of the welfare state. In Christendom, although the church pioneered services such as schools and hospitals it often did so not from a position of power but from the margins – most notably in the 18th and 19th centuries, through the voluntary sector. These projects were funded largely by private money and had little to do with the state. In character, they were philanthropic and were run mostly by volunteers.

Over time, many of the models and ideas that the church first developed were adopted by the state. The novel situation the church now finds itself in is that it is being encouraged to bid for funding for projects that a few centuries ago would have been financed not from the public purse but from the resources of churches and their congregations. The church was then largely in control of the way its projects were run and what they tried to achieve, and thus they made a political statement to the wider society about the church's values.

When the church accepts funding from government it is still making a political statement; but it has less control of the content of that statement. It reflects less the values of the church and more the values of the government. The church has to accept, by and large, government targets and will appear to be giving its blessing to many of the government's policy goals.

Church projects may also become dependent on the government, and if at some future date it decides to withdraw its funding, for whatever reason, a project may well fold. What did the apostle Paul say about not being 'unequally yoked'? Might not a contemporary political reading apply that injunction to political relationships? Having the church as a partner enables government to exert control over it. Already the argument has been heard that funding Muslim schools allows the government to restrain their more undesirable or worrying aspects.[45] If the church challenges the power-that-be in any way, or if they don't like what any section of the church is doing, they can always initiate moves to withdraw their funding.

For some Christians, the church risks endorsing the 'idols' of the system by taking on the values of the culture that surrounds it.

Conclusion

The message to local and national government from the churches has been presented as:

'Treat us fairly and you can rely on us to deliver good results. Partner with us and we rise to the challenge. Fund our work and we will not let you down. Celebrate, endorse and support our diversity and offer us equality. Judge us on our merits. Not on our beliefs.'[46]

An alternative message, however, might be: 'Even if you don't treat us fairly, we will do the best we can for you and deliver good results. Wherever we can we will seek to fund our own projects, because we seek the good of the wider society. If you do fund our work, be aware that we may act in ways that contradict what you stand for. Our doctrinal beliefs may be diverse but we are united in our commitment to justice and we recognise that sometimes this will put us at odds with you. So, you will have to judge us on our beliefs as well as our merits.'

One of the huge changes that occurred at the advent of Christendom was that the church became less of a critic or adversary of the state and more of an ally that endorsed what it did. As

---

[45] See, for example, David Cameron interviewed on BBC Radio 4's *Today* programme, 24 October 2004.
[46] Chalke, *Trust*, p. 44.

Christendom gives way to post-Christendom, we can see an opposite shift, from endorsement to challenge of the political system. The new deal represents a concerted effort still to endorse and support the structures and institutions of government, but we have to ask some serious questions about it. Not least, should the church be making the government 'feel comfortable', and should it want to feel comfortable with the government? The Faithworks agenda was a reaction to post-Christendom and the loss of power and privilege that has accompanied it. Specifically, it was born out of a feeling that Christian groups were being discriminated against when they applied for local authority funding. An appeal has been made to government for protection and support. But in Christendom, the price the church had to pay for its alliance with the state was often the compromise of its witness. Today's partnerships between agencies of the church and the state are another form of Christendom redivivus.

9

Future Imperfect

Post-Christendom is a transitional phase. What does the future hold? Will current trends continue? Will the new deal between church and state last? Must there always be some sort of alliance between the churches and government?

One fundamental question we have to ask is whether Christians will remain politically engaged at all. Is the present explosion of political activity no more than a brief phenomenon? The trend towards political engagement from the margins where the churches now find themselves seems to be strong, and even to be growing stronger – but history shows that sections of the church *have* certainly disengaged in recent times.

One example often cited is the 'Great Reversal'[1] that saw evangelicals withdraw from social and political involvement in the decades around the end of the 19th century. Although this was primarily the experience of Christians in the US, it also occurred in Britain. The reasons that have been proposed for this may offer some pointers as to what could cause Christians to withdraw from political engagement in the future.

The historian David Moberg has suggested that many evangelicals:[2]

---

[1] A term coined by the US historian Timothy L. Smith.
[2] David O. Moberg, *The Great Reversal: Evangelism versus Social Concern* (London: Scripture Union, 1972). For a discussion of the 'reversal', see John Stott, *Issues Facing Christians Today*, chapter 1, 'Involvement: Is It Our Concern?' (London: Marshall Pickering, 1983).

- Became preoccupied with 'defending' their faith against doctrinal error.
- Reacted against the 'social gospel'.
- Were disillusioned by the horrors and cruelties of the First World War.
- Began to embrace premillenialist beliefs that Christ would soon return.
- Identified their faith with their own culture and so saw reform as unnecessary.

The conclusion was 'a portrait of the religious-minded as a person having a self-centred preoccupation, coupled with an indifference toward or even a tacit endorsement of the social system that would perpetuate social inequality and injustice'.[3]

The description could also fit some Christians today, perhaps. But how likely is it that it will apply to Christians in the future?

Certainly, there appear to be major splits within the church around issues of doctrine. Within evangelicalism, there has been major debate amongst scholars in the last few decades over some central tenets of the Christian faith – and especially the idea of atonement.[4] This particular debate came to wider attention when Steve Chalke caused a furore by repeating a suggestion that certain interpretations of what happened on the cross amounted to 'cosmic child abuse'.[5] What distinguished this controversy from many others was that, for many people, it revolved around an understanding of ethical matters such as justice and violence. Contributors to the debate highlighted the important links with ethics,[6] but also stressed

---

[3] Milton Rokeach, quoted in Stott, *Issues Facing Christians Today*, p. 8.

[4] Evangelical scholars including Mark Baker, Robert Brow, James Dunn, Joel Green, Clark Pinnock, Stephen Travis and Nigel Wright discussed the basis of penal substitution and the importance accorded to it in evangelicalism.

[5] Steve Chalke and Alan Mann, *The Lost Message of Jesus* (Grand Rapids: Zondervan, 2004). This idea was proposed by Rita Nakashima Brock in *Journeys by Heart: A Christology of Erotic Power* (New York: Crossroad, 1988).

[6] A point made by people on both sides of the argument during public discussions in Westminster, and most notably by Anna Robbins and Stuart Murray Williams.

that certain readings of the Cross, such as 'penal substitution', 'lacked a persuasive socio-political theological outworking'.[7]

There is a strong political dimension to other issues that have recently caused major divisions within churches. For many (though by no means all), the Anglican communion's arguments over homosexuality and the appointment of women bishops revolve around questions of justice.[8] The distinctions made between matters of faith and doctrine on the one hand and 'works', including politics on the other, or between the 'spiritual' gospel and the 'social' gospel, are less and less clear. This suggests that a reaction against the social gospel, leading to a retreat from social and political involvement, is also unlikely.

Of course, it is impossible to say whether some cataclysmic event may not occur that will unexpectedly change things forever, in the way that the First World War shattered many hopes and illusions. No one can be sure that (for example) the effects of global warming or a future war will not change attitudes significantly. What we can observe, however, is that, whereas the First World War initially enjoyed strong support from the church,[9] Christians have increasingly over the decades that followed it warned and protested against the alignment of faith with war.[10] Others are campaigning against the suspected causes of climate

---

[7] 'Joint Evangelical Alliance-London School of Theology Atonement Symposium, 6–8 July 2005. A Statement by the Evangelical Alliance', undated.

[8] See, for example, the press release from Inclusive Church 'Yes to women bishops. No to a third province', 2 November 2004. For a good account of the way in which the various groups have campaigned, see Stephen Bates, *A Church at War: Anglicans and Homosexuality*.

[9] Some Christians opposed the war but there was also support, particularly from the established church following the German invasion of Belgium, in breach of treaty obligations. Even clergy volunteered to fight, and it has been reckoned that 4,618 were killed. See Alan Wilkinson, *The Church of England and the First World War* (London: SPCK, 1978).

[10] Philip Towle, 'The Anglican Church, the State and Modern Warfare', a paper given at the international conference 'Civil Society, Religion and Global Governance: Paradigms of Power and Persuasion', 1–2 September 2005, Canberra.

change. Christians will be less likely to become disillusioned if they have been working hard to prevent such disasters before they happen rather than being complicit in them. In post-Christendom, which is primarily the experience of western Europe, the Christian faith is also much less strongly identified with the nation state and its institutions. Christians are developing global perspectives, and this, too, suggests that major events that affect just this country may not have the same kind of spiritual impact.

As for the 'end times', the belief that the Second Coming is imminent (and that the establishment of the state of Israel was a fulfilment of biblical prophecy) seems to be politicising the (relatively few) Christians who subscribe to it, rather than prompting them to withdraw from politics (and in the US, where such beliefs are more prevalent, Christian Zionists continue to lobby their government very hard over the Middle East peace process).

It would seem, therefore, that a future withdrawal by Christians from political involvement is unlikely, at least for the reasons proposed by Moberg. But two other factors could still have a significant effect. It's conceivable that the church could be driven underground by persecution or, simply, that it could become so small and marginal that it becomes entirely inward-looking. At present, however, despite various crises and claims of persecution, there is little real evidence to suggest that either outcome is likely – and even those Christians who do take a bleak view of the future of the church in Britain appear to be becoming radicalised. Everything seems to point to the growing, not diminishing, politicisation of Christians.

Exactly what form this politicisation will finally take is as yet unclear, but it's worth looking at some of the trends that are developing in post-Christendom[11] to see if we can observe any themes. It will help us to assess which of the current trends in the church's political engagement are likely to continue, and maybe grow in importance, and which will die away.

---

[11] As highlighted by Murray, *Post-Christendom*.

From the Centre to the Margins

While government looks back to Christendom in search of a source of shared values for contemporary society, the larger trend is for the Christian story to move from the centre to the margins. With some exceptions, religious ideas are no longer at the heart of what government does. Christian faith is less and less identified with the surrounding culture.

We have seen how a political dimension of the Christian faith is emerging in post-Christendom that in Christendom was often suppressed. It is probable that as the church continues to read the Christian scriptures on the margins of society rather than at its centre, it will discover more and more a political interpretation of them, and especially of the life and teachings of Jesus.

The very concepts of evangelism, mission and the church are likely to become increasingly politicised. Already, their political nature and implications are being recognised publicly in contexts such as the government's proposal to ban incitement to religious hatred. But the Evangel of the Kingdom of God is also becoming politicised as Christians seek to apply it in ways that have important political consequences. It's likely that Christian stories will continue to be re-explained and reinterpreted, uninhibited by the traditional analysis of Christendom. There may be room for many different readings of texts that in Christendom had only one or two interpretations. Many of these will reflect the church's new position on the margins and will be more openly political, recognising the context in which they were written.

The church may also look in unfamiliar places for models for its political activity. When we consider the past, we tend to see it from the perspective of those who held power, who were at the centre of society. The church, too, has tended to look for examplars in the Bible whose position resembled its own at the centre of society, such as kings. But throughout biblical history, and indeed ecclesiastical history, there have been many other people who were politically active, often on the margins, and the church may increasingly look to their example. It may also seek inspiration from cultures less affected by Christendom, most notably from the ideas of liberation theologians.

The church may also find that, now it is on the margins, new methods of political engagement with government are possible and acceptable. In the first few centuries after the death of Jesus, public sacrifice was an important part of civic life and the refusal of Christians to take part in it registered as a political action.[12] When the church moved to the centre of society, political tactics of withdrawal, non-participation and civil disobedience were less practicable, as they seemed to present a challenge to the church as much as to government. In post-Christendom, such tactics will become more possible, more acceptable and more important for Christians.

From Majority to Minority

In Christendom, Christians (by which I mean people who, whatever their commitment, were familiar with the faith and understood the world in Christian terms) comprised the often overwhelming majority, but in post-Christendom they find themselves in an unfamiliar situation, as a dwindling minority amongst other minorities. This gives them more common experience with other groups who find themselves on the fringes of political life. Rather than a paternalistic perspective, which was often a feature of Christendom, Christians will increasingly see the world from their new position among the marginalised and disenfranchised.

As a result, they may become more critical of systems that allow majorities to rule over minorities. When they were in the majority, it was harder to identify with minorities, but Christians are now likely to be more sympathetic to political options such as systems of proportional representation that give a greater voice to smaller groups. Indeed, as the church moves further away from its old position of power, it is likely that Christians will pay more attention to constitutional arrangements. There are signs that para-church groups are doing this already. As the Bill to introduce devolution to Scotland was going through Parliament, Christians north of the border demanded that abortion issues should be dealt

---

[12] Chidester, *Christianity: A Global History*, p. 75.

with in Edinburgh, not in Westminster. When party lists were introduced for European elections,[13] they expressed concern that Christian voters would no longer be able to choose between candidates on the basis of their moral and ethical views. The Christian People's Alliance has campaigned in favour of proportional representation in Westminster.

But the move to the margins also presents a formidable challenge to the church given the nature of its political activity, which often at present involves petitions and other demonstrations of widespread popular support. The church will find it increasingly hard to get a hearing on the grounds that it represents a large number of people – or even the majority[14] – as the line that over 70 per cent of the population identify with Christianity carries less and less weight.

The fragmentation of Christian political perspectives, as well as of the church in general, is also discrediting the claims made by many groups about the numbers they represent. The Evangelical Alliance, for example, says that it speaks for over a million evangelical Christians in Britain,[15] and reiterates this claim whenever it makes a submission to government, yet its 'membership magazine' has a circulation of only 38,000.[16] The EA arrives at its total of over a million by adding together the estimated memberships

---

[13] In a party list system, voters vote not for a single candidate in their local constituency but for a list of candidates put up by their preferred party. They have to vote either for all of that party's candidates or for none of them, and are not able to say which individual candidates they prefer.

[14] Submission to the House of Lords Select Committee on the BBC Charter Review from 'senior members of faith communities', 2 November 2005.

[15] The exact wording that appears at the end of every press release is: 'The Evangelical Alliance UK, formed in 1846, is an umbrella group representing over one million evangelical Christians in the UK and is made up of member churches, organisations and individuals.'

[16] The Alliance describes *Idea* as its membership magazine and says, '36,500 copies are mailed to the Alliance's membership, with the rest sent to non-members or handed out at various Christian events' (information for advertisers taken from the EA's website).

of all the organisations and churches that belong to it, plus its individual members. This clearly leaves the way open for 'double counting', as many individual churchgoers will also belong to one or more organisations. While there may be a million people in Britain who could be described as 'evangelical' and who attend churches that could be so described, it is doubtful that quite so many would actually identify themselves as such – many would prefer the simple label 'Christian' – and even fewer perhaps would apply the term 'evangelical' to themselves in the sense that the EA defines it in its literature. Fewer still would actually align themselves with the EA as an organisation. In fact, it is likely that only a small proportion of those British Christians who could be described as 'evangelical' would consider that the EA represents them and their politics. As the number of people who go to church declines further, and their religious identities continue to change, such claims (and it should be noted that the EA is far from alone in making them)[17] will become less and less plausible.

Alliances with other groups are likely to be a growing feature of post-Christendom politics. When it was in a more powerful position, the church had less need of coalitions, but as a minority it needs to look beyond itself for political support (as is already openly acknowledged).[18] However, the alliances and coalitions that Christians will build are likely to be temporary, often based around single issues or campaigns. Those who the church stands with on one occasion will be people it stands against on another[19]

---

[17] For example, the Christian People's Alliance has claimed that nearly 100,000 people voted for its candidate for Mayor of London (see its submission to the House of Lords Select Committee on Religious Offences in England and Wales, 2002–3, made on 24 July 2002). It arrived at this figure by counting both first- and second-preference votes.

[18] Michael Schluter and John Ashcroft suggest: 'In democratic societies most reform requires majority support. It therefore requires influencing, persuading and working with individuals, groups and organizations who may not share our faith but who do share our concerns' (*Jubilee Manifesto*, p. 31).

[19] This has already happened in campaigns against the Racial and Religious Hatred Bill, when the Evangelical Alliance amongst others joined forces with secularists.

– though there may be exceptions to this, where Christians find themselves more regularly aligned with the more marginalised and vulnerable – and this will create a much more fluid situation. The church will reconsider who it sees as 'the enemy', and may well begin increasingly to identify 'the powers' as such, rather than 'secularists', 'humanists' or this or that lobby.

From Settlers to Sojourners

In Christendom, Christians felt at home in a culture shaped by their story. In post-Christendom, they are exiles and aliens in a culture where they no longer feel at home. Once, the church's political identity was bound up with governments, states and nations, but now it must discover a new one. We have already seen how, under the 'new deal', it is trying to acquire an identity as a provider of welfare, more professional, better motivated and better able than others to deliver what the government has undertaken to provide; but that identity is unlikely to be distinct enough. Moreover, the church's relationship with government – especially when it comes to meeting its targets and goals – is likely to be questioned increasingly as the priorities of the church appear to diverge more and more from those of the population at large. As Christians take a more global view, they will no longer see the health of the church in terms of the health of the country, and will no longer identify the common good so closely with the national interest. The church will feel much more free to recommend policies – for example, on immigration and asylum, international debt and international trade – that may be against the national interest but will benefit others overseas.

A new political identity may involve Christians making much more of a commitment to values such as justice rather than to a political party, institution or nation. In Christendom, national flags were hung in churches to indicate a political allegiance to the nation state, but now the church may develop its own political symbols. It may also begin to see new political meaning in existing Christian symbols such as the cross.

The church may also move further away from such roles as anointing heads of state and sometimes offering thanksgiving for success in war, and if such services are held in future at all they are likely to be multi-faith. Additional, Christian services may be held separately and these, like the services of 'remembrance' after the Falklands Conflict and the two Gulf wars, may be increasingly guarded, or even negative. There is likely to be a growing perception that wars involve Christians killing other Christians, and a growing awareness of the plight of Christians in situations such as Iraq, where the church has suffered significantly as a result of the invasion. As the church comes to see war as less and less justifiable, Christians may be compelled to think more deeply and creatively about alternatives.

There will also be a growing acknowledgement of the impact of national policies on the rest of the world. As the church sees the rest of the world less and less as 'pagan' or 'heathen', in contrast with 'Christian' Western Europe, it will be less and less ready to defend policies that hurt other nations.

This trend will be reinforced by the fact that Christians feel less obliged to defend the institutions around them. Institutions that were once considered 'Christian' will seem less so as the church moves further away from government – and also rediscovers the justice of Jesus Christ. The priorities of the criminal justice system, for example, may be seen increasingly as unnecessarily punitive, and in conflict with more radical Christian ideas of justice which involve a greater emphasis on the restoration of both victim and offender.

Christians' views of government will also continue to change. It's likely that the church will adopt an increasingly adversarial position as the government acts in ways it disapproves of. The injustice and violence of the state will become more obvious to those Christians radicalised by new understandings of justice. It is already noticeable that over the last century the church – even the Church of England – has become increasingly critical of the state.[20] Moreover, as government seeks to remove the church's

---

[20] See, for example, Towle, 'The Anglican Church, the State and Modern Warfare'; also Henry Clarke, *The Church under Thatcher* (London: SPCK, 1993).

remaining privileges to create a more equal society, some sections in particular of the church are likely to feel more hostile to government, and it is probable that more and more Christians will be open to the idea of disestablishing the Church of England. The government, too, will be more likely to entertain such an idea as it sees the special relationship between church and state as increasingly anomalous.[21]

From Privilege to Plurality

In Christendom, the church enjoyed many privileges, but in post-Christendom it is one community amongst many. As religious pluralism develops, its remaining privileges will appear increasingly unjustified and absurd and the calls for government to remove them will become louder.

This situation will be exacerbated by changing perceptions of evangelism and mission. Government may still be able to see advantages in (for example) granting tax exemption for charitable donations to support the advancement of religion, but as evangelism becomes increasingly politicised it will be harder to justify. Already, a campaign such as Make Poverty History (with which the church was deeply involved) has been banned from advertising due to its political content.[22] It is likely that local and central government will also seek to restrict certain forms of proselytising they see as divisive in the projects they fund.

The privileges that may soon be limited or removed include:

• Tax exemptions for the advancement of religion, and for evangelistic activities in particular.
• Funding for social action projects that involve vigorous proselytising.
• The right to discriminate in employment on the basis of sexual orientation or religious faith.

---

[21] Christopher Morgan, 'Brown would end PM's vote on bishops', *The Sunday Times*, 19 February 2006.
[22] Owen Gibson, 'Broadcast ban on Make Poverty History ad campaign', *The Guardian*, 13 September 2005.

- The right to discriminate in admissions to faith schools.
- Seats for 26 bishops in the House of Lords.
- The law against blasphemy.

The church may also find it hard to exercise privileges such as the primacy it enjoys in supplying hospitals, universities and the armed forces with chaplains – which increasingly will be provided by different faiths. The funding these positions receive from outside the church is also likely to be cut. Given the churches' diminishing influence, they will also find it difficult to acquire any new privileges, and any they gain will be short-lived. But there may also be calls from within the church to renounce existing privileges, as charges of double standards become more irrefutable – just as some bishops have called for the repeal of the antiquated law against blasphemy.

As the churches lose their privileges, Christians may be seen to have far more integrity in their political activity. In Christendom, the church's political witness was bound up with a specific idea of privilege and power that some saw as conflicting with Jesus' model of powerlessness and identification with the poor and the vulnerable. A fundamental dilemma for some Christians has been how to reconcile Jesus' teachings about power and about love of enemies with political activity in a governing role. In post-Christendom, Christians are being pushed into a position that seems to be more consistent with the message of the gospel. Some Christians may find that they are more comfortable in their political witness as a result.

Loss of privilege will also mean that vulnerability becomes part of the church's new identity. In particular, the church will be more exposed to the consequences of its own actions. In a sense, Christians have been reaping what they have sown politically, both by what they did in Christendom and also by what they have done in post-Christendom. Sometimes they seem to bring ridicule and hardship on themselves.[23]

---

[23] See, for example, the Evangelical Alliance's 'response' after the Co-operative Bank closed the account of Christian Voice. The EA stated that 'it cannot condone Christian Voice material which appears to make

Christians may also engage in further self-critical reflection as they come to terms with the fact that Jesus' ethics can be applied more fully to the public sphere than the church often admitted in Christendom. Already, the church is showing signs of a willingness to admit where it has got things wrong. In their recent report on prisons, the Catholic bishops observed that it was necessary to change attitudes within the Catholic Church towards people in prison.[24] There will be further questions about many of the contradictions in the political actions of Christians about the Church of England's established status. While any formal attempt to end this completely would land the government in a legislative minefield, it is likely that disestablishment will come about piecemeal.

From Control to Witness

The church's instinct to seek privilege, power and political influence seems to be deeply ingrained: a large number of Christians are aiming to exercise influence in and around government. But concerted efforts to change the law or wield any significant power will be less and less a possibility for Christians in post-Christendom. The church may be maturing politically but it is also shrinking and apparently becoming more fragmented. It certainly doesn't speak with one political voice, Christians will therefore need to think far more in terms of witness. Rather than lobbying directly for changes in the law, the church will need to consider other political strategies, such as:

- Taking part in political debates.
- Changing the terms of political debate.
- Making suggestions to government.
- Demonstrating models of best practice.
- Direct action and stands for justice.

---

[23] (*Continued*) generalisations and inferences about gay people in an unnecessarily provocative way' (5 July 2005).
[24] *A Place of Redemption*, Catholic Bishops' Conference of England and Wales, p. 4.

We have already noted that in post-Christendom the church is rediscovering the power of political witness through what it does on the ground. The Jubilee 2000 movement succeeded in changing the terms of the debate from *whether* debts in the developing world should be cancelled to *how* it should be done. Campaigns such as Faithworks have sought to demonstrate to government that the churches can deliver.

If the churches continue this change of emphasis, this will also mean a shift in focus from:

- *Short-term to long-term.* As Christians are no longer able to bring about short-term gains, they may see their witness as bringing about longer-term change.
- *Narrow to broad.* A preoccupation with government will increasingly give way to a broader concern with the cultural environment in which government operates and the agendas it follows.
- *Reactive to proactive.* Whereas to date a good deal of the churches' political action in post-Christendom has been reactive, a focus on witness will foster a more proactive approach.
- *Do-as-I-say to do-as-I-do.* There may well be a growing awareness that if the church is to lead, it will need to lead by example.

Accordingly, government will become less important for the political activity of the church, which will pay less attention to it. Christian engagement in politics will be less about changing the law and more about broader outcomes such as changing the surrounding culture. Its focus will increasingly shift to other institutions, from the United Nations, the G8 and the World Bank to businesses large and small, national and local media, arts organisations, schools and universities, local councils and community groups.

Two particular aspects of the church's witness will have a direct bearing on its impact. The first is the *quality* of its example. In Christendom, there was little need for the church to set a good example, since it was able to get what it wanted by other means. In post-Christendom, this becomes far more important.

The second is its *distinctiveness*. Increasingly, the church will consider what it is that makes its example different from those of other pressure groups. As we have already noted, it may struggle in this; but those Christians who are able to show that their ethics, beliefs and ideas in the realm of public policy have something innovative to offer will be the ones who stand out the most.

From Maintenance to Mission

In Christendom, the emphasis was on maintaining a supposedly Christian status quo, but in post-Christendom it is on mission within a contested environment. The ever-weaker association of social institutions and structures with Christianity, along with the movement we have just noted from control towards witness, could open an entirely new political agenda.

As we observed in Chapter 3, Christendom was characterised by approaches that tended to propose mediating principles that limited the negative effects of institutions and political practices, rather than their radical reform. Post-Christendom, in contrast, offers the opportunity to propose reforms that challenge social structures themselves. The church is already beginning to think more imaginatively and radically about the solutions it suggests. As such, it is likely to see itself increasingly as a political counter-culture to society and its institutions, rather than their guardian. Although some Christians are still defending social institutions they regard as under attack, such efforts seldom succeed. They may delay change in the short term, but political realities suggest that they will inevitably fail in the end. The church will be increasingly powerless to prevent change – and as it comes about, these institutions will seem less and less aligned with Christianity and so less worth defending.

Most notably, this means that the church will realise that government itself, no less than other institutions, is something to be challenged and reformed. In Christendom, government was something the church often sought to support and maintain. A new emphasis on mission, even towards government, will prompt the church to try to challenge and change it more than it has done before.

Increasingly, too, the church will see the political system as something to engage with and subvert rather than endorse and support. Increasingly, it may perceive it as illegitimate, as something that allows the oppression of minorities and perpetuates injustice. Given the diminishing allegiance of Christians to the state and their recognition that they are sojourners in a foreign country, there may be less emphasis on civic participation as a virtue in itself. This may mean, for example, that when Christians join a political party they will do so less to support it in what it does and more to reform it and change it. In elections, too, more Christians will consider 'spoiling' their ballot paper, or even not voting, as a witness to government that things need to change. In any event, Christians are likely to attach significantly less importance to elections as they take a broader view of politics.

From Institution to Movement

In Christendom, churches operated mainly as institutions, but in post-Christendom they are once again becoming a political movement. At first glance, it may seem that their political perspective is so diverse that they can hardly be considered a movement at all. Certainly the political voices are many and varied, but this may only be a reflection of wider and more general changes in churches. There is increasing lay participation as churches struggle to recruit clergy and find the means to support them. Denominational allegiances are weakening. There are disagreements over doctrine.

Nonetheless, there is a growing recognition that where Christians are divided over theology they can be unified around a political viewpoint: 'where the current view maintained is that we cannot often speak with one voice, we have an opportunity to prove that we are united to change society – that we have one heart for the marginalised. There will always be points of theology upon which we do not agree, but we can unite under the commandment of Jesus to love those rejected by the world.'[25]

---

[25] 'United We Stand: Building Trust'.

It is not that Christians will come together into one identifiable political movement – it's more likely that they will continue to disagree politically. But at the same time there may be a growing consensus about the values and ethics that should underlie political decisions. For example, it may even be that, while Christians continue to disagree over the morality of homosexual practice, they find that they agree more than they have hitherto about how gay and lesbian people should be treated. Conservative Christians have tended to oppose measures to formalise 'gay partnerships' on the grounds that they would 'undermine marriage'; but as civil partnerships become more accepted and legal marriage is no longer identified so strongly as 'Christian', Christians may more readily find common ground around ideas of fostering commitment in relationships, whether straight or gay.

Also, where Christians have hitherto been divided between those who hold a principled commitment to pacifism and those in the 'just war' tradition, they may find common political cause as they did in opposing the invasion of Iraq. The fact that the churches are less committed to the nation state may lead Christians to apply 'just war' criteria more rigorously and make them readier to unite in opposition to the use of force and the commercial arms trade and in favour of disarmament.

Rather than forming one great political movement, Christians will be involved in a complex array of campaigns, initiatives and coalitions from the local to the international level.

Conclusion

In this chapter, I have suggested that Christians are unlikely to withdraw from politics. None of the possible causes of evangelical disengagement at the end of the 19th century seem to apply today. There is less identification between Christianity and culture. The new theological movements that understand Jesus as a political figure also tend to reject premillennialist views and the separation of faith and 'works'. There is a growing realisation that it just doesn't make sense to divide the gospel into the spiritual and the social.

What is more likely is that Christian political perspectives will continue to develop, and so will their methods of engagement. The idea that Christendom can ever be restored is simply not credible, and the church's political activity will increasingly be driven by a desire for justice as it rediscovers the political dimension of the gospel. The church will be increasingly aware of a new political identity as a minority on the margins of our society. The character of Christian political involvement will be much more fluid – a movement.

Thus, there is good reason to believe that the new deal between church and state will not last. It may continue for a time in a more limited way, but even where it endures it is unlikely to be the dominant feature of relations between the two partners.

10

The State We Are Not In

The number of communicants on a wet February Sunday morning in the Church of England are more than the members of the Labour, Conservative and Liberal Democrat political parties. We are a mass movement by comparison.

Graham James[1]

How will Christians reimagine their political identity in post-Christendom? In this transitional phase, the identity of both the church and individual Christians is becoming increasingly political as the recognition grows that politics is not a narrow pursuit that only a few Christians engage in. The question is not whether Christians will be political but what their political expression will entail. Those who accept their new status will need to renegotiate how to be 'in the world' but not 'of' it.[2]

What Will the Church Look Like?

I will not attempt here to sketch out the form the church is likely to take in post-Christendom, as others have already done this;[3] but (among other things) it will probably be intricately intertwined with the political attitudes and activities of the churches. It's sufficient to note that the form churches take:

---

[1] Quoted in 'Defender of the Faith', *The Guardian*, 28 March 2005.
[2] Stuart Murray, *Church after Christendom*.
[3] See Murray, *Church after Christendom*, chapter 1, 'Church after Christendom: Belonging/Believing/Behaving'.

- Will depend to a degree upon political considerations.
- Will vary in how well they work politically.
- Will influence the political perspectives of the church.
- Will affect the quality of its political witness.

But the emphasis in post-Christendom will be less on form than it was in Christendom and more on the church's values and behaviour. Many Anglican churches have traditionally operated on the basis that their parishioners 'belong' (and have certain legal rights) regardless of their beliefs. Elsewhere, people who wished to belong to a church were expected to subscribe to certain beliefs. Believing and belonging may be more integrally connected in post-Christendom than they have been for hundreds of years.[4] And to this must be added the idea of 'behaving'.

Post-Christendom churches will be untidy communities where belonging, believing and behaving are all in flux rather than neatly fixed and integrated. Churches are likely to be defined less by what they believe and more by the values they hold and the way they behave. The communities that thrive will be the ones with core values or guiding principles – and many of these will be unmistakably political.

It has been suggested that a 'centre-set' model of the church is one that would work well in post-Christendom. This would have the following features:[5]

- It has a definite centre, comprising core convictions, forged by the story that has shaped the community.
- This centre is the focal point around which members of the community gather enthusiastically.
- Its core convictions continue to shape it and distinguish it from other communities in a plural and contested culture.
- It expends its energy on maintaining its centre rather than patrolling its boundaries.
- Its confidence in its core convictions frees it to be inclusive, hospitable and open to others, who are welcome to explore it.

---

[4] Murray, *Church after Christendom*.
[5] Murray, *Church after Christendom*, pp. 29–30.

• Those who 'belong' move towards the centre, however near or far away they are currently in terms of belief or behaviour.

This is a dynamic rather than a static model for a church, suitable for communities that expect constant interaction with others. Its appropriateness for the increasing politicisation of the church is clear – it could easily fit campaign groups that wouldn't necessarily be called 'churches'.[6] It could also describe smaller movements and campaigns involving local churches and Christians, such as those in defence of asylum seekers facing deportation. Nor is it limited only to Christians: such a model of the church could fit many other political initiatives, whether local or global.

But though in some respects this model resembles some existing Christian organisations that could describe themselves as 'movements', in other respects it is obviously different. The Evangelical Alliance, for example, describes itself as 'a movement for change' but it doesn't fit the model. Its core convictions are enshrined in a statement of belief, rather than in certain values and behaviour, and it has appeared to patrol its boundaries. At times it has looked as if it would exclude others who held divergent views – for example, on the meaning of Jesus' crucifixion[7] – and people who have disagreed with its line on homosexuality have had to resign their membership.[8] It is not obviously especially inclusive.

I noted in the last chapter how Christians may disagree over their approaches to war or homosexuality, say, but still be united in political activity opposing a specific use of force or demanding justice for gay and lesbian people. The successful movements in post-Christendom will be those that are able to hold together in

---

[6] Although many local churches and individual Christians might be involved in them.

[7] Its statement of faith was publicly said implicitly to endorse penal substitution, which some evangelicals felt unable to subscribe to.

[8] The Courage Trust was asked to leave the Alliance after it changed its stance on homosexuality. The Alliance has called this 'negotiated resignation' and denies that it constituted expulsion. See David Hilborn, 'Introductory Address to the Atonement Symposium at the London School of Theology', p.3.

this way people whose beliefs conflict. Indeed, this may be one of the distinctive characteristics of post-Christendom churches.

Other groups that describe themselves as movements, such as Faithworks, may conform more closely to the centre-set model of the church in post-Christendom, but they, too, often have membership schemes that emphasise belonging and make a distinction between those who are 'in' and those who are 'out'. They may even charge a fee to join and ask their affiliates to sign a charter and receive a certificate to indicate their membership. Nonetheless, Faithworks can still be said to represent a step towards how the church may be reimagined in post-Christendom. Unlike the Evangelical Alliance, its charter focuses on behaviour rather than doctrine – and it is certainly more inclusive, as its charter prohibits discrimination on grounds of sexual orientation.

However, while groups that call themselves 'movements' may differ in many ways from a centre-set model of the church, the individual campaigns they undertake may have far more in common with it. For example, their alliance with secularists during the campaigns against the Racial and Religious Hatred Bill show that even those organisations that patrol their borders rigorously are willing to be more inclusive when it comes to their political actions.

Of course, para-church groups, campaigns and coalitions are likely to remain distinct from local churches in post-Christendom; but the lines between them may become increasingly blurred. Some campaigns may have all the features of churches – and some churches may have all the features of political movements.

The Move toward Movements

The emergence of movements such as Faithworks, and the recasting of older organisations along similar lines, is an indication of the direction in which Christians are heading. It is also a signal that many Christians are recognising the advantages of reimagining the church in such terms.

- Movements are adaptable and can change far more easily.
- Movements provide a sense of direction and action.
- Movements provide a sense of identity.
- Movements look forward, not back.
- Movements are often more realistic and in touch with the world around them.
- Movements in many cases are growing at a time when the membership of both churches and political parties is in decline.
- Movements allow their members to move, closer to the centre or closer to the periphery, and even to be ambiguous about whether they are actually in or out.
- Movements focus on changing political values and whole agendas, rather than individual laws.
- Movements allow for variety and diversity of expression.
- Movements allow their members to be both proactive and reactive.
- Movements are often committed to radical reform.

The advantages of movements in post-Christendom are clear. But there are serious questions we have to ask about the extent to which they can be engineered and constructed in the way many Christians seem to want them to be. As we have already noted, there is a tendency in the church to want control; but in many respects movements will not flourish unless control is relinquished. They often appear anarchic. They often express moods and feelings that seem to emerge of their own accord and cannot easily be manufactured. As such, they are often the product of wider cultural changes.

The growing diversity in forms of church has been noted elsewhere.[9] The crucial political question, however, is what the values at the heart of the centre-set model will be. It is vital that Christians ask this as they work out what it is that will make them distinct from those around them in post-Christendom and what will form the basis of their identity.

In Christendom, Jesus as a political figure was often sidelined. In post-Christendom, the church is rediscovering the political

---

[9]   See Murray, *Church after Christendom*, chapter 3, 'Will It Emerge?'

Jesus and exploring anew the political dimension of what he had to say. In Christendom, the behaviour of those who began to recognise this dimension was often referred to as 'radical discipleship', but post-Christendom suggests that we are moving towards the abolition of such distinctions as the ideas of 'radical discipleship' enter the mainstream.

In Christendom, appeals were often made to the Hebrew scriptures and the writings of Paul for models of political engagement. These sources are not – yet – being abandoned,[10] but when Christians examine them they are doing so increasingly from a Christocentric position, which interprets them in the light of the political Jesus. Initiatives that take themes from the Hebrew scriptures, such as Jubilee 2000, the Micah Challenge, the Amos Trust and Operation Noah, seem to come up with far more radical solutions than might have been expected in the context of Christendom.

Many Christian approaches tend to treat the Bible as a handbook or a blueprint for society. In many ways this is a legacy of Christendom, of a time when the church had to be involved in ordering the world around it. At the coronation of the British monarch, senior leaders of the established church still present them with a Bible as a 'rule for the whole life and government of Christian princes.' It is still suggested that the Bible can 'offer a paradigm of a relational social order'.[11]

Such approaches may still be appropriate when the church speaks directly to government in post-Christendom; but they are less relevant for a church that is seeking to rediscover its own political identity, where politics is increasingly a matter of the churches' everyday life.

In the language of the New Testament, as sojourners rather than settlers Christians look set to rediscover what it means to be, first and foremost, citizens of the kingdom that Jesus preached. That involves a return to the roots of the faith, in the sense of

---

[10] See, for example, the concept of 'relationism' developed by the Jubilee Centre, which is based on Old Testament ideas (*The R Factor* and *Jubilee Manifesto*).

[11] Schluter and Ashcroft (eds.), *Jubilee Manifesto*, p. 19.

'radical' discipleship. In contemporary terminology, it may involve embracing such Christian ideas as:

- Nonviolence
- Powerlessness
- Reconciliation
- Equality
- Community
- Justice
- Forgiveness
- Grace
- Truth-telling
- Love
- Generosity
- Voluntary poverty
- Sacrifice
- Inclusiveness

In Christendom, although they were not always identified in those terms, many of these values were seen as private, other-worldly or spiritual. In post-Christendom, churches may be coming to recognise more and more that ethics are not merely personal or pie-in-the-sky but can have a very public application that is grounded in reality. These values, which emerge from an increasingly political understanding of Jesus, may be rediscovered by the church more generally in how it behaves as a political movement, but also more specifically in what it says to government.

Space does not permit us to explore all these values, but we can look at a couple. Although many Christians throughout Christendom have taken Jesus' rejection of violence[12] seriously, it is now being more readily and more widely embraced. In the past century, men such as Martin Luther King and Mohandas Gandhi have popularised it in the wider culture. There is a growing awareness that nonviolence does not mean inaction, but rather

---

[12] See, for example; Mt. 5:9; Mt. 5:21–22; Mt. 5:38–41; Mt. 5:43–46; Mt. 10:22–23; Mt. 22:40; Mk. 10:18; Mk. 11:25; Lk. 6:27–28; Lk. 9:54–55; Lk. 10:26–28.

means not being violent in the actions we *do* take. Many changes in government in recent history have been brought about more or less without violence.[13] Gene Sharp famously listed in detail 198 methods of non-violent action, ranging from methods of protest through to strikes, civil disobedience, sanctuary, the renouncing of honours, the use of humour, the destruction of property and the use of symbols.[14] In many respects, as the church moves further away from government, politics can be seen in terms of non-violent mechanisms for resolving problems that may otherwise end in violence.

Then there is the idea of forgiveness. Some amazing stories have come out of how Christians have responded to the injury or murder of relatives. The family of the police officer Stephen Oake said publicly that they forgave his murderer, Kamel Bourgass.[15] The Anglican church has apologised for the part it played in the slave trade. Increasingly, too, there has been talk of forgiveness at the level of government. The church has urged the forgiveness of the debts of the developing world and, outside western Europe, the idea of forgiveness has played a major part in 'truth and reconciliation' commissions in South America (for example, in Chile following the atrocities committed during General Augusto Pinochet's 17-year rule) and, perhaps most famously, South Africa.[16]

It is noteworthy that – in marked contrast to the new deal between church and government – these values are not:

• Concerned with professionalism or excellence.
• Primarily concerned with social cohesion.
• Particularly safe.

---

[13] For example, in South Africa, the Philippines, Czechoslovakia and the former USSR.

[14] Gene Sharp, *The Politics of Nonviolent Action: Part Two – The Methods of Nonviolent Action* (Boston: Extending Horizons Books, 1973).

[15] Helen Carter, 'Dead policeman was devoted officer and son of ex-chief constable', *The Guardian*, 16 January 2003.

[16] Desmond Tutu, *No Future without Forgiveness* (London: Rider, 1999).

- Always functional.
- Self-interested.

Values such as these may seem radical to many people. They don't always appear to make political sense, and are not promoted by a self-interested community that is demanding justice for its own benefit. They are not concerned with maintaining existing privileges or securing new ones, or with gaining new resources. Nor do they have much to do with ideas of social cohesion, social order or partnership with government. They are, however, linked closely with Christian beliefs, and a church that embraces such values is asking the world to judge it on its beliefs as well as on its values and actions – and certainly not on its ability to deliver the outcomes that government wants.

Most of all, these are distinctive values. Whereas a focus on excellence and delivery could transform the church into just another agent of government that sometimes does things a little better than the world around it, these values could mark it out as something quite rare.

Learning from One Another

But such ideas are only beginning to be rediscovered. It will not happen instantly – it requires a journey. The church will have to develop ways of exploring and discussing these values, and the habit of doing so, in order to form its unique political identity. The resources it will need to do this, however, may be less easy to come by in post-Christendom, so how can the church think creatively and with prophetic imagination? It will have to seek political inspiration from sources that relate more to its position at the margins rather than at the centre, as a movement rather than an institution.

There are a number of sources it could turn to for help.

Learning from history. There are many appropriate historical examples, from parts of the early church, the various monastic movements and groups of dissenters and radicals in Christendom.

Learning from other traditions. Different church traditions have different political insights that can be brought to bear:

- The Anabaptist and liberation traditions offer political interpretations and perspectives.
- The evangelicals offer a tradition of social and voluntary activism.
- Liberal elements of the church offer broader and more discursive perspectives with an emphasis on justice.
- Quakers and other peace churches offer non-violent perspectives.
- The established church in Britain, the various Catholic traditions and those that have historically been involved closely with governments around the world can remind the church of political realities – such as that politics is a necessary part of life but there are no easy solutions – and warn against ineffective strategies and risks of compromising the church's message.

Some traditions may have more to offer than others – and of course the church can learn from their failures as well as their successes.

Learning from other countries and cultures. Many groups around the world have been bold enough to take a radical stand informed by such values. For example, the World Council of Churches and Christian Peacemaker Teams have pioneered non-violent methods such as accompaniment programmes.

Learning from unlikely examples. The church may also need to look in some places that have not been explored before. Some may be very close to it, but Christendom made the church blind to them. Children, for example, were rarely considered as political models in Christendom, despite Jesus' insistence that the Kingdom 'belonged to such as these'.

One advantage the church has as a political movement is that it has the freedom to experiment, and this it needs to do – to try out new ideas and methods, make mistakes and learn from them. It also needs to foster debate – about how to read the Bible politically and how to interpret the text and apply it to its contemporary context. In short, it needs to develop its ideas of study, reflection and action.

Political Catechesis

As the church grows in its understanding of these values, it will also need to find ways to introduce them to others who want to join it. In Christendom, it often devised forms of training and initiation, and more recently it has come up with (for example) the Alpha and Emmaus courses – though these are notable for their complete lack of political content. Post-Christendom catechesis will require some exploration of 'behaving'. It will mean rehearsing the 'big story' and the core values of the community so that they can be internalised. Murray has noted that 'it may include a form of cultural exorcism, confronting the norms of a cynical, individualistic, patriarchal, consumerist culture, built on global injustice and sustained by institutional violence.'[17] Its political catechesis may involve identifying the idols of that culture that the Christian community refuses to bow to and pledges to expose.

One fundamental question is: What will denote membership of post-Christendom churches? Believer's baptism was important to many early Christians and has remained so to parts of the church throughout its history.[18] It has often been understood as a political statement, a sign of new citizenship of the Kingdom of God. But we have already noted that the idea of 'membership' is problematic. It sounds institutional. It has been suggested that a church that thinks in terms of membership will be more inclined to believe that it is the interests of its members that are paramount. It may also tend to see the Bible as a members' handbook.[19]

In contrast, people who are involved in movements tend not to be card-carriers. It is more likely that their 'membership' will be defined by behaviour – though symbols may also play an important role. The gold chains of the Jubilee 2000 Coalition and the white bands of the Make Poverty History campaign have already

---

[17] See further chapter 6, and Alan Kreider, 'Initiating attractive Christians: lessons from the early church', *Anabaptism Today*, 36 (2004), pp. 2–7.

[18] See Durnbaugh, *The Believers' Church*, p. 66.

[19] Presidential address by Dr David Stancliffe, Bishop of Salisbury, to the Salisbury diocesan synod, October 2002.

been seen on the lapels and wrists of many Christians, and other such symbols will doubtless appear. Perhaps Christians will increasingly adopt the white poppy, which symbolises a rejection of the belief that war is a necessary evil, rather than the traditional red one for Remembrance Sunday.

An organisation that doesn't have members is 'deeply subversive of contemporary culture'.[20] It is not inconceivable that parts of the church will be seen less and less as religious as they appear more and more political in their behaviour. After all, the early Christians were considered irreligious by some because their faith didn't square with the expectations of the time. Their religion was so alien to the prevailing culture that it could not be understood in religious terms. It is not unthinkable that such a situation may arise again.

In Chapter 4, we noted that evangelicals are seeing new opportunities for evangelism in political contexts. The credibility of the gospel is at stake, they argue: if Christians don't offer solutions to social problems, people will look elsewhere. From this perspective, political action is seen as a tool to create the conditions for a sympathetic response to evangelistic endeavours: 'it is both reasonable and right to seek to mould a society so as to minimise the conflict between Christ and culture.'[21]

In fact, the politicisation of evangelism is likely to go much further in post-Christendom, as evangelicals in particular recognise that their social and political action is actually part of the Evangel – the good news of God's lordship over creation. This would accord with some of the original meaning of the word, for the Evangel contained the idea of a messenger returning from battle, announcing that the victory had been won. There had been a change of regime. A new kingdom had been inaugurated.[22]

In Christendom, the Evangel became somewhat confused, because the new regime had joined with the old. Indeed, often the new regime didn't seem to be good news at all, because it

---

[20] Presidential address by Dr Stancliffe to the Salisbury diocesan synod, October 2002.
[21] Schluter and Ashcroft (eds.), *Jubilee Manifesto*, p. 27.
[22] Yoder, *The Politics of Jesus*.

employed violence, coercion, persecution and bloodshed. If this was the 'good news', it was surprising that anyone wanted anything to do with it. The Evangel that Jesus preached, however, was of a quite different sort – it promised liberation for the captives, sight for the blind, justice for the oppressed. As the political Jesus is rediscovered, so there will be a rediscovery by some parts of the church that the gospel is social as well as spiritual. It will have an increasingly hard political edge.

Worship and Liturgy

The fact that some parts of the church may come to be considered as less religious will not, of course, mean that they actually are. Nonetheless, there may be greater political content in church meetings and services. There is a strong Judaeo-Christian tradition behind this trend. In Micah, for example, God calls his people to remember their past, reminding them how he liberated them from slavery in Egypt and brought them to the promised land.[23] Just as some early Christians commemorated the death days of the martyrs as their birthdays, so the church may increasingly incorporate into its liturgies remembrance of acts of justice. Hospitality, too, may play a larger part in the life of the churches, as justice, 'sharingness' and mutual care acquire greater importance for them. Familiar religious symbols and traditions, too, may become more political.

New developments may include:

- The commemoration and celebration of political acts from the 'salvation story', such as the Passover, as well as those from Christendom and post-Christendom.
- Liturgies of repentance for the sins of the church.[24]

---

[23] Mich. 6:4–5.

[24] Rosemary Radford Ruether, *Women-Church: Theology and Practice of Feminist Liturgical Communities* (San Francisco, Harper & Row, 1985) contains an Ash Wednesday liturgy of repentance for the church's treatment of Jews, women, sexual minorities, racial minorities, the poor and its own believers.

- The exploration of the political dimension of liturgical events –
  seeing, for example, the Eucharist as a peace meal and Ash
  Wednesday as an occasion to repent of injustice.
- A critical assessment of the liturgies and creeds Christians use
  and the political message they communicate.
- A rethinking of the creeds Christians use, or the way they use
  them.
- The formulation of new creeds, and an examination of other
  traditions that have a heightened sense of the political.
- A review of what the church is praying for when it remembers
  'those in authority'.
- The selection more often in worship of scriptures with political
  content.
- The drawing-out of the political aspects of stories such as the
  Nativity and the Passion.[25]
- The telling of political stories.
- A review of how churches communicate with children. Many
  children's books relate biblical stories about the Kingdom of
  God in a way that entirely overlooks their political message.

The Priestly Role

The changing political identity of the church will bring into question its 'priestly' role. In Christendom, it was often called on to bless social institutions and the actions of government, giving them a divine sanction and authority. It still takes part today in:

- Coronation ceremonies
- Services of remembrance
- Christenings
- Marriages
- Funerals
- Chaplaincy in the armed forces

---

[25] For example, emphasising Joseph, Mary and Jesus' status as asylum seekers fleeing from Herod or the political reasons for Jesus' death.

But already in post-Christendom these things have become sources of tension. Some Anglican clergy have refused to baptise or marry people who they believe are not Christians. There was acrimony during the Falklands and Iraq wars over the nature and content of the services the church would hold for the armed forces.

There are a number of questions the church will need to face:

- In order to create a clear political identity, should it withhold from the wider society some of the 'services' it offers, such as baptisms and weddings?
- Should it hold services of remembrance? If so, what should it commemorate?
- If it does take part in state ceremonies, what approach should it take? Is the language of sacrifice, for example, appropriate to describe the deaths of men and women in war?
- Should its services recognise the impact of the events that are being commemorated on people outside Britain?

Conclusion

The church will take on a new political identity, but to reimagine itself more as a movement will clearly entail some hard choices. It may have to put aside its aspirations to be professional and efficient in favour of other marks of distinction, such as its radical stand for justice and its willingness to make sacrifices, take risks, admit its mistakes and go it alone. Many of these things may clash with the churches' current emphasis on trust. After all, a church that wants to be trusted may be afraid to experiment and reluctant to admit its mistakes. It may also have little incentive to be bold and radical.

One key question the church must face is whether it is going to sever some of its links with government of its own accord or whether it will wait for this to be forced upon it.

11

Enemy of the State

There are, broadly speaking, two attitudes that Christians can adopt to government. The first is to see it as a friend. This was the view generally taken by the church during Christendom. Of course, there was conflict at times, and struggles for power: governments did not always do what the church wanted – and vice versa. But the changes Constantine made inaugurated a deep and, according to some, mutually beneficial friendship. It seemed to secure protection for the church and an end to persecution. The organs of government were used to advance the church's goals. Doctrines were defended and moral standards were upheld. A sort of justice was implemented. Religious observance was safeguarded and sometimes enforced. The church enjoyed many of the benefits of the state's patronage.

The alternative approach has been to see the state in more negative terms – and even to regard it as an enemy. This is what many people have done who have been oppressed by governments around the world, including Christians suffering persecution. This is what many in the early church did, and also some Christians in Christendom. In 1646, the Fifth Monarchist preacher Christopher Feake declared that there was an 'enmity against Christ' in the aristocracy and the monarchy. Following the Reformation, the word 'Anabaptist' 'came to be used in a general pejorative sense to describe those who were believed to oppose the existing social and political order.'[1] Government was perceived as something that restricted Christians and took away

---
[1] Hill, *The World Turned Upside Down*, p. 26.

their freedoms. It waged war against them and killed them. It stood for injustice and oppression. It stood in the way of God's kingdom.

As we look back at Christendom, many commentators would suggest that often the 'friendship' was not one between equals. The church was compromised and constrained in its witness. It conspired in injustice and violence. As I have already suggested, one central difficulty was how to reconcile the life, death and resurrection of Jesus, and the kingdom he preached, with partnership with states, governments and political systems. The political remained a 'morally ambiguous realm': it was not 'insulated from the resurrection conquest of Christ and the signs of the coming kingdom', but nor did it belong to them.[2]

Although some Christians remain intent on pursuing such a partnership today, it is likely that many will see government less and less as a friend. This is a trend we can already observe, and there are a number of reasons why it will only grow more pronounced:

- Government will clamp down on some activities of certain parts of the church, such as proselytism.
- The injustice and violence of government will become more apparent to many Christians.
- Christians will identify increasingly with the powerless rather than the powerful.
- There will be less and less association of government and its institutions with Christianity.
- Christian influence on government will decline and it will act in ways that seem to be beyond the control of Christians.
- Government is likely to be seen as breaking trust with the churches and letting them down.
- Government will remove many of the church's remaining privileges.
- Government will impose more conditions on the funding it gives to churches.

---

[2] Oliver O'Donovan and Joan Lockwood O'Donovan, *Bonds of Imperfection: Christian Politics Past and Present* (Grand Rapids: Eerdmans, 2004), p. 2.

- Christians will more often employ theologies of 'the powers', which see government in largely negative terms.

As theologians who locate themselves within dissenting traditions have emphasised (and political theorists, too, have noted), there are some things that seem to be essential to most, if not all, governments – in particular, coercion, injustice and the use of violence. In Christendom, the church had to develop ways of dealing with the tension this created and so Jesus' teachings were privatised, relativised, reinterpreted or simply ignored. It applied different ethical standards to government and tried to mitigate the worst effects of government action, while at the same time justifying how Christians themselves could take part in the morally ambiguous functions of government. Christian political thinkers developed ideas such as 'just war' theory, set down the responsibilities of political leaders and drew boundaries around political authority and assigned it specific tasks. Whilst such political thought remains a valuable resource, in post-Christendom there is less of a need to come up with justifications for activities of government that appear morally dubious.

Law, too, was often regarded in Christendom as something that could support, protect or maintain the Christian faith. Although some Christians still hold such a view, it will fall out of favour in post-Christendom. Perhaps the most obvious change in the perception of government will be that it can no longer be identified with Christianity, or indeed any other religion. The state will be expected to be neutral on religious matters. Already some Christians and secularists alike look to government to be even-handed and treat all religions and belief systems the same. Government will be expected to safeguard their freedoms but is also likely increasingly to place restrictions on those elements of religion that are viewed as subversive to the social order, whether they are supposed to incite hatred, unrest or violence. This could include some forms of evangelism.

The church may well become more aware of governments as entities that themselves *do* violence. Already there is a growing realisation in contemporary Britain of the devastation states cause when they go to war – most recently, in the invasion of Iraq.

The effects of war are far more visible to us through media coverage that brings pictures of it into our living rooms. Christians have already been at the forefront of highlighting abuse in Abu Ghraib[3] and Guantanamo Bay. States do violence in other ways, too – through the prison system, for example, or against the environment – but the violence that may be most obvious to the church (because of its dialogue with other faith communities) is the state's response to religiously inspired violence and the threat of terrorism.

Government will also have to address issues of religious offence, and the violence that increasingly seems to be provoked by negative depictions of religion, whether in cartoons, plays, poems or other writings that are perceived as blasphemous. Some Muslims have called for a law that will provide protection for all religions, and the Vatican, too, has hinted that it may be in favour of such a measure. However, any moves in this direction will be fiercely resisted by others who attach more importance to free speech, and it's unlikely that any government will be able to come up with a legislative formula that pleases all the various interests. Many Christians are unlikely to be entirely satisfied by the outcome.

As the church has less say in what government does and less involvement in the affairs of state, it is likely that their importance for Christians will diminish and the churches' identity will be less tied up with them. In Christendom, governments were sometimes seen as agents of God's salvation or even equated with the Kingdom of God; but in post-Christendom Christians will greatly widen the focus of their political engagement as they become ever more aware that government is limited in what it can achieve and cannot be relied on to deliver what they want. There are many things that are only possible for governments when the political climate is right, and as the church matures in its understanding of politics from the margins it will perceive, too, that there are many social and international problems that governments cannot easily solve.

---

[3] Christian Peacemaker Teams in Iraq presented a dossier documenting 72 cases of prisoner abuse to the Coalition Provisional Authority, several months before the abuses at Abu Ghraib became public knowledge.

In fact, in post-Christendom the state may come to be seen far more as a cause of problems than a solution to them. Already some parts of the church believe that it undermines social institutions, and it may come to be regarded as an obstacle to God's kingdom rather than an aid to its realisation. Government will begin to seem less inevitable or desirable. The church may increasingly propose solutions to social problems that lie outside the immediate remit of government – such as responses to crime that look not to the courts as a first resort but to mediation in the community. It will become more aware of the injustice and violence of the state. In Christendom, when the authorities favoured the Christian religion, it was easy for the church to turn a blind eye to their use of force; but once it has lost its privileges it will see how coercive government is – and also, as Christians rediscover a passion for radical justice, how unjust and oppressive.

In Christendom, current political arrangements often shaped Christian ideas of justice – including what happened on the Cross. The law of the land was often identified with justice, approximately if not absolutely. Indeed, there are some who would still suggest that government is the institution that implements Christian ideas of justice.[4] In post-Christendom, however, justice and the law may be seen increasingly as separate things – and often as things that conflict. The contrast between the 'justice' the state administers and what Christians regard as justice may become more pronounced.

Nonetheless, the idea that law is something that restrains violence – for example, through the criminal justice system, backed up by the police, the intelligence services and the army – is likely to persist, and Christians will probably continue to appreciate the protection it affords as they start to feel more vulnerable. Yet they will also become far more aware both that it is inadequate as an answer to violence and that those who apply it often act unjustly and oppressively themselves. Although Christians may still see government as something that restricts or mitigates some of the impact of injustice, they will probably perceive it as being itself fundamentally unjust – a necessary evil, as some of the great

---

[4] Storkey, *Jesus and Politics*, p. 186.

political thinkers, including Augustine, have pointed out down the centuries. They are likely to conclude, as Christians have always done, that the law of the land has a function, but it will always be an imperfect one.

The new dispensation of post-Christendom means that the churches no longer feel the same pressing need to justify and explain their alignment with the authorities. But how appropriate is it to see the state as an enemy rather than a friend?

The Post-Christendom View of the State

Although the churches' political engagement may no longer be concerned primarily with government, they will still need to develop their ideas of government. As Christendom declined, different views of government prevailed, with particular disagreement between the dissenting churches and those more aligned with power. However, there may now be more convergence between Christians when it comes to their views of the state – at least when it comes to their outworking. In Christendom, it was a matter not only of explaining how the church should engage *with* the state but also, often, of working out how the church *was* the state.

We may observe the following contrasts:

In Christendom	In post-Christendom
The state is often identified as Christian.	The state is not identified with any one religion.
Government can often be controlled and influenced.	Government must be lobbied and witnessed to.
Church and state are more allied.	Church and state are more separate.
The state is more often supported.	The state is more often challenged.
The state is often seen in positive terms.	The state is often seen in negative terms.
Government upholds one religion.	Government is neutral on religion.
Law and justice go together.	Law and justice are more separate.
State violence is justified.	State violence is less justified.

Nonetheless, although they may see government in more negative terms, many Christians may stop short of regarding it as an enemy. There is a well-known scene in Monty Python's *Life of Brian* when Reg (played by John Cleese), the leader of the People's Front of Judea, is trying to whip up anti-Roman sentiment among his team of slightly hesitant commandos. 'What have the Romans ever given us?' he asks.

'The aqueduct,' somebody says, thoughtfully. 'And the sanitation,' says another. 'And the roads,' offers a third. Reg reluctantly acknowledges that there may have been a few benefits – but then, with growing enthusiasm, his comrades-in-arms reel off a litany of all the good things the Romans have achieved during their occupation. By the time they've finished, they're not so sure about the whole idea of insurgency after all and an exasperated Reg tries to rally them: 'All right, but apart from better sanitation and medicine and education and irrigation and public health and roads and a fresh water system and baths and public order, what *have* the Romans ever done for *us*?'

The Roman Empire was a very different beast from our governments today. It was ruthless, bloody and militaristic. It often practised vicious persecution, killed people by the tens of thousands and enslaved them by the hundreds of thousands, and appeared to pay little regard to the poor and the vulnerable. States in post-Christendom seem very humane by comparison: they redistribute wealth from the rich to the poor and provide health care for the sick and pensions for the old. And yet it has been pointed out that the way we respond to that scene in *Life of Brian* depends very much on our own perspective.[5] If we identify with the people who benefited from the Roman occupation rather than with those who suffered under it, it seems very funny. As post-Christendom unfolds, however, the joke may fall flatter, as the church is aligned increasingly with the marginalised, feels less affinity with the nation state and takes a more global view. What we must guard against is myopia and ethnocentrism.

---

[5] Tom Hurcome, 'Disestablishing the Kingdom' in Leech (ed.), *Setting the Church of England Free*.

From the perspective of those in the more deprived parts of the world, what does our government do?

- It makes decisions based primarily on its own 'national interest'.
- It maintains borders that prevent wider access to health care and many other important resources and benefits.
- It detains those who cross its borders without permission.
- It ensures that money is spent primarily at home, collecting some 40 per cent of national income in tax and allocating less than 1 per cent of that sum to overseas aid.
- It imposes its will on others, ultimately backed up by the threat of military force – and even, ultimately, nuclear attack.
- It takes life if it considers it necessary.
- It allows the people it governs to go on polluting the planet, and encourages the consumption (at home and abroad) that causes that pollution.
- It underwrites the commercial sale of arms around the world.
- It invests in and promotes its own culture, values, goods and services worldwide, often to the detriment of other cultures.
- It imposes barriers to trade, to favour the sale of its own country's goods and services.

A broader view reveals that the British government could be accused of operating a form of international apartheid. Overseas, hundreds of thousands of people die each day because they don't have access to clean water and basic medication, while this country hoards its material and human wealth within closely guarded borders – much of it acquired from other lands by means of questionable morality. With nuclear weapons, Britain threatens to kill far more people than the Roman state ever did.

How Valid is Such a View Theologically?

As the church comes to see government in more negative terms, it will increasingly look to traditions of Christian political thought that have a similar emphasis. Theologians who have taken such a line have sometimes regarded government as an enemy simply because that is a legitimate reading of the biblical texts. More recently, this view has become more widely accepted as theologians have stressed the idea of 'the powers' that lie behind not only government but other institutions, too.[6] In spite of Christian appeals for us all to trust our government, they can point out that it is difficult to find a single biblical verse that advocates this.

For those who, increasingly, see little or no connection between justice and government, a Christocentric reading of the Bible will be crucial. When God's justice is revealed in all its fullness in Jesus Christ, it becomes clear that government is not the agent of that justice – indeed, it is the state and the powers behind it that crucify the agent of God's justice.

In the Hebrew scriptures, of course, law had an important function of protection and restraint. When Cain killed Abel, the mark God put on his forehead limited the violence that might have ensued. The *lex talionis* – the principle of an eye for an eye – also prevented the downward spiral of escalating reprisals. All of this, however, will be placed in the context of the political Jesus, and his declaration of the new kingdom. While Jesus endorsed the principle of the *lex talionis*, he also made it clear that it was not enough. He urged in its stead forgiveness and what many would see as the creation of an upward spiral of peace. The new kingdom fulfils the law but also leads to its abolition, for when people work out their problems without reference to the law, the law becomes obsolete.

According to some theologians, since the justice of the new kingdom has nothing to do with coercion, no law can ever witness to God's kingdom. They can hint at it, point to it – but the nature of God's justice is such that it does not involve compelling people to behave in particular ways. Justice is a much more rounded concept. Justice is only done when people freely embrace it. In the New Testament, pagan 'justice' is exposed as unjust, because it crucified the Messiah.[7] Thus, the state will always be a very

---

[6] See, for example, Wink, *Engaging the Powers*.
[7] 1 Cor. 2:8.

imperfect agent of God's justice (though the New Testament does note is that it is a 'servant' of God who is the Lord of history[8]).

A good deal of political theology in Christendom treated governments in all cultures and at all times as the same, and in so doing elevated government in importance to a category all on its own. There are, of course, certain features that are common to most states – not least their use of violence. However, the nature of governments, states and political systems changes from age to age. They are not all identical. What one may do at one time and in one culture, others, at other times and in other cultures, may be unable to do.

It is important, too, to distinguish between the different elements of the state. The term 'the state' can be defined to be so comprehensive as to have little meaning. Of course, any state has administrative and organisational functions. In Britain, for example, it includes such elements as:

- The Cabinet (often referred to as 'the government').
- MPs, who sit in the House of Commons.
- The House of Lords (essentially a revising, but also a scrutinising, chamber).
- The researchers, library staff and secretaries who support MPs.
- The civil servants who prepare legislation and ensure that it is administered.
- The police and the security services who enforce the law.
- The armed forces.

In modern society, it is not so easy to delineate clearly where the state ends. There are others on the government's payroll, or at least supported by taxpayers' money. Church agencies, among many others, receive government funding. Government underwrites transactions by big business, and some industries such as the Post Office have yet to be privatised. Clearly, many of the people involved in this larger state don't actually govern. Indeed, some of the people recognised as wielding great power in Britain – such as Rupert Murdoch – are not only not in government but not even in Britain.

---

[8] Rom. 13:4.

In post-Christendom, the church needs to make a new assessment of the nature of the state. We have noted that the early church did not have a theory of the state as such. It often saw the state of its day as evil, but it explained why it was so: it was evil in that it was idolatrous and it resorted to coercion, violence and execution. So, too, today, Christians need to assess critically the activities of the state. Too often debates become polarised around the crux of whether or not it is acceptable for Christians to get involved directly in government. The post-Christendom response to the state ought to be more pragmatic and less theoretical, taking account of its different structures and elements and exercising discernment about its changing nature.

We may find it more helpful, therefore, to treat the government as one element in something much larger. The theologian Walter Wink has talked of 'the system'. The system – *ho kosmos* in New Testament Greek, which is usually translated as 'the world') – is, he says, simply the 'human sociological realm that exists in estrangement from God'. Wink and others have proposed an approach that focuses on 'the powers' that lie behind the system. The 'enemy' is not so much government or other social institutions as the powers that lie behind them.

Such an approach can be more 'joined up', but can also put government and the state in their rightful place. Engaging with government is one aspect of engaging with the powers that lie behind all social institutions. After all, it is not only government that does violence. Business does violence to the environment, to people's lives. Capitalism itself can be seen as systematised violence, and so can the legal system.

The New Idols

I said in the last chapter that the church must discern the values that underlie a state at any given time and in any given context. In an analysis that brings together sociology and theology, J.A. Walter has questioned the concept of secularism and asked whether post-Christendom can actually be considered 'secular' when there is still so much evidence of 'the sacred' (the 'cement' of our society, he says, which 'is or represents an object of worship'). He suggests that, rather than a secular culture, what we are surrounded by is a new religion and a new belief system. He suggests some contemporary idols, but also contends that often the sacred can become idolatrous. Idolatry is 'the granting of ultimate worth to the sacred and making it an ultimate concern.'[9] The word 'idol' signifies an object of love, admiration or honour taken to an extreme degree – in other words, something that is considered to be beyond challenge.

In trying to discern the nature of a government, therefore, it is helpful to identify its 'idols'. This task has to be done with great care.[10] Although everything can become sacred, not every institution actually *is* sacred. A society and system is distinguished by the shrines it sets up – and, of course, some parts of society may worship at different altars.

Christians, too, in post-Christendom are engaging politically with new objects of worship, to which they, too, are committed and which form the basis of their concern. They will also need to examine those 'sacred' things that the church 'worshipped' in Christendom and they are now 'worshipping' all the more in post-Christendom, such as:

- Acceptance of government funding.
- Engagement in and through political parties.
- Voting.
- The quest for political influence and power.

The danger in post-Christendom is that Christians will approach politics with the values and perspectives of Christendom and in so doing will focus on mediating principles rather than radical reform. They will accept uncritically those things that are sacred to the new religious system – and sometimes bow before them. We have already raised the question of how far the new deal between church and state will blunt the church's radical agenda. The

---

[9] J.A. Walter, *A Long Way From Home: A Sociological Exploration of Contemporary Idolatry*, p. 14.

[10] Walter, *A Long Way From Home*, p. 15.

church appears to be endorsing the political system and seems to be employing its methods quite uncritically. Walter, however, suggests that the sacred provides 'illegitimate' answers to the pain of human existence and 'blinds human beings to the need for radical change'.[11]

Government May See the Church as an Enemy

If the church acknowledges that it has treated such 'sacred' things with a misplaced reverence and takes on the role of iconoclast instead, it is also quite possible that government will see it much more as an enemy than a friend.

Even if the church is more reticent, there has already been open acrimony between church and government, when the Thatcher government launched scathing attacks on the Church of England. That particular denomination still periodically comes in for criticism from MPs – in 2006 it was accused of being 'politically motivated' by a group of Conservatives professing a Christian faith over its decision to disinvest its funds from companies profiting from Israel's illegal occupation of Palestinian territory.[12] As churches become more political across a wider range of issues, there is certainly more scope for them to draw criticism from elected politicians.

We have already noted that government recognises the negative effects of religion as well as the positive ones when it comes to social capital, perceiving that religion has the potential to divide as well as unite. Under the threat of religious extremism and fundamentalism, it is quite possible that government will damn all religions without discrimination – or, at least, all those radical believers who dare to challenge it.

---

[11] Walter, *A Long Way From Home*, p. 13.
[12] 'Church stand on Israel', letter to *The Times* signed by Alistair Burt MP, David Amess MP, David Burrowes MP, Stephen Crabb MP, David Davies MP, Greg Hands MP, Gary Streeter MP, Ed Vaizey MP and Ann Widdecombe MP, 24 February 2006.

As with the early church, opposition from government could be provoked by a misunderstanding of the church as much as by what it is actually saying or doing. It is possible, too, that the church could be made a scapegoat for problems and failures elsewhere. However, the likeliest causes of government hostility may be that the church:

- Challenges the political system, suggesting non-voting, civil disobedience and other methods outside the usual political channels.
- Challenges the government increasingly over the positions it takes.
- Exposes the idolatry of the political system, questioning the assumptions of decision-making based primarily on 'the national interest'.
- Refuses to meet targets set by government.
- Increasingly takes a position that challenges the social order rather than defends it.

As we noted in the last chapter, religion has come to be seen as a threat to governments and the social order in a number of ways. For one thing, religious belief is finding expression in violence in new ways, and there is confusion as to why it has come about. Some people talk of the danger of extreme religious beliefs. Others blame poverty and hardship. Others still blame the imperialistic policies of the West.

However, we can also explain the motivation behind this terrorism in terms of the idols of the system. There are cultures that are refusing to bow to the idols of our culture, and some will resist violently, though others do it without violence. The reason for 'the clash of civilisations' is that they clash over the dominant values of the two different societies. They clash over the 'sacred', the idols of the system. Democracy, capitalism, militarism, the nuclear family – there are many such idols, and some cultures will not accept them because they claim ascendancy over their own idols. The terrorism is a misguided attempt at iconoclasm. (The West's attack on Islam can also be seen as iconoclasm, but that is outside the scope of this book.)

What are the Chances of a Holy War?

An important difference between the circumstances of the early church and post-Christendom is that the modern state makes promises. It promises the potential to change things and influence things. It urges people, including Christians, to engage with its democratic systems and mechanisms, and assures them that if they do, they can have a stake in government, and even a share of political power. Whether this is the reality or not is another matter, but this is what the state promises. As the church moves further to the margins, it will become ever more aware that in fact this is not true in any meaningful sense. And now that many in the church are engaging politically it is not just possible but highly likely that Christians will become disillusioned with government and the political system. This is, after all, the trend in the wider society.

If and when that does happen, the church will turn to other methods of political engagement outside the system. It, too, may even begin to resort to violence.

It is possible that parts of the church will choose violence for several reasons:

- Many of the church's political activities already bear the hallmarks of violence, even if they do not employ physical force. Some of the language the church uses (for example, in denouncing homosexual practice) verges on the violent, and it also shows a readiness to use the compulsion of the legal system to get what it wants. *Jerry Springer – The Opera* was met with threats not merely to prosecute BBC television executives under the law against blasphemy but even, reportedly, to kill them.[13]
- We have already seen cases in the US where Christians have bombed abortion clinics. Elsewhere in the world Christians continue to be involved in violence. There are, for example, conflicts between Christians and Muslims in places such as the Moluccas, and in Nigeria and elsewhere Anglican conservative Christians have threatened violence against Muslims.[14]

---

[13] 'Merry hell', BBC News Online Magazine, 8 December 2005.
[14] Archbishop Peter Akinola said: 'May we at this stage remind our Muslim brothers that they do not have the monopoly of violence in this

Christians could conceivably resort to violence in this country as well.

- As the church moves further to the margins, Christians are feeling increasingly vulnerable and fearful, and sometimes fear can lead to irrational responses. The anger generated by the churches' loss of privilege or by instances of perceived blasphemy or discrimination could drive some Christians to extreme actions.
- Christians have already suggested that they should make a stand against blasphemy 'like other religions have done'. Sometimes reference has been made to acts of violence by groups of Muslims or Sikhs.
- There are passages in the Bible that appear to endorse violence.
- Some theologies of the Cross emphasise the idea of retribution, and this can encourage a belief in 'redemptive violence' – that good triumphs over evil ultimately through the use of force. This is why apparently sterile debates about penal substitution are important, because they have moral and ethical implications for (for example) the criminal justice system and the so-called war against terror.[15] It is not that we need to get our doctrine *exactly* right but that the wrong theology can react with religious zeal to produce very dangerous results.
- Many Christians do not subscribe to a theology of 'the powers' and may therefore come to see the state as 'the enemy', rather than the spiritual forces that lie behind it.
- There are signs of the emergence in Britain of an 'other-wordly' faith that looks forward only to heaven, not to 'a new heaven and a new earth'. If, for example, a premillennialism again takes hold that despairs of this world, it is not inconceivable

---

[14] (*Continued*) nation. Nigeria belongs to all of us – Christians, Muslims and members of other faiths. No amount of intimidation can change this time-honoured arrangement in this nation. CAN may no longer be able to contain our restive youths should this ugly trend continue' ('Reaction of the President of the Christian Association of Nigeria, The Most Revd Peter Akinola on recent events in Nigeria', Anglican Communion News Service, ACNS 4113, 21 February 2006.

[15] See Barrow and Bartley, *Consuming Passion*.

that some Christians may try to hasten Christ's return by starting its destruction themselves. Some already make a connection
between the restoration of the state of Israel and the Second
Coming, and even link opposition to Israel with hostility
towards the church.[16]

Christendom, of course, was marked by violence – often perpetrated by the church, against governments, against Christians,
against non-Christians, for example in the various crusades and
inquisitions and in the Reformation – and some of its attitudes
and approaches persist. Indeed, violence with religious connections has been a feature of recent and local conflicts, such as the
Troubles in Northern Ireland. It may even become more prevalent
in post-Christendom.

Of course, it may not always be easy to distinguish clearly
whether it is 'really' Christians who are carrying out acts of violence. Certainly, many in the church will claim that those who
have embraced violence are not Christian at all. Members of the
British National Party (BNP), for example, have been observed
joining Christian Voice's protests against *Jerry Springer – The
Opera*. The far right is increasingly employing religious language
and imagery in its own campaigning, and talking of 'defending
the Christian culture' of Britain.[17] However, the fact that such
groups can find not just common cause but common arguments
with some Christians should in itself be enough to generate great
alarm.

Whether or not Christians are responsible, violence that is
thought to be perpetrated by Christians could result in some very
repressive legislation as fears of religious terrorism grow, and this
could indeed lead to real persecution of the church. This could in
turn radicalise more Christians, increasing the likelihood of
Christian violence, and could thus initiate a vicious circle.

---

[16] Comments made by Paul Diamond at 'Freedoms We Treasure', a day
conference organised by Deo Gloria Trust examining religious freedom
in contemporary British society, 20 May 2003.
[17] Andrew Grice, 'BNP to use prophet cartoon in campaign', *The Independent*, 22 February 2006.

Which methods Christians resort to in response will depend a great deal on how they believe God achieves his purposes, and how they interpret Jesus' teaching on the Kingdom of God, especially with regard to violence. A Christian commitment to non-violence will be extremely important in post-Christendom.

12

A Loving Witness

We have considered the possibility that in post-Christendom some Christians may respond to the growing hostility of government with violence. If they do, they will be a small minority. Others will continue to campaign peacefully, some on issues of justice for the vulnerable and the marginalised, some in defence of the church's old privileges and others again to try to repair the 'new deal' with government. Already some Christians are aware that the deal is fraying as the church finds itself at odds with government, and are working to try to maintain or restore the friendship. They realise that Christianity is being lumped together with other religions and may be being judged unfairly, and are seeking therefore to explain what the faith is about and how it is distinctive.[1] They emphasise the personal motives of Christians and the benefits their faith offers to society.

As we have already noted, there are serious questions about the desirability of these attempts. Even those who think primarily in terms of what the church needs may see that it is healthier for it to keep its distance from government and that there are advantages, too, in seeing government in less positive terms.

- It does not risk compromising the more 'prophetic' voice of the church.
- The church has more freedom to propose radical reform rather than simply addressing the negative effects of current policy.

---

[1] Press release from Faithworks, 'Faithworks announces measures to deal with fear of faith', 17 October 2005.

- The church can look at government more realistically and acknowledge its limitations more easily.
- The church will be better able to recognise the injustice and idolatry of government.
- The church will have a better understanding of justice.
- The church will be much more easily distinguished from government.
- The church will not have to justify those actions of government that conflict with Christian beliefs.
- Christians should not in any event be allied with power and privilege but should be more closely identified with the powerless, the marginalised and the persecuted.

The church will need to come to terms with its increasing alienation from government because, whether or not individual Christians see more advantage or disadvantage in it, it is going to happen anyway. The question is: What then is the most appropriate way for the church to respond?

At the end of the last chapter, I suggested that a commitment to non-violence would be extremely important. In the early church, at the celebration of the Eucharist Christians stood to recite a prayer for the blessing of the church and the welfare of the Emperor,[2] just as today many churches still pray for the Queen and her ministers. For the early Christians this was a rather more radical act, given that the Empire often persecuted them and put them to death; but it was not a compromise of their witness, but an essential part of it. Paul had instructed the Roman Christians to bless those who persecuted them,[3] in accordance with Jesus' command to love our enemies.[4]

In Christendom, Christians in positions of power often did not take such teaching seriously when it came to politics, though it was obeyed by some dissenting movements that were oppressed by both church and government. Love in Christendom was often relegated to the private sphere and became romanticised. Today,

---

[2] Chidester, *Christianity: A Global History*, p. 68.
[3] Rom. 12:15.
[4] Mt. 5:43–44.

too, it seems to many something soft and ill suited to the political realm. But for those who have accepted it as a political necessity, it has proved to be a radical path. Jesus' death on the cross was not only a political event engineered by the powers, it was an act of love in which Jesus made himself utterly vulnerable. The call of the gospel – also often privatised in Christendom – was for the church to respond to its persecutors with love. Indeed, what was supposed to make Christians distinctive was their love.[5]

In post-Christendom, the notion of love in a political context raises some challenging questions with regard to the political behaviour of many Christians:

- How loving is it to base political decisions primarily on what is in the church's interests?
- How comfortably do calls for a 'level playing-field' sit with a gospel message of love that often entails putting the interests of others first?
- Does love require the relinquishing of privileges – even to the point of preferring the special treatment of others?
- How does the kind of love that Jesus demonstrated square with attempts to gain political influence?
- Does love lead Christians to accept a position of powerlessness?
- Does love require the church to be more honest about its failures and inadequacies?

Ask Not What Government Can Do for You

'Ask not what your country can do for you, but what you can do for your country.' John Kennedy's famous exhortation may resonate with the church in post-Christendom more than it could have done for hundreds of years before now. The primary question that many Christians are asking now, from their place at the margins, is 'What can we get government to do for us?'; but increasingly the church will need to ask, 'What can we do for ourselves?' It may even ask: 'What can we do for government?'

---

[5] Jn. 13:35.

Christians and politicians alike are already recognising the importance of such questions as the church displays more of the features of a political movement. Gordon Brown, both in private meetings with people such as Jim Wallis and in his public speeches, has highlighted how he needed the help of the churches to secure debt relief for Africa. Although in Make Poverty History churches (among others) were urging the British government to deliver debt relief, they were also helping to create the necessary political conditions for it to happen. Brown told the churches, development agencies and others involved in the campaign that they had to create a groundswell of public support to put pressure on the other leaders of the G8. Jubilee 2000 had begun by asking what government could do for it and, by implication, the people of the world's poorest nations. A decade later, Make Poverty History ended with campaigners being asked what they could do for government.

The new deal between church and government has sought to highlight the important work of Christians, and this is crucial, and will become more so as post-Christendom develops. But we have seen that old habits die hard. Often appeals from Christians to government have appeared to be largely self-interested. The church has got used to being in a position of power and influence where, if it can't actually make the law, it can certainly try to shape it. In Christendom, government and politics were frequently seen as a solution to the church's problems and a means of carrying out its mission. Even in post-Christendom the first response of many Christians to a political problem such as perceived discrimination or lack of funds is to appeal to the appropriate authorities. However, the church is going to become increasingly aware that government will neither save the church nor even be much help to it in solving its problems or fulfilling its mission.

The church will have to look more and more to its own actions for answers if it cannot rely on government. In Christendom, it did not often lead by example, but now that it lacks any real political power it will have to do just that if it wants to be a witness. As the church's relationship with government becomes more adversarial, love could guide it in a number of important changes in approach. It could also, as it happens, address many of the problems the church faces of liquidity, vulnerability, authority, credibility and identity.

Liquidity

As we have already noted, many churches are facing a cash crisis, with dwindling congregations, mounting pensions bills and infrastructure that costs a small fortune to maintain. Government funding for their projects is attractive when they need as much money as they can get. We have seen how this can compromise churches in several ways. They may have to adopt the values, goals and targets of government at a time when the priorities of government and those of the churches are increasingly divergent. The dash for cash may subdue their prophetic voice. It may also undermine their loving witness, as the bigger churches, and especially the established church, often seem to get preferential treatment. Christians may also be tempted to exaggerate the case that 'faith works' and overlook the fact that other, non-faith-based agencies can also deliver – and often do it far better.

But it may also be that the very acceptance of government funding detracts from the loving witness of the church, because it makes Christians merely the deliverers of services rather than their providers. Churches and para-church groups may literally provide the services, but they are not generating the resources that pay for them. The finance comes ultimately from the taxpayers, and it is government that is actually making the services happen. A more loving witness would be for the church to concentrate less on securing government funding and more on giving of itself. This would show love not only to the community around it but also to government.

This may seem unrealistic at a time when many churches are in financial difficulties, but the fact is that the church as a whole has massive resources at its disposal. The commissioners of the Church of England alone manage assets of over £4 billion. If there are two million Christians in Britain, with an average annual income of £20,000, there is potentially £40 billion a year that the church can call on.

Nonetheless, there is no doubt that many churches are in decline and they will have to make some hard funding decisions. There will come a point when the church recognises that it needs to liquidate far more of its assets. Some small steps have already been taken in this direction. Despite opposition from traditionalists,[6] some bishops have already moved out of their palaces in order to cut overheads, and some assets are being sold off. But the new deal with government, which gives some access to resources, is perhaps putting off the inevitable.

Many proposals for cutting costs just seem to tinker at the margins. It has been suggested that the General Synod of the Church of England should meet once a year instead of twice, that clergy should get better management training and that other cathedrals and places of interest should follow the example of St Paul's and charge an entrance fee. It has been suggested that the Anglican Church should appoint a professional head of finance, practised in turning around organisations in crisis.[7] But such measures do not address the underlying realities.

The churches in general, and the Church of England in particular, need to make some hard decisions about such fundamental matters as whether they can afford full-time, professional clergy. Denominations will need to explore pooling their resources and working more closely together. More assets will have to be sold or given away. The Anglican Church may even need to rethink its parish system. It has been keen to emphasise that through such structures it can identify with the whole population of England, but it can derive authority from another source, and that is the quality of its witness.

Vulnerability

If the church feels vulnerable, a loving response may be to accept its new condition but also to recognise that others are also vulnerable, and often more so than it is.

---

[6] See, for example, George Trefgarne, 'Sell churches, keep bishops' palaces', *The Daily Telegraph*, 19 January 2004.

[7] Trefgarne , 'Sell churches, keep bishops' palaces'.

What should the church's witness be when it comes to other religions? Often it has complained that followers of other faiths receive preferential treatment, but rather than opposing this, it would be more loving to listen to their concerns and appeal to government on their behalf, to try to ensure that they at least receive equal treatment, if not (as an even smaller minority) special safeguards.

In 2004, a row broke out over a planning application for Northern Ireland's first purpose-built mosque, in Craigavon, three miles outside Portadown. There had been an increasing number of attacks on the 200 Muslims in the area, and some families had been burned out of their homes. Friday prayers had been taking place in a community centre since vandals burned a temporary mosque five years before. When plans to construct a new one, funded by the Muslim community, on land donated by a Muslim, were blocked, local churches intervened and soon representatives of the Muslim community in Craigavon had discussions with leaders from the Methodist, Presbyterian, Church of Ireland, Catholic and Mennonite churches, facilitated by the Northern Ireland Council for Ethnic Minorities. After the churches agreed to speak out in favour of the Muslims' right to build a mosque in Craigavon, the borough council eventually granted planning permission.[8] Despite the deep religious divisions in Northern Ireland, Catholics and Protestants were able to unite in advocacy for another faith.

Such an example shows how distinctive a political contribution Christians can make when they put aside their fears and seek to love the minorities around them. Other approaches might include:

- Lobbying for religious freedoms and protections for other religious communities in Britain.
- Speaking up for people persecuted around the world for their religious beliefs, regardless of whether they are Christian or not.

---

[8] 'Craigavon: Religious liberty in the shadow of Drumcree', *Lion and Lamb*, issue 37, autumn/winter 2004.

- Calling on broadcasters to give other faiths airtime and not just Christianity.
- Calling on the government to direct its resources less towards churches and more towards other religious communities.

Such tactics would make an important political statement domestically, and could also make an impact in other countries, where Christianity is still strongly associated with the foreign policies of states such as the US and Britain, and in particular their recent military interventions in Afghanistan and Iraq.

The overwhelming majority of Muslims and Christians reject both the use of terror and the reactive politics of revenge. If they spoke with a united voice, it could make a powerful impression on government and could persuade it to develop new tactics that didn't rely on force to resolve conflicts. And how would the extremists, who like to cite the abuse of Muslims as justification for their actions, react to a country that favoured Muslims rather than Christians?

A loving response may also entail Christian organisations relaxing their employment policies somewhat. In many cases, they have practised discrimination in the name of maintaining a distinctive 'Christian' ethos, but this may rather reflect the problems they are having in actually being distinctively Christian. Perhaps a truly Christian organisation would not discriminate in that way, but would feel secure in the distinctive values it holds rather than the ability to control its religious make-up.

Authority

We have already noted that in post-Christendom it is going to be far harder for the churches to base their authority on weight of numbers, and this is increasingly being recognised. Appealing to what Christians do, rather than how many there are of them, could help to make up the deficit. For example, rather than complaining that many churches feel discriminated against when they apply for local authority funding, Christians may find that their arguments for equal treatment have a good deal more moral authority if they offer to give up their existing privileges. This would show that the church was prepared to identify with the vulnerable – the people it claims it wants to help. This is a truth the church may be beginning to learn. For example, as the debate over incitement to religious hatred grew hotter, the former Archbishop of Canterbury Lord Carey made public his belief that the time was right to repeal the law against blasphemy.[9]

Love in practice could also provide common ground for a diverse church in the way it tackles political issues. We have seen how competition for government funding has divided churches. An end to the quest for funds from central and local government would not automatically end that competition, but it would change the context in which it took place. It would mean for a start that churches and para-church groups were not vying with each other to meet the goals and targets of the state. Any competition would instead be to find money from sources other than government, such as increased giving by local congregations – which would be far healthier as it could (for example) be a stimulus to increased giving by Christians and greater commitment. The goals and targets of projects would come more under the control of the churches, and Christian action in the community might then actually become a cause of unity, and so of enhanced authority, rather than disunity and disagreement.

There is, perhaps, one more area where loving behaviour may give the church renewed authority. As Christians have rediscovered the political dimension of their faith, they have often faced accusations of naivety in their policy prescriptions, and it's certainly true that churches and para-church groups have offered simplistic, 'pat' answers to social problems that others have wrestled with for years. This has been a constant source of frustration for Christian MPs, who struggle to explain the complexity of many issues to their fellow believers. The church must recognise in post-Christendom that it is merely cutting its first political teeth. Nonetheless, if it can talk of the lessons it has learned in

---

[9] Tania Branigan, 'Ex-archbishop backs axing of "redundant" blasphemy laws', *The Guardian*, 21 October 2005.

action on the ground in its own community, it may be able to show from its concrete examples that it has some credible answers and models of best practice to offer.

One difficulty it faces, however, is, again, that as long as it is dependent on government funding and has to meet government targets, the church may be constrained in its creativity. It is those projects that are pioneered at a healthy distance from government that are most likely to generate ideas that government will want to imitate or learn from.

Credibility

There is a growing awareness in post-Christendom of the importance of the example the church sets. Duncan Forrester saw a crucial connection between the vision the report 'Faith in the City' had for the nation and its thinking concerning the church. He suggested that only when the church was serious about setting its own house in order could it 'call on the state to do justice and love mercy'.[10]

It was a characteristic of Christendom that, though the gospel is based on love, much of what the church did, particularly through the organs of government, didn't seem to be very loving. Its political actions were closely aligned with coercion and violence. In post-Christendom, the message of love could still be compromised by the church's apparent self-interest, defence of privilege and alliance with power; but displays of true love that renounced privilege and pursued the interests of others would give the gospel much greater credibility in the political arena.

The church has lately addressed the problem of trust, but in fact it has always had such problems. In 1606, a man was presented to the church courts for saying that he would rather 'trust a thief than a priest, a lawyer or a Welshman.'[11] What makes the present situation rather different is that churches cannot rely on their privileged status any more when people's trust fails. Rather than launching a public relations campaign to improve

---

[10] Duncan Forrester, *Theology and Politics* (Oxford: Blackwell, 1988).
[11] F.W. Fincham, quoted in Hill, *The World Turned Upside Down*, pp. 28–29.

their image, churches could find that renewed trust was a natural consequence of the example they set of love in practice.

One major threat to the church's witness is internal division – not only over the different positions Christians take in their political campaigning but also over issues within the church that have a strongly political dimension, such as homosexuality. Much of the church's internal politicking resembles the party politics of the world around it. It also displays many of the attitudes of Christendom – for example, a desire to control rather than to witness. There can be no doubt that a change of approach, to the practice of love, would go a long way towards repairing the damaging splits in Christian ranks.

With little sign of an end to doctrinal disagreement, the church will need to find better ways to deal with differences of opinion. Christians will have to be willing to live with this diversity. I have already suggested that political causes such as justice for gay and lesbian people and opposition to war may provide a source of unity even though the Christians concerned still differ over the rightness or wrongness of homosexual practice or the use of force in general. But the more that para-church groups are able to relax their control of doctrinal purity, the more credibility they are likely to have. Until now, it has often been supposed that the opposite is true: that the more tightly controlled an organisation is, the more united it will appear and the greater its credibility will be. This mentality is ill suited to the diversity of post-Christendom – and it is also ill suited to a context of movements, which are doctrinally very diverse.

Identity

The current, church-led campaigns such as Faithworks that are seeking to impress on the government the differences between the various religions only go to show that churches are finding it hard to be distinctive. This is not just because Christians have lost their privileges, or because government tends to lump all religions together under the heading 'faith'. The problem is also that the church itself is not sure what makes it distinctive. Churches and para-church groups often behave like other pressure groups, pushing their own political agendas and asserting their rights.

Rather than asking the government to recognise the uniqueness of Christianity, the church could try to distinguish itself by how it behaves. An approach based on love would mark it out as something very different, not only from government but also from most other pressure groups. The church could truly claim to be a movement that exists for the benefit of its non-members. Such an approach could also make the church a model of political action. There is a growing acknowledgement of the many social-action projects it undertakes locally,[12] and increasing awareness that it can set an example to government. If Christians can show how to achieve reconciliation where there is conflict and how to care for the poor and the vulnerable, this in itself will be a powerful political statement. It could go some way to re-establishing the church's credibility.

In the last chapter, I noted that in Christendom ideas of justice were confused. One idea of justice as something voluntary and unforced that makes things right came into conflict with a punitive idea of justice based on sanction. Post-Christendom allows the church to rediscover itself as an agent of God's justice in the former sense – a community that 'does justice' in a different way to the state and can witness prophetically to the state about justice. The church can say: 'Give us your prisoners, give us your poor, give us your homeless children and we will look after them.' The law tells us only what has gone wrong, not how to put it right. In this respect, the biblical concept of justice is far more empowering.

In practical terms, this may mean concentrating further on the churches' existing projects such as remand fostering schemes, pregnancy crisis centres, housing co-operatives, credit unions, urban regeneration schemes and a host of other such initiatives. However, it may also involve something more radical that is not always to the liking of government. For example, church communities may increasingly become places of refuge for fugitives from

---

[12] See Steve Chalke and Tom Jackson, *Faithworks 2: Stories of Hope* (Eastbourne: Kingsway, 2001).

the 'justice' of the state. Thus, in 2004 a 23-year-old woman called Josette Ishimwe took refuge in a church in Bristol to avoid being sent back to Rwanda, where she had seen her parents being hacked to death. When her final appeal for asylum was rejected, she was taken in by Richard McKay, the priest of St Nicholas of Tolentino Church, and some of his parishioners. Father McKay would not allow police or immigration officials to enter his church when they came for Ms Ishimwe, and he said he was prepared to go to prison in her defence.[13]

Conclusion

At the 2005 Live 8 concert in Hyde Park, Kofi Annan addressed the vast crowd from the stage. 'Thank you for standing with the poor' was his brief message.

But was the crowd really 'standing with the poor'? There was much talk of the 'eight rich white men' who were meeting in an expensive hotel in Scotland, but a good deal of attention was also being paid to the rich, mostly white rock stars who were enjoying the applause in London. When the concert was over, the crowd went home. Perhaps they sat down with a cup of tea. Then they went to bed. Were they still in solidarity with the poor then?

It is important to call on political leaders to help the poorest and the most vulnerable, but it is also important that we practise what we preach. The emphasis on 'moments' rather than 'movements' concentrates attention on (usually political) events and demands that policy-makers effect change. It can be a substitute for change in ourselves. The most powerful political statement is truly to stand in solidarity with the poorest and most vulnerable. In this, the church asks for no privileges or favours. Nor does it make any demands of the state. Rather, it seeks to witness to government and demonstrate God's love to it. Its political effectiveness is measured not by its ability to dominate or control others but by the quality and integrity of its approaches.

---

[13] 'Asylum seeker in "sanctuary" bid', BBC News Online, 28 October 2004.

The church can be reimagined as a political community, but a political community that does not merely replicate the politics of the world around it but lives out a new and unique kind of politics. This means that we have to rethink who we are, who our enemies are and what our mission is. It means we have to consider a witness that incorporates such values as love, generosity, grace and forgiveness as political as well as personal virtues. In pre-Christendom, the church's witness was its primary political expression, but the forms such a witness can take vary greatly with the political context. Today, the church has more opportunities to witness than ever before.

In Micah 6:8, the people of God are instructed 'to act justly and to love mercy and to walk humbly with [their] God.' God has treated them with liberating justice, and now they are urged to pass it on. Their acts of justice and righteousness are to be a response not to coercion by the state but to the gratitude and love instilled by what God has done for them. This idea of justice was also manifested in the Crucifixion, when Jesus acted out of love and invited our response. In a similar way, the church's engagement in future may take the form of political invitations extended to government, which encourage a response. It may act out of love toward government, seek the good of the communities around it, and indeed those abroad, and urge government to take note of its example. In many respects, this is a 'faith works' agenda, but it is not one that aims to follow the government's lead or seeks it as a partner. Rather, it urges government to consider imitating the church.

The question is: How appealing will that invitation be? Clearly, its effectiveness depends to a great extent on its integrity and the quality of the church's witness. It is an agenda that relies not on the professionalism or efficiency of the church in meeting the government's goals but rather on its authenticity and creativity.

People are afraid to make themselves vulnerable. They are frightened of letting go of assets and power. Yet the witness of love is what is needed to restore the church's unique identity, as well as its integrity, authority and credibility. Only then can it hope to reverse its decline and begin again to grow – both in the faithfulness of its witness and in numbers.

13

Getting Our Hands Dirty

A charge that is frequently levelled at people who see government in more negative terms is that they have no realistic proposals for political engagement. They are accused of withdrawal and sectarianism. In Christendom, such a charge was often a self-fulfilling prophecy. Often, the reason that Christians were suspicious of the state and didn't engage with it was that the state was already suspicious of them and its repressive measures made engagement difficult. In post-Christendom, the church's position is rather different, but even so it is far more realistic for the churches to accept their new place on the margins of society than to imagine that they can gain significant political influence by getting close to government. Those that pursue the latter goal may not be facing up to political reality.

However, seeing the state in more negative terms does not necessarily lead to disengagement, and nor does it mean that Christians have fewer political options. Those who are committed to friendship with government will have one set of political methods at their disposal but will find others denied to them. The same will be true for those whose approach is more adversarial. To 'loving enemies' of government, these strategies are particularly appropriate:

- They can negotiate with it.
- They can subvert it.
- They can challenge it.
- They can appeal to it.
- They can withdraw from it.

In Christendom, it was often harder for a church, operating in and around government, to pursue such strategies. Its witness was compromised. Often it could negotiate only from a place where government had a high degree of control and influence. Subversion would involve breaking deals. Challenge might be seen as disloyalty. Attempts to undermine government would be difficult. Appeals to government often had to be made on the basis of mutual benefit. Withdrawal was virtually impossible. The church's options were clearly far more limited in Christendom than they are now.

Christians are likely to choose different methods of engagement at different times, depending on their situation. Many of these will involve witnessing to government, rather than trying to use it to gain control. However, seeing government in more negative terms does not necessarily mean that Christians will not have relationships with policy-makers. What it does mean is that they will be warier of becoming (to use a biblical phrase) 'unequally yoked' with government.[1] As Murray has noted, the new situation requires not 'pietistic withdrawal' from society 'but fresh thinking about *how* representatives of marginal churches with countercultural values engage in political and cultural debate.'[2]

Christians have not always been good at working out how to engage, however. Indeed, they have often attempted to gain power or influence without actually giving much thought to the means they use to get it. But the church's new position on the margins, where it has to operate through the democratic system like almost everyone else (and as a shrinking minority), means that it has to consider and get used to new approaches. It will take time to adjust to this situation. One temptation will be to adopt uncritically the methods of other pressure groups, and even political parties. But each of these involves certain assumptions about power, as well as particular goals, whether the church acknowledges this or not. How, then, do Christians decide which methods are legitimate and appropriate? Should they rule out some

---

[1] 2 Cor. 6:14.
[2] Murray, *Church after Christendom*, p. 24.

activities and concentrate on others? Should they stand for Parliament? Should they seek power? How do such strategies square with a reading of the gospel that emphasises powerlessness, or with a theology of 'the powers'? These are the kind of questions the church needs to ask itself.

The Movement of Ideas

The churches are likely increasingly to resemble an often chaotic political movement, with many campaigns going on at any given time, from the local to the international level. As a movement, rather than an organised lobby group or institution dedicated to changing specific laws, its impact is going to be wide – sometimes altering whole agendas. While occasionally the churches may focus on particular legislation, their influence on it will be limited. The general thrust of their political engagement will be much broader.

In the first chapter, I quoted Tony Benn's quip on his retirement from the House of Commons. It expressed a seasoned politician's conviction that it is movements that bring about real change. Often they dictate the agenda of government, and the choices governments face. It will be primarily in this way that the church will operate politically in post-Christendom.

It has been two hundred years since the abolition of the transatlantic slave trade in the British Empire. Many Christians still look back on William Wilberforce with fond admiration, as a shining political example to follow (though of course he was not without his failings – for example, in 1819 he approved of the Peterloo Massacre and backed other repressive measures against radicals). However, Wilberforce was himself part of a huge movement, which originated centuries before with Christians who called for an end to slavery, and worked for it, at a time when most of the institutional church was quite happy to accept it (and, indeed, endorse it) as a fact of life.

During the Reformation and the English Civil War, a diverse mix of groups such as the Ranters, the Diggers, the Levellers, the

Quakers and the Anabaptists stressed the fundamental equality of all people and challenged both slavery and the subordination of women. To most Christians, on both sides of the Reformation and the civil war, these views were extreme. The Anabaptist William Gouge shocked his congregation in the 1620s when he told them: 'Teach that all are alike and that is no difference between masters and servants.'[3] Nonetheless, it was their scandalous witness – often inspired by their understanding of the teachings of Jesus Christ – that eventually triumphed, as first Enlightenment thinkers and then evangelicals[4] took the same stand these 'purists' had taken so many years before. Interestingly, it was often Quakers and Methodists – that is, adherents of relatively new, unpopular and radical expressions of Christianity – who inspired the campaigns for abolition around the world. Wilberforce himself, though an evangelical Anglican, was converted through John Wesley's ministry and was urged by Wesley to campaign for the cause of slaves. Wilberforce was the politician who brought to its conclusion something that other Christians had set in motion long before,[5] and behind his breakthrough was a much broader movement towards respect for what we now call human rights.

In post-Christendom, Christians may come up with new ideas that seem just as outrageous as the abolition of slavery did in the sixteenth and seventeenth centuries, and yet in the fullness of time these may move into the mainstream. Indeed, the 'fullness of time' may come far more quickly. Agendas in contemporary politics can change in just a few years. After all, the proposal to cancel much of the debt of countries in the developing world seemed outlandish to many in 1990, but by 2000 politicians and civil servants were discussing how best to do it. Likewise, in only 2000 a ban on smoking in public places was for many politicians unthinkable – but in 2006 it came into force throughout Scotland.

---

[3] In Hill, *The World Turned Upside Down*, p. 35.

[4] Who can also be seen as a product of the Enlightenment. See Bebbington, *Evangelicalism in Modern Britain*.

[5] Philip Wogman, *Christian Perspectives on Politics* (Louisville: Westminster John Knox Press, 2000), p. 45.

Those who doubt the impact that Christian ideas can have should reflect on the comments of the influential left-of-centre journalist Will Hutton, writing about Jubilee 2000 in the *Observer* in 1999.

'I doubt many readers know the Old Testament books of Leviticus, Exodus and Deuteronomy any more than I do,' he wrote, 'but … at the end of an increasingly secular century, it has been the biblical proof and moral imagination of religion that have torched the principles of the hitherto unassailable citadels of international finance – and opened the way to a radicalism about capitalism whose ramifications are not yet fully understood … The Left of Centre should take note; it is no longer Morris, Keynes and Beveridge who inspire and change the world – it's Leviticus.'[6]

However, Christians must recognise that they need to work with others if they want their ideas to make an impact. They will still need to work with the Wilberforces – or, as Jim Wallis might have it, the Gordon Browns – of this world. The campaigns and movements they are part of may cohere around some central values and ideas but they will nonetheless be untidy affairs, bringing together individuals and networks with very different perspectives and involving a great deal of negotiation, adjustment and compromise with both politicians and other campaigners.

A centre-set model of the church, as explained in Chapter 10, allows for alliances with others without a loss of identity – indeed, politics becomes a fundamental part of the church's identity. It also means that it can break down the sacred-secular divide and make new alliances with those it has previously shunned. In post-Christendom, the church is already showing signs of enjoying that freedom, making common cause even with humanists and secularists. However, in order to be true to its gospel witness it will need to take care that it does so because it finds there is common ground, and not simply because it wants the influence that comes with weight of numbers.

---

[6] Will Hutton, 'Debt-relief campaign Jubilee 2000 can now claim its great victory, thanks to Leviticus', *The Observer*, 3 October 1999.

Engaging with the System

In the future, the churches will focus less on gaining control of the levers of power and more on subverting power and the systems through which it is exercised, holding the powerful to account and shaping the contexts in which they operate. Drawing on the idea of 'the powers' that lie behind systems, institutions and governments, the church will involve itself in identifying, examining and exposing the 'idols' of the political system. If idolatry is defined as that which demands our worship apart from God, contemporary idols include:

- 'The national interest'.
- The nation state.
- Consumerism.
- Militarism.
- Individualism.
- Marriage and the family.
- Choice.
- Power.
- The environment (both to those who exploit it and those who protect it).
- Prosperity and wealth.

As we have already noted, however, there will also be times when the churches need to make specific suggestions to government about how it should tackle injustice. In particular, they may be keen to advocate ways that move away from coercion and violence towards more unorthodox but still credible methods of dealing with such things as crime, the threat of terrorism and environmental degradation.

Post-Christendom affords new opportunities. In Christendom, the church was limited in what it could do. 'Just war' theory was an attempt to encourage governments to find an alternative to war, but it also proposed circumstances in which war was justified as the lesser of two evils. In post-Christendom, churches will need to decide which elements of the political thought of Christendom are worth keeping and which should be discarded. But there is no longer the same pressing need for them to provide legitimacy for violent activities – indeed, they could oppose the state completely. Christians may find themselves increasingly offering and suggesting non-violent, solutions where options seem limited and governments look as if they will resort to the use of force.

As I said in the last chapter, the strength of the church's witness will depend to a great extent upon whether it can point to its own example. When war is threatening, the church may be able to point to alternatives that governments haven't tried – like the accompaniment programmes of the World Council of Churches and Christian Peacemaker Teams. It may be able to join forces with others who also advocate such methods and can offer their own examples, and with them be able to change the terms of the debate. Likewise, in the area of economics, the church could point to different ways to do business.[7] In the area of criminal justice, it could promote the ideas of restorative justice and reconciliation between victim and offender, which could allow the government to relinquish control and move from being the inflicter of punishment to becoming more of a facilitator of justice.

This requires a change from reactive protest to the proactive proposal of alternatives. Given its distance from government, the church will not need to offer guidance on how (for example) politicians should govern, or under what circumstances they might try to justify war.

The Way of the Cross

Such an approach however, may mean that the church has to take a longer-term view. It may come to see success and failure in terms more of the consistent faithfulness or otherwise of its witness than of whether it delivers the immediate political outcomes that the church has often sought historically.

When Charles Bradlaugh was elected to Parliament in 1880, he refused, as an atheist, to take the oath of allegiance, which

---

[7] See Michael Northcott, *Life after Debt: Christianity and Global Justice* (London: SPCK, 1999).

involved swearing 'by Almighty God'. He was unseated by an angry House of Commons, arrested by the Serjeant at Arms and imprisoned in the Tower of London. Both the Archbishop of Canterbury and leading clergy in the Catholic Church denied his right, as an unbeliever, to be a MP. When he was re-elected; he refused again and again was unseated. In the end, he consented to swear the oath – but the Speaker of the House of Commons would not let him do it. Finally, in 1886, a new Speaker, Sir Arthur Wellesley Peel, did not object, arguing that he had no authority to interfere with the taking of the oath. In the short term, Bradlaugh's principled stand was an apparent failure – yet his long-term achievement was significant, for his actions paved the way for a change in the law that allowed Members of Parliament to affirm, rather than swear, their allegiance to the Crown.[8]

The churches will be aware that even when their faithful witness seems to result in political failure it may eventually bring about change. This will resonate with many Christians who in post-Christendom will rediscover the political dimension of Jesus' own death – an apparent political failure that Christians believe was part of a larger strategy of success. We have already seen that in pre-Christendom Jesus' death was central to the political understanding and identity of many Christians. In Christendom, it was often an embarrassment, and certainly was rarely held up by those in positions of power as a good example to government. In post-Christendom, however, Christians will recognise anew that Jesus' death was also a political statement and indeed a model of faithful witness and engagement.

Elections

It may surprise some readers that I have left it until now to consider Christian involvement in electoral politics. I have done this for a number of reasons:

---

[8] See http://www.libertarian.co.uk/lapubs/legan/legan009.htm.

- In Christendom, the focus was on government; in post-Christendom it is less so.
- Post-Christendom is a transitional phase which we are only just beginning to understand, and the church must learn more about its new political identity before it can determine the most appropriate way to engage electorally.
- Politics is about a broad agenda of which electoral politics is just a small part.
- Participation in elections is declining and so decreasing in significance.
- It is a particularly controversial area for Christians.

Nonetheless, despite the trends, electoral politics in some shape or form is likely to remain a reality for the foreseeable future. In a democratic society such as ours, there are all kinds of elections that Christians may participate in:

- To the boards of companies.
- To the boards of charities.
- To committees.
- To the boards of governors of schools.
- To local councils.
- To regional assemblies.
- To the Welsh Assembly and the Scottish Parliament.
- To the House of Commons.[9]
- To the European Parliament.

Election to each of these bodies confers widely different responsibilities and powers, and in each one different people play different roles. Nonetheless, for a number of reasons elections may also prove increasingly problematic for Christians.

First, as a political reading of the Bible, and especially of the life and teaching of Jesus, becomes more prevalent, it will be hard to find examples of people who are commended for seeking power. Power-seeking is rarely held up as a laudable, or even legitimate, goal for the people of God. The Kingdom of God appears to be at

---

[9] There may soon be elections to the House of Lords, though at the time of writing its members are all appointed.

odds with the quest for power and influence. There are repeated warnings against kings in Scripture, and Jesus appears to face temptations to seek political power which he rejects. The gospels even record that he was one of two candidates in a small referendum conducted by Pilate and he lost.

A negative view of the political system may also further discourage engagement in electoral politics. Becoming a politician is in many respects a career decision like any other. There is a standard route to becoming a Member of Parliament. You decide that this is the career for you, you join the party that is most aligned with your values, you become an activist, raise your profile, attend party conferences, get involved in your local constituency party and go leafleting. Possibly you stand for the local council and become a councillor. Eventually you are approved as a candidate for your party and you then look around the country for a seat to contest. You probably fight for one or two unwinnable seats. You then find one that is winnable and, if all goes well (and you kiss a few babies), you find yourself in Parliament.

From a Christian perspective, this process is problematic. It tends to treat constituents as instruments for political advancement and demonstrates little commitment to a particular area. The adoption of party lists for elections to the European Parliament, the Scottish Parliament and the Welsh Assembly also further remove politicians from the people they are supposed to represent.

Christians are also likely to come to see political office as less important than in the past. Increasingly, there will be a perception that the real politics is done elsewhere, and the limits of the power and influence of elected politicians will become obvious. Some people will still seek to become MPs out of a desire to help their constituents and to be an influence for good; but the churches will no longer go to the same lengths to try to get Christians elected.

Elections as Martyrdom

Elections may come to be seen in another light, however. They may be viewed less as a way to get Christians into positions of

power or influence and more as a way to bear witness to a different set of values and bring new ideas to public attention. From this
point of view, winning or losing an election will not be the crite-
rion of success or failure. Indeed, standing as a candidate may
even be regarded as a contemporary form of martyrdom.

As we noted in Chapter 2, for some early Christians martyrdom was a way to confront the powers and their system of injustice with an alternative set of values. In theory, other ways to do
this were open to them. They could have joined in violent revolt.
They could have amassed wealth and worked their way into the
political classes. However, the way many chose was to 'speak
truth to power' and bear witness to the new kingdom before the
authorities of their day.

In our contemporary context (with the stakes, of course, significantly lower), Christians may also engage in electoral politics
with a view to political witness rather than the pursuit of power.
In a modern democratic system such as ours, candidates can take
part in hustings and are welcome to go door-to-door canvassing,
put information through people's doors and speak to the local
press and may even be granted a free mailshot to every home in
the constituency. These are all good ways to engage politically,
whether one is elected or not. Christians may stand for election,
but on the basis that:

- They wish to influence political debate with a different set of
  values.
- They are not seeking to get elected.
- They are not judging their success by the number of votes they
  receive.
- They are not standing on a party manifesto.
- They want to draw out and draw attention to what is good and
  true in their opponents' positions, as well as their own.

Indeed, it is doubtful that on such a basis a Christian would get
elected. It is even less likely that they will be elected if they ask subversive questions that challenge the idolatry of the political system, such as how government might discard the idea of the
national interest, how it might make the resources of this country

available to the rest of the world, how it might work to reconcile victims and offenders, how it might move beyond competition between nations and how it might set an alternative goal to economic growth. Anyone who suggests that it is immoral to close our borders to the rest of the world has no hope of being popular.

Not-voting

In Christendom, the church's mission often involved using political processes to gain power and control. In post-Christendom, its mission may be to use those processes to enrich and change the terms of debate. Indeed, Christians will increasingly come to see politics and the political system as a mission field in themselves. For example, those who join a political party may do so less because they agree with what it stands for than because it is part of a system that needs to be engaged with, challenged and subverted.

Most commentators interpret the growing 'democratic deficit' in negative terms and attribute it to a mix of apathy and cynicism – the system, after all, depends for its legitimacy on mass participation. The government and a number of denominations and para-church groups have all run campaigns to register voters and persuade them that their cross will count. Churches are eager to emphasise that voting is a virtuous exercise (an idea that still goes largely unchallenged in the national media). The Baptist minister Jesse Jackson is amongst those who have come over from the US to mobilise the black vote in Britain, and the major church denominations and their leaders in this country are no less keen.

However, Christians will become increasingly aware that a trip to the polling station also implies support for the system. Whether it be the fledgling democracy of Iraq or the Mother of Parliaments in Britain, when people go to vote they implicitly endorse both the way a particular kind of politics is being carried out and the values on which it is based. Non-participation, on the other hand, sends a powerful political message that the system needs to be changed. The theologian John Howard Yoder has shown how declining to vote in elections can be a form of both Christian witness and political action.[10]

Thus, although the church has been keen to 'get out the Christian vote' so that Christians can exert their political influence, it may well be that increasingly they decline to vote or 'spoil their ballot papers' as a way of expressing themselves politically. If they regard the system, as well as government, is perpetuating injustice and something to be subverted, they may see voting, too, in negative terms, as something that endorses the system.

Seeking Political Power

In the 2003 European elections, the UK Independence Party won a number of seats in the European Parliament – and this presented them with a major conundrum. Indeed, it seemed to signal the beginning of the end for the party. The problem was that they didn't believe in the European Union. They had stood for election and got elected, and suddenly found themselves part of a system they had previously railed against, whose corruption they claimed to have exposed. To many people, they seemed hypocritical and absurd.

In post-Christendom, the pursuit of political power may be a rather futile exercise for Christians, and it may also undermine their witness if that witness is based on calling those in power to account, and on identifying with the poorest and the most marginalised. Moreover, if Christians compete with each other for political power by standing as rival candidates in elections – as, indeed, they already often do – it will further undermine the church's witness. It will mean, too, that 'the enemy' is no longer the powers but a fellow believer – which in the eyes of many Christians would hand the victory to those very powers.

Whereas in Christendom the church was comparatively insulated from the consequences of its political decisions, in post-Christendom it will be far more exposed to them. It will be less

---

[10] Yoder, *The Politics of Jesus*.

easy to separate words and actions. The church will have to justify
the positions it takes by what it does – this is where its authority
increasingly will come from. But this may also oblige the church
at times to break the law. For example, if they campaign against
what they believe are unjust asylum policies, churches may need
to offer sanctuary to asylum seekers and even to bar access to
them non-violently. It is not yet clear how many forms the
church's civil disobedience could conceivably take – for example,
it might even consider helping people to enter the country ille-
gally. The government might see this as the asylum system breaking down, but the churches would see it as faith working for those
who need refuge.

At other times, however, the government will recognise that
Christians have pioneered successful solutions that it wants to
support or copy. Likewise, even if it is characterised as an enemy,
there will be things that government does to which the church will
be sympathetic. It will be the coercive, unjust and violent elements
that the church wants to challenge.

In Christendom, the church in general was not anxious to
embrace hardship. A few Christians did – the Franciscans, for
example, took a vow of poverty – but it was a fundamental principle of Christendom to try to gain as much power, privilege and
influence as possible.

It has often been asked why Christians in the West today do not
face persecution. The answer that is often given is that we live in a
'Christian' society where we enjoy freedom of religion. Others
suggest, as we have noted, that a time is coming when this will
change and that freedom will be suppressed. Whether or not this
is the case, there is a third answer: that the church has lost its radical edge and so there is no reason to persecute it.

I have argued that in post-Christendom the political authority
of the church will rest not in the political positions it is able to
hold so much as its authentic witness. A feature of both the early
church and Christendom was that it was only those whose
witness was authentic and whose stand was radical who were
persecuted. Those who fitted in with the status quo and sacrificed
to the idols had no reason to worry. It was those who renounced

the idols and followed Jesus radically who suffered as a consequence.

Political thought in Christendom took centuries to develop – and even then the issues were not resolved to everyone's satisfaction. We shouldn't expect that in post-Christendom we will find all the answers we need quickly or easily. Nonetheless, the Christian view of the state is eschatological. We believe that the state as we know it will one day disappear when the rule of Jesus Christ is finally consummated. This doesn't mean that the church can abdicate its responsibilities here and now, but it does mean that, as it gets involved and makes compromises and mistakes, it has this ultimate hope on which it can rely.

Select Bibliography

Anstey, Robert, *The Atlantic Slave Trade and British Abolition, 1760–1810* (London: Macmillan, 1975)

Bainton, Roland, *Christian Attitudes toward War and Peace: A Historical Survey and Critical Re-evaluation* (Nashville: Abingdon Press, 1960)

Barrow, Simon and Jonathan Bartley (eds.), *Consuming Passion: Why the Killing of Jesus Really Matters* (London: Darton Longman Todd, 2005)

Barth, Karl, *Church and State* (London: SCM Press, 1939)

Bartholomew, Craig, Jonathan Chaplin, Robert Song and Al Wolters (eds.), *A Royal Priesthood? The Use of the Bible Ethically and Politically* (Carlisle: Paternoster 2002)

Bartley, Jonathan, *The Subversive Manifesto: Lifting the Lid on God's Political Agenda* (Oxford: BRF, 2003)

Bates, Stephen, *A Church at War: Anglicans and Homosexuality* (London: Hodder and Stoughton, 2004)

Bebbington, David, *Evangelicalism in Modern Britain: A History from the 1730s to the 1980s* (London: Unwin Hyman, 1989)

Berry, R.J., *The Care of Creation: Focusing Concern and Action* (Leicester: IVP, 2000)

Brown, Peter, *The Rise of Western Christendom: Triumph and Diversity AD 200–1000* (Oxford: Blackwell, 2003)

Bryant, Chris, *Possible Dreams: A Personal History of the British Christian Socialists* (London: Hodder and Stoughton, 1996)

Cahill, Lisa Sowle, *Family: A Christian Social Perspective* (Minneapolis: Fortress Press, 2000)

Cardenal, Ernesto (ed.), *The Gospel in Solentiname* (Maryknoll: Orbis, 1982)

Chidester, David, *Christianity: A Global History* (Harper San Francisco, 2000)

Crossan, John Dominic and Jonathan L. Reed, *In Search of Paul: How Jesus' Apostle Opposed Rome's Empire with God's Kingdom* (Harper San Francisco, 2004)

Durnbaugh, Donald F., *The Believers' Church: The History and Character of Radical Protestantism* (Scottdale: Herald Press, 1985)

Eller, Vernard, *Christian Anarchy: Jesus' Primacy over the Powers* (Grand Rapids: Eerdmans, 1987)

Elliott, Neil, *Liberating Paul: The Justice of God and the Politics of the Apostle* (New York: Orbis, 1994)

Ellul, Jacques, *Anarchy and Christianity* (Grand Rapids: Eerdmans, 1991)

—, *The Ethics of Freedom* (Grand Rapids: Eerdmans, 1976)

—, *The Meaning of the City* (Grand Rapids: Eerdmans, 1970)

—, *The Politics of God and the Politics of Man* (Grand Rapids: Eerdmans, 1972)

Hampsher-Monk, Iain, *A History of Modern Political Thought: Major Political Thinkers from Hobbes to Marx* (Oxford: Blackwell, 1993)

Hauerwas, Stanley, *After Christendom? How the Church is to Behave if Freedom, Justice and a Christian Nation are Bad Ideas* (Nashville: Abingdon Press, 1991)

Hay, Donald A. and Alan Kreider (eds.), *Christianity and the Culture of Economics* (Cardiff: University of Wales, 2001)

Herzog II, William R., *Parables as Subversive Speech: Jesus as Pedagogue of the Oppressed* (Louisville: Westminster John Knox Press, 1994)

Heslam, Peter (ed.), *Globalization and the Good* (Grand Rapids: Eerdmans, 2004)

Hill, Christopher, *The World Turned Upside Down: Radical Ideas during the English Revolution* (London: Penguin, 1984)

Horsley, Richard and Neil Asher Silberman, *The Message and the Kingdom: How Jesus and Paul Ignited a Revolution and Transformed the Ancient World* (Minneapolis: Fortress Press, 2002)

Horsley, Richard, *Paul and Empire: Religion and Power in Roman Imperial Society* (PA: Trinity Press, 1997)

Horsley, Richard (ed.), *Paul and Politics: Ekklesia, Israel, Imperium, Interpretation. Essays in Honor of Krister Stendahl* (PA: Trinity Press International, 2000)

Kraybill, Donald, *The Upside-Down Kingdom* (Scottdale: Herald Press, 1978)

Kreider, Alan, *The Change of Conversion and the Origin of Christendom* (PA: Trinity Press, 1999)

Marshall, Paul, *Thine is the Kingdom: A Biblical Perspective on the Nature of Government and Politics Today* (Basingstoke: Marshalls, 1984)

MacMullen, Ramsay, *Christianising the Roman Empire, AD100-400* (Yale University Press, 1984)

McLellan, David (ed.), *Political Christianity: A Reader* (London: SPCK, 1997)

Moberg, David O., *The Great Reversal: Evangelism versus Social Concern* (London: Scripture Union, 1972)

Murray, Stuart, *Church after Christendom* (Milton Keynes: Paternoster Press, 2004)

—, *Post-Christendom: Church and Mission in a Strange New World* (Milton Keynes: Paternoster Press, 2004)

Myers, Ched, *Binding the Strong Man: A Political Reading of Mark's Story of Jesus* (New York: Orbis, 1988)

Nash, David, *Blasphemy in Modern Britain: 1789 to the Present* (Aldershot: Ashgate, 1999)

O'Brien, Mark, *When Adam Delved and Eve Span: A History of the Peasants' Revolt of 1381* (Cheltenham: New Clarion Press, 2004)

O'Donovan, Oliver, *The Desire of the Nations: Rediscovering the Roots of Political Theology* (Cambridge University Press, 1996)

Smith, James K.A., *Introducing Radical Orthodoxy: Mapping a Post-Secular Theology* (Milton Keynes: Paternoster Press, 2004)

Storkey, Alan, *Jesus and Politics: Confronting the Powers* (Grand Rapids: Baker Academic, 2005)

Villa-Vicencio, Charles, *Between Christ and Caesar: Classic and Contemporary Texts on Church and State* (Grand Rapids: Eerdmans, 1986)

Wallis, Jim, *God's Politics: Why the American Right Gets It Wrong and the Left Doesn't Get It* (Oxford: Lion, 2006)

Walter, J.A., *A Long Way from Home: A Sociological Explanation of Contemporary Idolatry* (Exeter: Paternoster Press, 1979)

Weller, Paul, *Time for a Change: Reconfiguring Religion, State and Society* (London: T & T Clark, 2005)

Wink, Walter, *Engaging the Powers: Discernment and Resistance in a World of Domination* (Minneapolis: Fortress Press, 1992)

Wogaman, J. Philip, *Christian Perspectives on Politics* (Louisville: Westminster John Knox Press, 2000)

Wright, Nigel, *Disavowing Constantine: Mission, Church and the Social Order in the Theologies of John Howard Yoder and Jürgen Moltmann* (Carlisle: Paternoster Press, 2000)

Wright, N.T., *Jesus and the Victory of God* (London: SPCK, 1996)

—, *What St Paul Really Said: Was Paul of Tarsus the Real Founder of Christianity?* (Grand Rapids: Eerdmans, 1997)

Yoder, John Howard, *The Christian Witness to the State* (Eugene: Wipf & Stock, 1998)

—, *The Politics of Jesus* (Grand Rapids: Eerdmans, 1972)